A WORLD TO CARE FOR

A WORLD TO CARE FOR

THE AUTOBIOGRAPHY OF
HOWARD A. RUSK, M. D.

A READER'S DIGEST PRESS BOOK

RANDOM HOUSE NEW YORK

Library of Congress Cataloging in Publication Data

Rusk, Howard A   1901–
A world to care for.

Autobiographical.
I. Title.
R154.R92A3   610'.92'4 [B]   72–5263
ISBN 0–394–48198–4

Designed by Carl Weiss

Manufactured in the United States of America
by Haddon Craftsmen, Scranton, Pa.

24689753

First Edition

DEDICATION

*To my beloved wife and children
with heartfelt gratitude
for their unswerving support,
patience and understanding
without which this book
could never have been written,
because there would have been
no story to tell.*

ACKNOWLEDGMENTS

AFTER SPENDING ALMOST HALF A CENTURY in the practice of medicine, it is obviously impossible to thank individually all the people to whom I am indebted. First and foremost, however, I want to express my unending appreciation to my patients, whose courage and spirit have been a constant source of inspiration through the years. I also want to thank my professional colleagues, not only for their loyalty, dedication and empathy, but particularly for their imaginative developments of innovative techniques and programs that established new parameters for serving the disabled. And I can never say enough about the many benefactors who believed in our program and who have, over the years, given unselfishly of their time, effort and financial resources and helped make this crusade become reality.

Many wonderful men and women helped make this book possible. I want to pay special tribute to two brilliant publishers and wonderful friends, DeWitt Wallace of the *Reader's Digest,* who initiated this project and backed it from the beginning, and Donald Klopfer of Random House, who has been unstinting in his support over the years. I also want to express my appreciation for the counsel of the late Robert Haas, who urged me many years ago to record this story. In preparing the text I want to thank Thomas M. Coffey, and especially Bruce Lee of the *Reader's Digest,* for their expert assistance. Others helped, too, in compiling the research and helping to organize the manuscript. They include Mary Cartagena, Rose Elfinbein, Margot Lundell, Jo Ann Schuman, and Margaret Trenkamp—for their hours of yeoman labor I shall be forever grateful.

—HOWARD A. RUSK

....

𝔉OREWORD

....

"It was a warm summer's day, only two months after I had graduated from Tufts University in 1966, and I was water-skiing with two college friends on Lake Cochituate, near Boston. The motorboat pulled me into shallow water, not far from shore, and somehow I lost my balance, pitched forward, and hit bottom.

"The water was only three or four feet deep, so there shouldn't have been any problem, but I couldn't lift my head above the surface. I was floating face down and suddenly afraid I was going to drown.

"My two friends in the boat circled back quickly, and when they saw me with my face in the water, they turned me on my side so I could breathe. The next thing I knew, I was lying on the beach. I didn't feel any pain, but I couldn't move anything below my neck. When I tried to move my hands and arms, they flopped around crazily, out of my control.

"I remember a man coming over and saying, 'Don't move him.' I was frightened now, but not panicky. I knew something strange had happened to me, and I told myself I had been shaken up when I hit bottom. I'd be all right in a little while.

The thought that something dreadful had occurred never entered my mind.

"At the Leonard Morse Hospital in the town of Natick, Massachusetts, where I was taken, they X-rayed me and told me my neck was broken. Even then the full meaning of it didn't really hit me. It takes a while for it to sink in.

"They transferred me to Boston University Medical Center and Dr. Edward Spatz, a neurosurgeon, operated to relieve the pinching of my vertebrae on my spinal cord. Afterward, they put my neck in traction, so I couldn't move even that. I knew then what it really meant to be helpless. I kept feeling little itches on my nose and forehead and it almost drove me crazy not to be able to scratch my own face.

"With every passing day, the significance of my injury became more inescapable. The first time the nurses helped me sit up it took three hours of preparation. I thought to myself, 'Oh my God, I'll never be able to do even this for myself. All my life I'll be completely helpless and dependent on other people.' When my father came to the hospital to take me for my first automobile ride, he brought a lift with which to hoist me off the wheelchair into the car. I hated the experience. Never again would I be able to drive. Or do anything else. In the back of my mind were horrible questions like, Why did this have to happen to me? Why not someone else? And how can I ever possibly cope with it? But something else in my mind prevented these questions from coming forward and overwhelming my emotions.

"By this time, my ability to move my wrists and raise my hands had returned. But I couldn't lower them. Gravity did that. Within another month or two, I could also move my arms; though I had some motion in my fingers, I couldn't close them. I gradually had to face the fact that this was as much

muscular control as I was ever going to have in my whole body. A horrendous thing had happened to me. I was a quadriplegic, and my arms and legs would be paralyzed for the rest of my life."

Those are the words of Robert Heist, who arrived at the Institute of Rehabilitation Medicine in New York City about four months after his 1966 accident. His father drove him down from Wayland, Massachusetts, the Boston suburb in which they live, and Dr. Howard Rusk went out to their car to meet them when they arrived. As Rusk recalled the moment, *"That young man was just about as helpless as a human being can be. The only things he had going for him were a family that truly loved him, plus his own intelligence and determination."*

During the next nine months, Robert Heist went through the institute's complete program of physical rehabilitation. Doctors and therapists evaluated every muscle in his arms and shoulders with even a trace of capacity left in it, and they put him on a course of exercises designed to maximize those few physical powers he had not lost. Then they taught him, one step after another, a whole new set of procedures for daily living. He learned how to use one of his partially manipulable hands to help the other, how to substitute shoulder strength for arm strength, how to use his arms to control or move his body, how to get back and forth without help between bed and wheelchair, how to feed and dress himself, how to control his bodily functions, how to write with a special pen which fitted onto his hand. Finally, he learned how, despite his quadriplegia, to safely drive a hand-controlled car.

When Rob Heist left the institute in the fall of 1967, he was proficient at all these things and many more. He bought a car, got a job as a department trainee for the John Hancock Insur-

ance Company in Boston, and began driving himself back and forth to work every day, even though Wayland is about eighteen miles from his office in the center of the city. His promotion has been rapid. He is now staff assistant for John Hancock's Contract Services Department. He still drives to work every day, winter and summer. He goes to basketball, baseball and hockey games. On weekends he bowls with friends. In the summer he takes his friends out on his motorboat, a Boston Whaler, which he handles himself. He has an ambition to work his way up into an executive career with the John Hancock Company, and with his intelligence and personality there is no reason why he shouldn't succeed. Despite his disability, he is a very able man.

Not everyone in Robert Heist's condition is rehabilitated so successfully. Thanks to his determination to help himself, and to a total training program, he has overcome quadriplegia to become a well-adjusted, responsible and productive member of society. That's what medical rehabilitation is all about. And basically, that's what this book is about. It's the story of rehabilitation as Dr. Rusk has seen it develop in the last quarter of a century, a fascinating account of a new branch of medicine which will give hope and life to millions of people around the world.

THE EDITORS

A
WORLD
TO
CARE
FOR

CHAPTER

. . . .

I

. . . .

IT HAD BEEN A ROUGH TWENTY-FOUR HOURS. I had gone
to the hospital at three o'clock the afternoon before to see an
old friend who had suffered a massive stroke. Strokes always
disturbed me; the patient's future was so bleak. Even if he
recovered, the chances were that he'd spend the rest of his
life in bed or in a rocking chair, half paralyzed, and possibly
unable to speak. It was a terrifying thought, for in those days
there was very little we could do to help stroke victims. But
for my friend, the question of what we could or could not do
didn't arise, and I stayed with him until he died early the
following morning.

Afterward, I did the only thing a doctor can do when he
loses a friend and a patient. I turned away from death, back
to life; I made hospital rounds, saw my other patients and
went home about noon.

It was a cold, damp, December day, and I felt that a good
hard ride across the Missouri countryside on my favorite
horse was what I needed to get the kinks out of my body. But
when I returned home I sensed something terrible had happened. Everyone in the family was ghostly white. The radio

had just announced that the Japanese had attacked Pearl Harbor. Instinctively I knew that from this day on, my life was to be drastically changed.

I closed out my practice of internal medicine in St. Louis and joined the Air Force (at that time still a part of the Army) as a medical service major in August 1942, just when World War II was becoming most ferocious. In the Pacific the U.S. marines were invading the Japanese stronghold at Guadalcanal; German Field Marshal Erwin Rommel was pushing the British back toward Alexandria in North Africa; and the German army in Russia was meeting unexpectedly fierce resistance at Stalingrad. My first assignment was safely remote from all this—at Jefferson Barracks, Missouri, just outside St. Louis—but while I had absorbed enough R.O.T.C. training in college days to give me some preparation for the shock of military life, I was quite unprepared for many of the situations I was to encounter.

The thing that hit me hardest was that I was no longer master of my own life. The morning I reported to the base commander at Jefferson Barracks, the first thing he said to me was, "You're out of uniform, Doctor."

I couldn't imagine what he meant. I thought I looked quite sharp and military. My shoes were glossy; my uniform was well pressed; I even had my necktie tucked into my shirt. But therein lay my error. "You've got your tie tucked in under the fourth buttonhole," he said. "On this base we tuck it in under the second buttonhole."

Though my necktie offense was not very great, I felt chastened when I left his office, and with another newly inducted doctor, started down the steps toward the door. There, on a landing, we came to a soldier in perfect uniform. His shoes sparkled, his pant-legs were razor sharp, and his tie was tucked in below the second button. Quickly, I saluted. So did the officer beside me. Then both of us took a second look at the soldier. It was a dummy that the base commander had placed there to demonstrate how he wanted his men to dress.

I smiled sheepishly at the other officer. "I'll never mention this to anyone," I said, "if you don't."

"Agreed," he said.

The next thing I had to do was to report to the commander of the base hospital, Colonel James McDowell, a surgeon who had spent most of his career in the regular Army, and who believed, as did the base commander, in doing things by the book. His first words to me were, "Let's see your orders, Major."

I blinked. "What orders, sir?"

"Your mimeographed orders. The orders that told you to report here today."

I had been told by telephone to report. I didn't recall receiving any mimeographed orders. Then suddenly I remembered. Two or three weeks earlier I had gotten some mimeographed sheets in the mail, but they had looked like junk, so I had thrown them away without reading them. Colonel McDowell wasn't very pleased to hear that, but nevertheless he appointed me Chief of Medical Services of the 1,000-bed hospital.

Jefferson Barracks was an old Army base that dated back to before the Civil War, and it looked as if nothing much had been done to keep it in shape since then. I think the only reason for its being an active base was that, when it became evident the war was approaching, the Army had to use every available facility, and the Air Corps, being the newest and smallest branch, was relegated to some of the most dilapidated bases. The hospital itself, though enormous, was what they used to call a "theater-of-operations" type of installation, the kind of hospital you might find just a short distance behind a battlefield. It was a huge maze of shedlike wooden barracks perched on cement blocks with open space beneath and connected by what must have been five miles of corridors in which a person could get hopelessly lost.

There were five units—medical, surgical, venereal, and dermatology, plus one small section for civilian dependents of the officers and men on the base. The operating theater, if you could call it that, was in the oldest part of the hospital, and it was totally outdated except for certain pieces of equipment which had recently been installed.

One of the first things I did was to go through the storage section to see what we had in the way of medical supplies. Among the items I found were three or four hogsheads of quinine left over from World War I and three or four hogsheads of Dovers Powders, a medicine which one would have to be elderly to remember—a combination of opium and one of the salicylates used in the old days for flu and fever. One of the first things we did was to try an experiment with common-cold patients, giving one group nothing but aspirin, another group sulfadiazine, and a third group Dovers Powders. The aspirin and the sulfa group recovered at about the same rate, but it took the Dovers Powders group about three days longer because the drug constipated them so badly it took a blasting charge of cathartic to get them flushed out and back to duty.

We learned two things from this rather crude bit of clinical research. First, we could throw away those three or four hogsheads of Dovers Powders. And second, that remarkable as it was for some things sulfa did not cure the common cold.

Aside from its size, another thing I noticed immediately

about the Jefferson Barracks hospital was that it was almost unbearably hot. The base commander, a strict regular Army man, was tough, and he wanted his troops to be tough. He believed that if they were going to endure combat, they should be able to endure the St. Louis heat. He ordered long drill sessions, parades, physical exercises, cross-country runs, and ten-mile hikes. But most of the draftees had been civilians only a few days earlier and were in poor physical condition. They began collapsing in bunches, and we had an epidemic of heatstroke so severe we could hardly find enough ice in which to pack those kids. We were alarmed, but when we complained about the situation we were informed that the training program was a military, not a medical, matter. There was a terrible scrap, and it looked as if the commanding officer, as usual, would be the winner. But then a dreadful thing happened. Two or three of these heatstroke patients died, and the training program was modified until the worst of the summer heat had passed.

This was only the first of many incidents that dramatized the complexity of the new problems I would be facing in military medicine. For example, I was learning some lessons about spinal meningitis. In my sixteen years of civilian practice, I had seen only one or two cases of meningitis, but within the first two or three weeks in service, I encountered at least a half dozen cases and found out in a hurry the importance of quick diagnosis. If the meningitis patient's adrenal glands cease to function because of the severity of the infection, it is likely that he'll be dead in a few hours. But if we could immediately fill a man with enough sulfadiazine to prevent a crisis and keep his adrenals functioning, we could almost certainly save him, and of those we saved, a large percentage had no residual effects.

Or we would have a man brought in from the drill field who had suddenly passed out and gone into shock. He might be a strong, strapping nineteen- or twenty-year-old, and we'd find that he was suffering from a perforated stomach ulcer, or a massive gastric hemorrhage. On questioning him we'd learn that his symptoms had arisen within a few days of his arrival, and it soon became evident that the physical problems of such men grew out of psychological factors—usually the trauma of facing Army life. More and more the medical profession has come to recognize the possible relationship between ulcers and anxiety, and wartime military service provides anxiety to the nth degree. When a soldier has hanging over his head the knowledge that eventually he's going into combat and will have to kill or be killed, it becomes, for certain individuals, an unmanageable phenomenon. We soon realized that if we wanted to bring these patients back to health, we would have to do much more than cure their ulcers.

Another problem that nagged me constantly was one which might not, at first glance, appear very serious. It was how to handle convalescent patients. For the medical service staff in a 1,000-bed hospital full of nineteen- and twenty-year-old soldiers, this problem could be very acute. Time was bound to hang heavy on them as these youngsters began to feel better. Bored and restless, the convalescents would get in the way or get into mischief. You couldn't blame them. If a man was in the surgical section, for instance, he might be in one ward while his condition was acute, then move to the next ward as he improved, and finally to a ward where he could carry his own trays and get along without much nursing. An effort was made to keep together those who were at the same general level of convalescence; but this wasn't always practical. Often, in a ward where there were some very sick patients, you would have others engaging in bois- terous horseplay, pushing each other around, wrestling in the aisles. Obviously, this posed something of a dilemma.

In mid-September, we had to get the hospital shined up, because an inspector was due to arrive from the surgeon general's office in Washington. That was the Army surgeon general, not the air surgeon. The organizational pattern was so involved at that time the Air Force didn't even have control of its own medical section. Though we were in the Air Force, we had to follow directions from the Army. So we prepared for this inspection and prepared well, because it was important to keep the Army off our backs. The inspec- tor was a wonderful physician, Colonel (now Brigadier Gen- eral) Hugh Jackson Morgan, who had been professor of medicine at Vanderbilt. I had known him casually at the American College of Physicians and we got on well together. But at one point during his visit, as we were going through my wards, swarms of these convalescent soldiers, in their purple bathrobes and gray pajamas, kept walking by us, and I can remember how Colonel Morgan stopped and looked at them, shaking his head.

"This is awful," he said. "Something has got to be done about it."

Needless to say, I was in complete accord. These boys were a constant threat to the orderly functioning of the hospital. But Colonel Morgan was looking at the matter from still another, more serious angle.

He told me that the Air Force, even though it is the smallest of the three services, has an average of fifty thousand men in its hospitals every day. "You may not know it," he added, "but it's touch and go as to which side will win this war. And when there are fifty thousand men out of action every day, do you know what that does to your training program?"

It was as if he had switched on a light. For the first time it dawned on me that the problem of convalescent servicemen was important, not just to me and to the Jefferson Barracks hospital, but to the whole country. The time these men were wasting was time we could not afford to lose during a war which was the biggest, most horrendous in the history of mankind.

"If you get any ideas about it," Colonel Morgan said, "please let me know."

Within a few days, I did get an idea. It was simple, yet it seemed so sensible I decided to try it right away. I reevaluated all of my patients, and in about 90 percent of the cases—if their fevers were down and they looked and felt all right—I simply released them. When I was through, that hospital was running so smoothly, I was proud of myself. No more crowds of healthy boys in purple bathrobes getting in the way. Now we could concentrate on caring for the patients who were really sick.

This happy situation didn't last long, however. Within forty-eight hours, 90 percent of the men I had discharged were back in the hospital. And they were not gold-bricking, they really needed care. I was embarrassed and chagrined. Once again it had been brought forcibly to my attention that there was a great difference between military and civilian medicine. In military medicine I couldn't tell a patient, "Go home and take it easy for a week or ten days, then come to see me at my office and I'll tell you when you can go back to work." In the military, either a man was in the hospital or he was out. If he was in, he was a patient; if he was out, he was a soldier. And as a soldier, he did whatever his outfit was assigned to do that day, whether it was a run through the obstacle course, followed by a long parade, or a ten-mile hike with a full pack. The men I had discharged, though they had recovered from their illnesses, were simply not yet strong enough for such activity. So I was forced to the conclusion that a man couldn't prepare himself for strenuous training routines by playing blackjack in the hospital sun parlor or listening to his bedside radio. But on the other hand, what else was there to do in a hospital? I didn't have an answer.

CHAPTER

. . . .

II

. . . .

AFTER MY EMBARRASSING MISTAKE in discharging patients before they were ready for duty, I became almost totally occupied with the enormity of the convalescent problem. In time I worked out the beginnings of another plan and made an appointment to explain it to the base commander.

"Since we can't just release these boys from the hospital," I said, "why can't we start a program of activities to keep them busy while they're convalescing. Not just exercises, but some kind of constructive training to keep them from wasting their time."

"Great idea," he said, "that's exactly what we need. Why don't you go ahead and do it?"

My hopes rose immediately. "We'll need some personnel assigned to it."

His face clouded and he shook his head. "Well now, wait a minute," he replied. "We're short-handed already. I don't know where we'd find any extra men for that sort of program."

My happy dream diminished. Though I had been thinking in terms of several men, I decided I had better lower my sights. "Even if we could get only a couple of men to begin it . . ."

He looked doubtful. "You could go to Personnel," he said, "and ask them."

Without a specific order from the base commander, I knew what the answer would be from the Personnel section, and that's the answer I got. They had no men for me. I went back to the hospital feeling discouraged.

Then I ran into a major who was the executive officer to the hospital's commanding officer and a real old-timer. He had been a sergeant major in the regular Army and knew all the angles. When I told him my predicament, he had an immediate answer. "Why don't you look around among your patients? If you find the men you need, keep them in the hospital. Assign them to work in the program."

For the next couple of days, I must have looked like the grim reaper, going through the wards staring at everyone, deciding who my victims would be. Soldiers can instinctively sense when an officer is looking for volunteers, and it was amusing to watch them slink away when I glanced at them. It wasn't long, however, before I found a couple of fellows who seemed ideal. The first was a man named Raymond Lewis, who had been a teacher, was very energetic, and tremendously interested in visual aids and all kinds of teaching methods. As I gradually learned, he was a sensitive, intelligent man, and he was a patient because he was having trouble with his feet. Anyone accustomed to sitting in a classroom was likely to have trouble with his feet after being introduced to obstacle courses and ten-mile hikes. But he was recovering nicely, and he would have no trouble getting around the hospital, doing what I had in mind for him. Then I encountered another patient named Leo Vishneau, who had been a court stenographer before entering the service, and who was the best typist I'd ever seen. You couldn't dictate fast enough to keep up with him.

Our embryonic team thus assembled, we sat down to decide what to do first. Physical-conditioning exercises seemed to be the logical starting point. But how should we design the exercises? If we designed them for patients who were just beginning to convalesce, they would be too easy to benefit patients who were back on their feet and preparing to return to duty. Yet, if we worked out a strenuous routine, the early convalescents wouldn't be able to handle it. We finally settled on a simple system of tags. If a man had no tag on the end of his bed, it meant he was not yet well enough to be in the program. A red tag meant he was just well enough to begin it, and though he would start with the others, he would drop out after five minutes. When he graduated to a blue tag, he could go on for another ten minutes. And when he got the green tag on the end of his bed, he was able to go through the full exercise routine, at least once and sometimes twice a day.

This all sounded fine to us. But as we might have realized, some soldiers don't exactly love calisthenics, a fact that was immediately illustrated when one of my ward officers called me and said, "I have a patient who refuses to do your exercises, or have anything to do with your program. What do I do? He's disobeying an order, but he's a patient, after all, and he might claim he's too sick for calisthenics. Do you want me to report him for disciplinary action?"

That was the last thing I wanted. The program would never work if it depended on the threat of punishment. "I'll come over and talk to him," I said.

After two minutes with this young man, I realized I had

a very difficult case on my hands. He was a tough kid from Brooklyn, and when I tried to explain to him nicely how the program would help him, how it would speed his recovery and help prevent a recurrence of his condition, he looked at me as if I were a naïve little boy. He didn't say it, but I knew he was thinking, Nuts to you. The truth was that he was no longer suffering from any illness; he just didn't want to leave the hospital and return to duty. I couldn't say this to him, however, because I couldn't prove it.

I turned to the captain in charge of the ward. "We'd better reexamine this man," I said. "Maybe he shouldn't be in the program."

We took him into the examining room and I found him to be strong as an ox and sound as a dollar. But as every doctor knows, even the healthiest of human bodies has certain vulnerable areas, and one of them is in the lower left quadrant of the abdomen, where the sigmoid colon makes ready for the final exit from the body. If you roll it under your fingers with a lot of pressure, it's not very comfortable. When I got to examining this man's abdomen, I gave his sigmoid a real workout, rolling it on my fingers about half a dozen times, until he was nearly jumping with discomfort.

"You see," I said to the captain, "he has a very tender, irritable colon. He really isn't fit for the exercise program. He needs drastic therapeutic measures. I want him to have complete bed rest. I don't want him to get up even to go to the toilet. He'll have to use a bed pan and a urinal. And I want you to put him on a Sippy diet."

A Sippy diet is one in which a person gets four ounces of half milk and half cream every hour, sixteen times a day, which includes the middle of the night. The fellow was delighted with his victory, and the milk-cream combination tasted good to him the first couple of times. But when he began calling for the bedpan and the urinal he found service wasn't very good, either on delivery or pickup, because everyone in the ward knew he was gold-bricking. By the following morning he was sick of his diet and by that afternoon he was desperate. He now hated the milk and cream, he hated the bed, he hated the routine, he hated the fact that he couldn't go to the movies or the PX; he was so thoroughly miserable he asked if he could see me again.

When I came to the ward three or four hours later, he said, "Doctor, you were so right about your diagnosis. My stomach was very sore yesterday, but this treatment has helped me tremendously and I feel like a new man." I reexamined him (with considerably less pressure), pronounced him improved, but not yet cured. "I think you'd better have at least one more day of this regimen," I said.

When I saw him the next day, he said he had been thinking about the exercise program and he really wanted to get into it. "But you know, there are some fellows around here," he said, "who don't quite go along with a program like that. They don't understand it. If you have any trouble with these goof-offs, let me know and I'll take care of them."

The incident sounds amusing now, but it was crucial then. Had we let this man get away with his gold-bricking, or had we resorted to punitive measures, the program wouldn't have gotten off the ground.

It was progressing nicely when another difficulty arose. My two staff members, Raymond Lewis and Leo Vishneau, had recovered so completely, it was ridiculous to keep them in the hospital as patients. Yet if I discharged them, they would return to their original units and I'd lose them. By this time, they didn't want to leave the program any more than

I wanted to see them go, and once again I went to see the wily, knowledgeable executive officer.

"I've been thinking of your problem," he said. "I can tell you, you're not going to get any men assigned to you in the routine way. But there are other ways. You're chairman of the C.D.D. Board, aren't you?"

I was, indeed, chairman of the hospital's Certificate of Disability Discharge Board, which meant it was for me to decide whether a man should be released from the service for medical reasons.

"If you were to bring these two fellows up before your board," the executive officer said, "and find them unfit for military service, they would be automatically and immediately transferred to the hospital patient detachment. Then they'd be under our jurisdiction. The next day, you could call another meeting of your board and 'un-C.D.D.' them. In light of further evidence, you might find that they are able to continue their military duties, after all. And since they would already have been assigned to our hospital unit . . ."

About twenty minutes later, these two strong, healthy invalids, Lewis and Vishneau, were standing before my board, looking very unfit to me. By the following day, when they reported for duty as the first men assigned permanently to the convalescent program, they were looking quite fit. That was how the convalescent program began.

A few days later, when I was making rounds, I came to a boy who had a broken leg, plus pneumonia. I stopped to say hello, but he was so angry he scarcely spoke to me.

"What's the matter with you?" I asked.

"I hate this place," he said, "and I especially hate the orderly in this ward. He did me a dirty trick this morning."

Knowing the kinds of practical jokes one can encounter in

hospitals, I waited with some trepidation to hear what had been done to this poor fellow who was flat on his back and couldn't move.

"There was a spider web over my bed," the boy continued, "and that damned orderly came by with a broom and swept it down."

That didn't sound so dreadful to me. "We've got to keep the place clean," I said.

"But I can't move," he said. "All I can do is lie here looking up at the ceiling, and the one thing I've enjoyed in the last three weeks is watching that spider make her web, catch flies, and have young spiders. That web kept growing bigger and better every day and now it's gone."

This gave me a sudden idea, which was so obvious I felt stupid for not having thought about it before. We were in the Air Force, and in the Air Force, aircraft identification is so important everyone has to take a course in it. If these boys were so bored they were staring at the ceilings, why not give them something useful at which to stare? The Air Force already had sets of exact models of the various German, Japanese, British, Russian and American planes. We got forty to fifty of them and hung them from a rope, on a pulley arrangement, that was stretched the length of the ward directly above the heads of the beds. Now when a boy stared at the ceiling, he was studying aircraft identification, whether he knew it or not. Every half hour or so, someone would pull the rope one way or the other, and above each bed was a new plane to study. We soon found that after ten days or two weeks in our hospital, a patient was more skilled at aircraft identification than anyone who had taken the regular course in the subject.

This was our first proof that we could actually teach practical courses in the hospital as if it were a school. We then organized a course in military courtesy, which I don't suppose was very popular, but the boys accepted it politely. They knew it might save them a dressing down in the future. Next we got in touch with the base camouflage officer, Captain William Pahlmann (who is now one of the finest interior decorators in New York City), and he came to give a series of lectures and demonstrations in camouflage that were so clever he got everyone interested.

From there we went on to academic courses like meteorology, trigonometry, calculus, and American history. It was our aim to provide the boys in the hospital with any subjects their units might be studying in ground school. This, I think, was the concept that eventually made the program so successful. Now when the boys went back to duty, they were better prepared for it. Our re-admission rates were decreasing, and I was beginning to think we might have an answer to the problem Colonel Morgan had posed about the millions of man-hours going to waste in all the service hospitals.

In November of 1942 there was a meeting of the Southern Medical Association in Richmond, Virginia, which I was planning to attend. Before leaving St. Louis, I wrote a one-and-a-half-page summary of what we were doing at Jefferson Barracks, and on the way to Richmond I stopped at Washington to see Colonel Paul Holbrook, a dynamic internist from Tucson, Arizona, and Colonel Walter Jensen, a career medical officer who was executive officer to the chief of the Air Force's medical branch, Brigadier General David N. W. Grant.

When I showed my little summary to colonels Holbrook and Jensen, they both said it made sense and that General

Grant should see it. As it happened, the general was on the same train I took to Richmond and I got a chance to talk with him. I told him we had a program at Jefferson Barracks in which he might be interested, and asked if I could consult him about it on my way back through Washington. Two days later I was in his Washington office handing him my little page-and-a-half memorandum. I remember watching him as he sat there reading it. He wore little pince-nez glasses, and when he finished, he glanced up momentarily, then went back to the first page and read it again. When he finished, he took off his glasses and gazed out over the Potomac River for what seemed to me about an hour and a half but must have been only a couple of minutes.

Then he turned to me and said, "This could be a great program. I want it started in every one of our Air Force hospitals. And I'm going to order you to Washington to be responsible for it."

I didn't realize it at the time, but that moment was to change my life. A short time after my interview with General Grant, I was in Washington, sitting at a card table with a half dozen sharp pencils and two or three tablets trying to figure out how one went about starting a program of the size the general wanted. I knew nothing about military procedure. I had never even written a directive. Fortunately, my colleagues were very helpful. My first task was to think of a name for the project. "The Army Air Force Reconditioning and Recreation Program" sounded good to me, so I worked up an innocuous little announcement that such a project was under way and put the announcement on the headquarters bulletin board.

When I arrived at my office the next morning, two ladies from the Red Cross were there to see me, elderly ladies whose determined expressions indicated I was in trouble. One of the women brought out a copy of a congressional bill, and with a flourish, laid it on my desk. "We saw your notice on the bulletin board," she said. "You say you're organizing an Air Corps Reconditioning and Recreation Program. Apparently you don't realize that the Red Cross is responsible for recreation. It is not your prerogative. Congress has designated the Red Cross for this, as you'll see when you read this bill."

I didn't have to read the bill to know that I wanted no trouble with the Red Cross. "Well," I said, "I can assure you we don't intend to step on anyone's toes. From what I've been able to see, there's more work in this field than all of us can handle, even if we devote twenty-four hours of every day to it. But I'm sure our duties won't be overlapping. We have in mind a therapeutic type of recreation. Our aim is to help make these boys better soldiers—it will be really more like training than recreation. If it will make you ladies fell any better, we'll change the name of our project."

Their faces lit up immediately, and then and there, the Air Force Reconditioning and Recreation Program died, to be replaced by the Army Air Force Convalescent Training Program. It couldn't begin, though, until a directive had been issued, and since I didn't even know how such a directive should begin, it was fortunate for me that a major (now dean of the College of Medicine at Ohio State) named Richard Meiling came along at that time. He spent the day with me, and we came up with a simple, generalized three-paragraph directive which became our authorization for launching the program in 253 Air Force hospitals.

The directive did raise one obvious but unavoidable problem. It meant extra duty for some medical officer at each hospital, and the likelihood was that whoever got that extra duty was already pretty busy. Most likely he would resent the added burden. If so, we'd be starting our program by making enemies of the men we needed most. At this crucial moment, I was again fortunate. I had assigned to me a man named Captain Alfred Fleishman, an excellent writer and one of the best public relations men I've ever known. He began by selling the program to the doctors who would be in charge of it at the various hospitals. He sent them letters, notes, and news releases; he even published a little monthly newspaper about our progress. Pretty soon, these doctors who were setting up convalescent programs for us began sending Captain Fleishman items for the newspaper about what they were doing and what new ideas they were incorporating—everything from victory gardens on the hospital grounds to engine-repair programs in the hospital sun rooms.

About this time, I also learned that I was authorized to write letters of commendation, so whenever the Convalescent Officer in any of the various Air Force hospitals submitted a worthwhile idea or showed some initiative, I would write a letter to his commanding officer, commending him for his outstanding work and asking that the letter be incorporated in his official service record. If there was any resentment among the doctors when the program began, I don't think it lasted long, especially after it became evident that it really worked.

One of our first successes occurred when the patients in our Coral Gables, Florida, hospital started a hydroponic garden—a large tank filled with a chemical solution in which vegetables and other plants can be grown. As it happened, General H. H. Arnold, the commanding general of the Air Corps, became ill for a short time in early 1943 and was a patient at Coral Gables. When he saw the hydroponic garden, he said, "Maybe that's how we can get fresh vegetables to our troops in Asia." American forces in China and Burma had not been able to eat the vegetables there because of parasitic and contamination problems. Within a few months, they were eating hydroponic vegetables.

Despite our successes, we faced many difficulties, one of which involved the Sioux Falls Air Base in South Dakota, which was in a low, swampy area a few miles outside of town —a horrible location. It was all "theater-of-operations" construction—plain wooden barracks perched on concrete blocks. But it was an important training base because it was the home of a large radio school, one of only six such schools in the Air Force, and its six-week course was so intensive that if a boy missed as much as two days because of sickness, he simply couldn't catch up. He would have to wait another six weeks and repeat the whole process.

A hospital could be an ideal place to learn radio code. The base surgeon, a wise man and an excellent doctor, realized this and wanted to wire the hospital wards so that Morse-code lessons could be broadcast every day from 9 A.M. to 5 P.M. There would be different lessons at different times for each achievement level so the boys would be able to study their code and do their paper work in bed. But the base surgeon's problem was that he hadn't been able to get the wiring done. He couldn't get anyone assigned to the project and wondered if I would talk to the commanding officer about it.

When I walked through the hospital, I had to sympathize with the doctor's situation. They called the Sioux Falls base Pneumonia Gulch, because there were more pneumonia and upper-respiratory-infection cases here than in any other Air

Force hospital. The base also had a commanding officer with a reputation for opposing new ideas, and I didn't have much confidence in my ability to persuade him to change his ways. Nevertheless, I made an appointment to see him.

His name was Colonel Cody. He was another old-time regular Army man who had been assigned to the Air Force, and though he was only five feet, four inches tall, he was tough and able. I explained our program carefully, and while he listened politely, he didn't seem impressed.

"It sounds interesting," he said, "but I haven't any men I could assign to it. They're all busy."

"The reason I think it might be important," I said, "is that all those boys in the hospital are losing time and having to repeat the entire course. I'm sure if they could study in the wards, a lot of them could graduate with their classes."

The colonel didn't waste a lot of time thinking about this. "Frankly," he said, "I've got so many other things to be done with higher priorities that I can only tell you I'm not interested."

When I stood up to leave, I felt completely defeated. Just before I turned to go, I said rather apologetically, "I'm sorry to bother you, sir, but I came here to try to establish the program because General Grant is deeply interested in it, and so is General Arnold."

I'm not yet sure just why I threw in that last name. I wonder if it was as innocent as it seemed at the time. General Grant's name was hardly likely to impress a tough old soldier like Colonel Cody. After all, Grant was just another doctor, general or not. But General Arnold was another matter.

"Does the old man know about this program?" Colonel Cody asked.

"Indeed he does." I said. "That's why I'm here."

"Well, why didn't you say so?"

"Anyway," I replied, "I've enjoyed talking to you, Colonel Cody. I'm leaving this afternoon for Scott Field [another radio-school base in Illinois]. I'm sorry you can't manage the program I had hoped to establish here. I'll just have to explain your difficulties when I turn in my report."

"Oh my God," he said, "you can't do that."

"I'll have to," was my reply. I was a rather brash new major, I'm afraid.

He steered me back to my chair. "What did you say you'd have to have?"

"Well, we'd have to get all those wards wired, and we'd need at least six teachers to begin the program. Probably double that when we get going. I'm sorry you don't have the men to spare." I stood up again. "I understand they do have enough men for it at Scott Field."

"Wait a minute," he said. "Can't you stay over for another twenty-four hours?"

I shook my head. "They're expecting me at Scott tomorrow morning."

Cody rose to the bait. "Let me tell you this—within a half hour I'll have people assigned to wire those wards. When you get to Scott Field tomorrow morning, you'll have a telegram from me that the wires are in, the instruments there, the men assigned, and the program in operation. Sioux Falls is going to be the first radio school in the Air Force to adopt your Convalescent Program."

I left there delighted, not only because Colonel Cody had given me what I wanted, but because he had also, without knowing it, given me a wedge to use at Scott Field, where the commanding officer was even tougher than Cody. He began shaking his head negatively before I was even through explaining the program.

"We don't have time for that," he said. "We've got other things to do. We're running a training program here, not a convalescent program."

"I understand," I said, "but I wanted you to know about the program, because Colonel Cody in Sioux Falls is tremendously interested. I was up there only yesterday and he's already assigned people to go to work on it. He's determined that his will be the first and best convalescent training program in any of the radio schools. And he particularly wants me to report that to General Arnold."

Again it was the magic word, and I got immediate action.

We were not always that successful, of course. Shortly after the program began, we became excited about the idea of early ambulation after surgery, which was a new concept at the time. As a result, Dr. Donald Covalt, who was the Convalescent Officer for the Air Force's largest basic-training installation at Miami Beach and its surgical staff, evaluated a group of two hundred and fifty men, all of whom had been operated on by the same surgeon for simple, indirect, inguinal hernias. Half of them were instructed to get up the day of their operation; the other half were allowed to stay in bed for the conventional period of two weeks. The boys who walked early were quickly doing much more than walking. Dr. Covalt soon had them playing volleyball on the beach, taking long hikes, and participating in all kinds of strenuous activities. They seemed delighted with it. But then, one afternoon in midsummer, Dr. Covalt telephoned to say that we might find ourselves in a spot of trouble.

"A small, wire-haired general has just dropped in to look

at what we're doing," Covalt said, "and I don't think he liked it."

The man to whom he referred was General Norman Kirk, who had stopped in Miami Beach on his way back from Africa to Washington. President Roosevelt had just chosen him as the new surgeon general, and Covalt had very proudly shown him all his patients playing baseball and volleyball right after surgery. The general's reaction had not been a happy one.

"He's rather red-faced," Covalt reported. "When he saw the way those boys were running around, I thought he was going to have a stroke."

"What did he say?" I asked.

"He didn't say a word. He simply turned and walked away."

General Kirk was sworn in as surgeon general the next week in Washington. The first order he issued was that all hernia patients were to be kept in bed for two weeks, kept in the hospital for thirty days, and then given at least thirty days' home leave before returning to duty.

It looked as if our early ambulation program had come to an early end. However, most of us were civilians in uniform —doctors first and soldiers second—and we were more interested in medical care than in orders from above. I don't know whether it was right or wrong, but we soon began giving General Kirk's order a symbolic interpretation. For a while it took our hernia patients several days to complete their two weeks in bed, but soon they were completing the two weeks in one day. Not once did we suffer any repercussions from disobeying General Kirk's order. I'm sure he had more important duties to attend to. Meantime we kept track of the original two hundred and fifty hernia patients, and the long-term results were so encouraging that we were soon putting boys on their feet right after appendix operations and other types of surgery. That first solo walk may not be much fun, but by now it has been well established that early ambulation reduces pain, sedative requirements, and other complications. Today it is a generally accepted practice.

At the same time, the educational part of the convalescent program was growing, and we were soon teaching about three hundred and fifty different subjects in more than two hundred hospitals. We even had aircraft engines in the sun parlors for the boys to assemble and disassemble, and we set up all kinds of procedures and standards to make sure our classwork complied with Air Force requirements.

Despite such success, many of us felt our program was grossly inadequate. This feeling became intensified when wounded boys from the battlefields began being packed into our hospitals by the planeload. Suddenly we were faced with men with broken bodies and, all too often, broken spirits. We concluded that our program was a schoolboy project in the context of what needed to be done for the severely wounded—the amputees (the double, triple, and quadruple amputees), the paraplegics and quadriplegics, the blind, the deaf, the disfigured, the emotionally disturbed. These men would need complete rehabilitation, whatever that might be—I wasn't sure. Just exactly what could be done for them? And did the Air Force have the facilities, or the inclination, to do as much as possible for them?

It was horrible to realize that there was no precedent for rehabilitation programs on a large scale in the military. And as far as I knew, there were no extensive civilian programs, either. What should we do next? When I walked through the wards, looking down at row after row of severely wounded men, I knew we had to do something. But I had no idea which way to turn. I began to wonder what had brought me to such a challenging dilemma. It seemed that all of my life's experiences were coalescing and coming to the surface, and it must have started way, way back in my early life.

CHAPTER

. . . .

III

. . . .

I WAS BORN ON APRIL 9, 1901, in Brookfield, Missouri, a
prairie railroad town of five thousand people in those days.
It was a division point of the Chicago, Burlington & Quincy
Railroad, about halfway between Hannibal and St. Joseph—
or halfway between the worlds of Mark Twain and Jesse
James.

My father had left his native Ohio to come to Brookfield
in 1890. As the oldest of eight children in a family which
scratched a living out of some rather poor farmland near a
town called Fairpoint, he had wanted to go to medical
school, but there was only enough money to send him to one
year of teachers college, after which he began teaching in a
country school. Before long he came to the conclusion that
his prospects were limited in Ohio, and gathering together
his savings, the bulk of which was a pair of fifty-dollar bills
that he put in his shoes, he set out to seek his fortune in the
West. When he arrived in Chicago, he spent so many hours
walking around sightseeing that when he took his shoes off
at bedtime, he found he had worn sizable holes in each of
them—and in each of the fifty-dollar bills.

Sending the damaged bills back to his hometown Ohio bank (which later replaced them), he continued on to Brookfield and went to work in a furniture and undertaking establishment, where he soon became a partner. A few years before the turn of the century he met my mother, whom he married after a courtship of only a few months.

My mother, whose maiden name was Augusta Eastin Shipp, was a tall, beautiful girl, eleven years younger than my father. She had grown up in Lincoln County, Missouri, the daughter of a grocery salesman who rode the rough trains in that area, covering all the little towns. Her grandfather had been one of the first doctors to practice in Pike County, Missouri; he contracted pneumonia and died at the age of thirty-five after riding out to see a patient during a blizzard. Having come to Brookfield to live with an uncle and aunt while attending a small seminary, my mother was nineteen when she met my father. My parents' first child, a boy who would have been three years my senior, died in birth because complications developed and the family doctor didn't have the training or facilities to cope with them. There was no hospital in Brookfield at the time, and when I was born, my mother was desperately afraid that the same thing might happen. But I survived, though homely, jaundiced and not too strong.

We lived in a frame house that my father had rebuilt on the north side of Brookfield, near two lovely parks. When I was eleven, I started developing an interest in medicine. For some reason, I had always liked all the strange-looking bottles in which medicines were kept. Soon I found myself fascinated with the whole idea of doctors and medicine and curing people.

By this time we had a hospital of sorts in Brookfield.

Actually, it was no more than just an old frame house with six or eight rooms, where doctors could take patients suffering from serious illnesses and perform rudimentary surgery. The kitchen had been converted into an operating room, and there were a half-dozen beds downstairs with three or four more upstairs. To get a patient up and down the stairs, someone had to carry him in his arms or transport him on a kitchen chair. And while most of the doctors had primitive X-ray machines in their offices, there was very little equipment in the hospital.

I used to hang around both the hospital and the office of one of the doctors in town, a fat, jolly man named Thomas P. Fore, who took a liking to me. At least, he seemed to tolerate me, and one day he even took me into the hospital with him to watch some minor surgical procedure. I was entranced.

"Howard," he said, "I'll make a deal with you. After this you can come in and watch surgery if you'll stay afterward to scrub the operating room and clean the instruments."

That was the beginning of a wonderful friendship. From then on I was his firehorse, running errands for him, scrubbing for him, and getting things ready for him in emergencies. In one of his emergency cases, maybe a year or two after I began helping him out, I learned my first important medical lesson.

He called one day and told me to get down to the hospital right away. "A farm boy has been shot," he said. "The family is bringing him in, and I want you to be there when they arrive, because I'm on a confinement case and I may be delayed."

I ran all the way to the hospital and arrived just as a Model-T Ford pulled up with one tire flat and the radiator boiling. I remember that the man driving it had sandy hair, and a sunburned neck, and was wearing a turtlenecked sweater under a spotted canvas sheep-lined coat. In the back was a boy, obviously his son, with the same sandy hair and wearing the same kind of sheep-lined coat. His face was gray and he was perspiring heavily, but otherwise he seemed to be intact. I thought he was just frightened, so I decided to cheer him up.

"Don't be scared," I said. "You're not bad hurt."

"Not bad hurt!" he cried, throwing open his coat to let me see. "All my guts are out!"

He had shot himself in the belly pulling a shotgun through a fence, and disemboweled himself. I was so startled and frightened I picked him up, though he was as big as myself, and carried him without help into the hospital. I had him in bed and all ready when the doctor arrived to start taking pieces of shell and debris out of him. It was useless, of course, because there were no antibiotics in those days, nor proper instruments for that kind of surgery. As I watched the doctor work, I kept thinking of the stupid thing I had said and was chagrined and ashamed. By the time he died, about three hours later, I had made up my mind on one thing: I would never again start talking until I knew the facts.

I had another firsthand medical experience about this time that shook me up considerably. Our family doctor, Dr. Howard, had taken a short course one week from a nose-and-throat specialist in St. Louis. He decided I ought to have my tonsils out, so I went to his office on a Saturday morning. Another doctor, named Brownfield and a railroad surgeon, acted as anesthetist, dropping ether as it was needed to keep me asleep.

I went to sleep under the ether thinking this was a relatively simple matter. Both doctors, as well as my parents, had assured me there was nothing to it. But it took Dr. Howard about an hour and a half to get my tonsils out, and by the time I regained consciousness, I was so sick they had to take me home in a carriage my father kept for occasional use as a funeral coach. I couldn't swallow solid foods for ten days, and later Dr. Brownfield said to me, "Howard, I worried a good deal about you during that operation. I gave you more than two cans of ether and once I thought you were gone. I kept thinking how aggravated your mother would be if you died having your tonsils out." Medical practice could be quite casual in those days.

Brookfield, Missouri, is typically American, fairly prosperous, with a solid, concerned citizenry. Yet it was not until the early 1950s that the ridiculous little hospital I remember from my boyhood was replaced by a new well-equipped one. Despite such inadequacies, which were common to most towns at the time, the town gave me a wonderful boyhood, and in many ways you might say I actually lived the Huckleberry Finn story. My father had a stable in town where he kept two big black hearse horses, a cow, and Old Frank, our family driving horse. A hired hand named Mr. Brammer took care of the stable, milked the cow, brought the milk to the family and all that sort of thing. I can see him now, pouring the milk through a strainer, which was as close as it came to pasteurization.

For amusement, we found pleasure in pastimes which today would appear too old-fashioned for the young generation. We had wonderful times at dances and picnics and sleigh rides—bobbing for apples and picking berries. When we felt especially wicked, we smoked corn silk—at least the boys did. A girl would have had to be an abandoned creature in those days to smoke, and if there were any among the girls with whom I grew up, I wasn't aware of it.

My parents were strict. They imposed a ten-thirty curfew during my high school years, and though it cramped my style and I used to complain, I obeyed it. My mother was a member of the Christian Church, and my father was a Presbyterian. There also were revival meetings in the country with evangelists like Billy Sunday, but my family had nothing to do with them because my mother did not believe in that kind of religion. It was too flamboyant, too much like show business. But we kids liked to go, perhaps for the same reason my mother didn't.

I wasn't a great student at Brookfield High School—just a bit above average. There were too many outside activities attracting my attention, one of which was football. Our team was eager enough, but we had no real coach, and there were only seventeen gawky, gangling boys on the squad, including my best friend, Wes McAfee, and me. Since this didn't constitute two full teams, we couldn't even divide up for a proper scrimmage. We had no uniforms, and I'm afraid we looked like Coxey's Army when we trotted onto the field.

The big game of the year was Excelsior Springs, which outnumbered, outweighed, outblocked and outtackled us. The first play of the game I was knocked flat on my back and I got knocked flat again just about every play thereafter. Some of our boys were smarter. They would hit the ground for protection as soon as the ball was snapped, but I was fool enough to try to stand up and take it. We weren't saved by the final gun until the score had reached sixty-some to nothing, and by that time I was a mass of bruises. But I did receive some consolation. A much-respected sportswriter for the *Kansas City Star*, a man named Clyde McBride, had seen the game, and when the season ended and the time came to choose the Missouri All-State high school team, he nominated me as first-string center. "Rusk played on the worst team I ever saw," he wrote, "and he took the worst beating I ever saw. For that beating, he deserves this dubious honor."

If football was something of a distraction, it was not the most important one. In 1917 the outbreak of World War I preoccupied everyone. I was only sixteen, but I wanted very much to enlist. The marine sergeant who ran the recruiting station in Brookfield stayed in a rooming house next door to us, and he was signing up everyone he could find. He easily convinced me it was my duty to go to France, and I told him I would be on my way as soon as I got my parents' consent. I was much less persuasive with them than he had been with me. They said I could go, all right, but not until I finished school, or until I was old enough to exercise my own judgment in the matter. By that time, of course, the war was over.

A very poignant incident took place in Brookfield in connection with the end of the war. A tall, rather shy man named Charlie Spurgeon, who wore pince-nez glasses and worked as a clerk in the H. Tooey Mercantile Company, had gained a certain amount of notoriety by telling the fellows at the Elks Club he was a close friend and classroom seatmate of General John J. Pershing, the commander of the American Expeditionary Forces in France. The boys would ask him questions about Pershing and he would tell them how he and "Black Jack" did this and the other thing when they went to rural school together in a neighboring village. It was possible, of course, because Pershing had been born in Laclede, Missouri, only five miles from Brookfield, but he was now such a famous hero there was doubt in some minds whether a timid fellow like Charlie Spurgeon could possibly have known him so well. After the war, in the summer of 1919, some of the townsfolk decided that this great military hero should be invited back for a celebration at his birthplace, so a committee was formed and Charlie Spurgeon was chosen as chairman.

To the surprise of many, General Pershing accepted the invitation, and on the day of his arrival, two high school bands, plus everyone in town, were at the station to greet him. Everyone, that is, except Charlie Spurgeon. As the train came in, the bands played, the flags waved and the firecrackers exploded. The general, tall and ramrod straight, came down the steps and began shaking hands with the assembled dignitaries. But as he did so, he kept looking around.

"Where's Charlie Spurgeon?" he asked.

Someone said, "We don't know. He's the chairman of our committee, but he didn't show up."

"Well he's the man I want to see more than any other," Pershing said. "Let's go find him."

For all of his celebrated toughness, Pershing must have been a sensitive man. He apparently remembered how shy Charlie Spurgeon had been and figured the poor fellow had stayed away from the station fearing he would not be remembered. Before beginning any of the ceremonies, Pershing and some of the committee members drove to Charlie's house and there they found him.

"You old son of a gun," Pershing said, "why weren't you at the train?"

Charlie Spurgeon broke into tears. "Well, General," he said, "you know how I feel about you."

Pershing took him by the elbow. "You get in that car," he said. "I want you to be right by my side every minute I'm here."

General Pershing made Charlie Spurgeon's life that day, and from then on, Charlie was king of the town. When he spoke, the boys at the Elks Club listened.

That year I graduated from Brookfield High School, and in the fall I enrolled at the University of Missouri. I traveled to Columbia quite stylishly in a little Ford with white wire wheels. My father's business was booming. He had five or six farms, and like so many other people at the time, he was pyramiding his savings at an amazing rate. I had what was for those days a very liberal allowance—$75 a month. I went out for the freshman football team, made friends and was invited to join one of the old, respected fraternities, Phi Delta Theta. I lived at the fraternity house and had a grand time, especially since there were lots of beautiful girls around the place. That first year at the university was wonderful, and so was the second. I was going to college the way every kid wishes he might go to college.

Then, in 1921, came the first great postwar depression. My father suddenly lost all of his farms. He found himself so deeply in debt he had to liquidate his business. And to pay off the bank, he had to sell everything but the furniture. He was so broke it seemed to me I should quit school and go to work to help support the family. But my mother wouldn't hear of it. "I'll sell the furniture," she said. "I'll do anything to make sure you stay in school."

Thus, it was under quite different circumstances that I returned to the university for my junior year. Luckily I was able to get two jobs. I washed glassware in the bacteriology laboratory of the medical school, a most unpleasant occupation, since many of the test tubes contained bacteria that would make a sewage disposal plant smell like a rose in comparison. Then at night I worked as an orderly at the county hospital, which was two miles across town, and which I had to reach without the benefit of my long-gone wire-wheeled Ford. I did some laboratory work at the hospital, but mostly I took bedpans and urinals to the patients. I learned one trick as an orderly that proved profitable. I kept my bedpans on the radiator, so they were always warm. For this, my patients were so grateful they would often tip me a dime or even a quarter. One night a man gave me a whole dollar. It was the biggest amount I ever got, and in those days it meant I could take my girl out to dinner and even have enough left to tip the waiter.

By this time I had fallen deeply in love with Gladys Houx, the most wonderful girl in the world. That's what I thought of her at the time, and that's what I still think of her today, after being married to her for forty-six years. Our courtship was not easy because money was scarce and I got very few windfalls like that dollar tip. But Glad was understanding and we became engaged at the end of our fourth year in college. I should say that first *I* became engaged. It took a while to convince her that she was engaged. And I didn't have too much time to do this because, of course, I had to find a summer job. Fortunately I found one, at the Missouri State Colony for the Feeble-Minded and Epileptic at Marshall, Glad's hometown. There were about twelve hundred to fifteen hundred patients and only two doctors, one of whom doubled as the administrator. I think it was there that my interest in the handicapped developed, although it didn't begin there. It began, strangely enough, at my college fraternity house, where we had a houseboy who had lost a leg. He used to thump around on crutches, trying to do his work, and it was so pathetic to watch that we got together a committee, of which I was chairman, to take up a collection and buy him a leg. I can still see his face when we presented it to him. That leg meant everything to him, but it also meant a lot to me because it made me feel the crucial importance to a handicapped person of something the rest of us took for granted —the ability to walk.

The patients at the hospital for the "feeble-minded and epileptic," a horrible phrase, had much in common with my friend the waiter even though their handicaps were different. They could do a lot for themselves if someone would just give them a start. I remember one little boy who seemed to be totally helpless. All day long he would lie in his crib and keep brushing at his ear. Finally I caught on to the possibility that there might be something in his ear. When I syringed it out, I found five flies and twenty dead gnats. It's a terrible story, and it demonstrates the full horror of neglect. Nobody at that institution was to blame for the child's condition. The staff was so small that there just wasn't time to give proper care to all the patients. But after I saw the improvement in that one little boy as a result of such a simple procedure, I was alerted to check all the children. I was amazed to find how many were in need of similar help.

Epilepsy in those days was deadly serious; patients used to have violent attacks because we didn't yet have the wonderful anticonvulsive drugs of today. Luminal, a barbiturate, was the best then. It had been developed in Germany just before World War I, but we couldn't get it until some time after the war ended. The first shipment of it, several hundred pounds, came to America by submarine and was sold at tremendous prices. I remember the day we got our first small consignment of this new injectable drug. One of our patients, a teenage boy, was then in the throes of continuing epileptic seizures, known as status epilepticus, which is often fatal.

The doctor in charge said to me, "I want you to go up and sit with that boy and give him injections until he either stops breathing or stops having convulsions. I'll give you two helpers to hold him down."

The two helpers were inmates, both mentally retarded. I asked the doctor, "What's the dose?"

He said, "I have no directions and I have no idea. I think you should start with a modest dose and keep increasing it until something happens."

I sat beside that boy all day and all night, with my two "assistants" holding him down on the mattress while I gave him ever-increasing amounts of a new drug about which I knew almost nothing. I was thoroughly frightened. But after twenty-two hours, during which I had injected what seemed to me an enormous quantity of sodium luminal, the boy's convulsions stopped and he was on his way to recovery. When I saw the convulsions ease I suddenly began to feel like a doctor. It was a great sensation.

But not all of my adventures at this time were medical. My father was still in a desperate financial condition and had to find some way to make a living. Finally he decided to run for clerk of the county court, a most unpromising decision because the man who was then clerk had held the job for sixteen years and was a member of one of the oldest political families in Linn County. My father's chances looked so slim that my friend Wes McAfee and I pitched in to help. I think we must have visited every farm in Linn County as well as every village and town. We shook every hand we saw. We waved signs. We passed out leaflets and five-cent cigars that were lethal, and we talked until we were hoarse. We really worked, and to everyone's surprise, my father won the election by seventy votes. His victory was fortunate for me because, without the salary he earned as county court clerk, I could never have gotten through medical school. It was a very small salary, yet somehow my father managed to pay my tuition and help me with the bare necessities.

At the end of my fourth year in college, which was my second year as a medical student, I transferred from the University of Missouri because it offered only a two-year medical course. My grades were good enough, so I could go almost any place within reason, but I chose the University of Pennsylvania on the advice of my bacteriology professor, a colorful teacher named Mazyk P. Ravenel, who asked me one day, "What is it you want to do in medicine?"

"I want to treat patients," I said. "I want to look after people."

"Then the best place for you to go is the University of Pennsylvania," he said. "That's my school. I once taught there and I can tell you it's a fine medical school with a great tradition. The oldest medical school in the United States."

With his backing, I applied for admission to Pennsylvania and was accepted. The summer before I came East, Glad and I became formally engaged, and spent all of our free evenings together. I was very excited about my acceptance at the University of Pennsylvania, but it did create a problem for us. We hated the thought of being separated, but Glad was clever enough to work out a partial solution. Having just graduated after majoring in social work, she got a job as a caseworker in New York City with the Brooklyn Bureau of Charities. It paid the enormous sum of one hundred dollars a month. So we both traveled East that fall, Glad to Brooklyn and I to Philadelphia. It didn't make us next-door neighbors but it did put us reasonably close to each other.

In Philadelphia, I began managing the commissary for our

medical fraternity, which gave me room and board. Every six
weeks or so, Glad and I would rendezvous for a weekend in
New York. Glad went without lunch to scrape up funds, and
the only way I could finance my share was by selling blood.
I had an odd blood type, so I got fifty dollars for each pint,
but I could do it only once every six weeks. I'd give the blood,
get the money, and run for the train to New York, where a
friend of mine, who was a resident at St. Luke's Hospital, had
an extra bed I could use. It was not an ideal arrangement,
because St. Luke's is far north on Amsterdam Avenue, and
Glad lived many miles away, in the center of Brooklyn. After
we went to the theater, it took about an hour to take her
home by subway, and then almost two hours to get myself
back to St. Luke's.

There was one consolation, however: we couldn't spend
much money while we were riding the subway. We didn't
dare spend more than a small portion of my earnings, so
Glad and I would pool our funds. If we went to the theater,
we sat in the top balcony. We loved to dance, but when we
went dancing the waiters glared at us because we never ordered anything to eat, only ginger ale. Prohibition had just
come in, and I suppose we could have gone to speakeasies,
but even if we had wanted to, we couldn't have afforded it.
I well remember a Sunday afternoon when we went to a tea
dance at the Biltmore Cascades. After buying our tickets, we
had maybe a dollar left over. We hadn't eaten lunch, because
we were saving money for the dance, and to make things
worse, a huge, fat man at the next table ordered a double
portion of bay scallops. They were brown and succulent, and
as he sat there slowly dipping them in tartar sauce and
popping them into his enormous mouth, their aroma drifted
right over to us. I was gnashing my teeth in hunger, but with

a dollar, we just couldn't order any food at the Biltmore. Finally I grabbed Glad by the hand, pulled her out of the cabaret, and rushed her to a hamburger stand, where we could at least eat enough to stop the hunger pains. By then I was so hungry I miscalculated the change in my pocket, and when I got back to Philadelphia at three thirty the next morning, I didn't have a nickel left for carfare. I had to walk all the way to the campus.

For Christmas that year, Glad was determined to get me what I needed most—an overcoat. The only one I had was out of style and almost out at the elbows. So she saved her lunch money until she had twenty-five dollars, which she gave to my roommate with the specific instructions that he buy me a coat. Instead, he bought me a little case of surgical instruments, and when I opened this present, presumably chosen by Glad, I didn't know what to say. What was a third-year medical student supposed to do with surgical instruments? Glad was heartsick when she found out. The instruments couldn't be exchanged, the money was gone, and I was still shivering in my threadbare old coat.

After the first year in the East, Glad and I traveled by train to Missouri together. When I returned to Philadelphia that fall for my senior year at the University of Pennsylvania medical school, Glad remained in Missouri; her family refused to let her return to Brooklyn. I didn't see her again for a whole year, and a lonely year it was, since I didn't have enough money to go home for Christmas.

The following summer I graduated and went home. Actually, I didn't do it in that order; I returned home and then graduated because, not having seen Glad or my family for such a long time, I couldn't wait three more weeks after finishing my final examinations just to attend commencement exercises. Someone had to be there to accept my diploma, however, or it would not be given. Fortunately I found out that the janitor who kept the animal house also kept a cap and gown in his closet because every year there was someone like myself who didn't want to hang around for the ceremony. This janitor had probably received more M.D. degrees than any doctor in the country. I asked him if he would like to receive mine.

"For five dollars," he said, "I would be honored."

Since he furnished his own cap and gown, and included in the five dollars the cost of mailing the degree afterward, it was a great bargain. I immediately contracted with him to be my stand-in at graduation, and it worked well except for one thing. Some time later, when I encountered one of my classmates at a reunion, he was still talking about how drunk I was at graduation. My friend the janitor had bought whisky with the five dollars and by the time he answered the call to march up and accept my diploma, he was staggering.

Before returning to Missouri, I had already been accepted as an intern at St. Luke's Hospital in St. Louis. But that didn't mean my financial problems were eliminated—far from it. As interns, we were paid twenty-five dollars a month plus room, board and laundry. That was about the going rate for good hospitals in 1925. Many teaching hospitals paid their interns nothing and prided themselves on it. Under those circumstances, it was almost impossible for medical students to get married. Even after seven years of training and internship they were usually broke. Fortunately times have changed for the better: an intern in New York, for instance, gets a little over nine thousand dollars a year, compared with the three hundred dollars I got. As a result, something like 90 percent of the medical students today can marry before they graduate. They're obviously living happier, more normal lives because of it.

That is not to say I was unhappy with my life as an intern. The chief of staff was a big, jovial, able surgeon named Harvey Mudd. We all loved him. He had a good staff, and we had fun and learned a lot, too, even though we had very little money for recreation. Those were prohibition days, and we liked to have a cocktail before dinner if we were not on duty. It took a bit of ingenuity, but we managed it. Inside the hospital pharmacy there was a locked section in which they kept the alcohol. One of the interns, who later became a department head at Mayo Clinic, got a very bright idea. The two of us went in, and while I engaged the old pharmacist in conversation, my friend used a bar of soap to make an imprint of the key to the alcohol locker. We had a duplicate key made to this inner sanctum, and since we already had a key to the pharmacy itself (so we could get any drugs we might need at night), we were ready for action. One of us would stand guard while the other went into the alcohol locker with two flat bottles tied to his belt and a rubber tube under his coat. All that was necessary was to give a tremendous suck on one end of the tube and the alcohol began flowing into the bottles. Back in our quarters, we would add the alcohol to a bit of glycerine, oil of juniper, oil of coriander and oil of orange, and we had a gin that was quite delicious —as long as we drank it with enough canned fruit juice or sweet soda.

The work was hard and the hours were long. We did all the scut work—that is, the routine laboratory work, blood and urine tests, medical histories and physical exams—plus scrubbing for surgery. There were no antibiotics in those days, so diseases like pneumonia, which is not very worrisome now, was a real scourge. The mortality rate among pneumonia patients was more than 33 percent. There was no specific treatment for it, but we knew about three types of pneumococci that were sensitive to an antiserum we had. For patients who had an unresponsive type we resorted to what was euphemistically called "expectant treatment." We tried to get all the foods and fluid we could possibly get into the patient, even though he was racked with coughing and fever, and then we waited hopefully for the crisis. For some reason I never understood, it usually came on odd days: the third, fifth or seventh. When it was due, we'd sit with the patient through the night to give him stimulants when the fever dropped. It seems primitive now, but it was all we could do.

Glad was living with her parents back in Marshall, Missouri, about two hundred miles from St. Louis, and she was able to come to the city and stay with friends only once that year. I got to see her a few times on my nights off. We didn't have much money, but we were invited to parties, and on occasion we went to movies at the considerable cost of twenty-five cents each.

Still, the time passed so quickly I realized to my astonishment one day that I had better figure out what I was going to do next. My internship was nearly finished. Glad and I were eager to get married, and as usual, I was broke. Finally, a physician who was not a regular at St. Luke's, but who had a few patients there, offered to take me on as his second assistant at a hundred and fifty dollars a month. That was about six times what I had been getting, but it still wasn't much when I figured that out of it I would have to pay for my own food and lodging, plus having to support a new wife. I accepted the job with the stipulation that I could take patients on my own after office hours.

By a stroke of luck, I had two or three patients of my own, and after the first two weeks, more patients began coming to me. Since I had the right to use his office and equipment, the doctor I worked for watched with decreasing enthusiasm as my after-hours practice grew. Eventually the situation became so difficult I offered to resign, but he wouldn't have it. "You've agreed to stay for a year," he said. So, for a year I stayed, and at midnight on my last day I departed.

Glad and I had been married on October 20, 1926, three months after I began practicing. To pay for our wedding and buy a car, I borrowed a thousand dollars from my aunt, Keziah Hall, my father's oldest sister, who ran a nurses' registry in St. Louis. Although Father hadn't been able to afford to study medicine, when he prospered in business he helped his two brothers and a sister through medical school. His oldest sister remembered this when I needed money.

We were married in Marshall at an evening ceremony in the charming old stone Presbyterian church to which Glad and her family had belonged ever since her grandfather came to Missouri from Virginia. I borrowed a white tie and tails that were fairly close to my size, and with lots of safety pins holding the rig together, I made it safely down the aisle. It was a lovely wedding, the candlelight was soft and warm, and we were joined by family and friends from all over Missouri.

We left on our honeymoon in a secondhand Model T, with our baggage held onto the running board by one of those accordion baggage racks. We went down to the Ozarks for a few days, then to St. Louis, where a friend let us use his apartment. Despite the dirt roads, we had only one mishap on the trip. I had bought that particular Model T because it had an electric cigar lighter, the first I had seen, and as soon as we got on the highway I couldn't wait to take out a cigar and show my new bride what a fancy fellow I was. I unwrapped the stogy, and casually flipped the lighter switch. Suddenly, there was a short circuit, and a few moments later I was burning my hand pulling the red-hot wires out of the dashboard to keep the car from bursting into flames.

During our honeymoon, we also had to find a place to live. I went to the owners of a large apartment building called the Ranlagh-Wilmar, a place with about a hundred and fifty small units, and offered to rent one of their single-room efficiency flats provided they named me the house doctor. They agreed, and the idea must have amused them. I can see why now. As soon as we moved in, I learned that being a house doctor is about as rewarding as being a house detective. Most of the patients I treated had suffered minor household accidents, or had fallen down after too much to drink, or had lost a family fight. I didn't make enough on them to pay the rent, which was between fifty and seventy-five dollars a month. Whenever I think of that apartment I can smell paint remover and wax because, for the first six months, we sat on orange crates and ate from packing boxes while we refinished several pieces of antique furniture we had bought. My own contribution to the furnishings was a small hooked rug I had made during my internship.

When we could afford it, we left the apartment house to move into a little home of our own, and after living there for a year, I made a deal with another doctor. In exchange for space in his office I would do his laboratory work. But within three or four months, my practice had grown so much that I was able to pay off the money I had borrowed from my aunt.

On the advice of a very wise doctor named William Mook,

I started doing some teaching. Dr. Mook had said to Glad, "That fellow can't just see patients. He's got to be in a teaching atmosphere."

I began doing some research, and eventually I got interested in urticaria, or hives—not just the ordinary hives one can get for an hour or two after eating strawberries, but those God-awful, continuous, itching hives, which are so distressing and for which we had no drugs at that time. I had several patients who were suffering terribly from them, and one, in particular, was a very dear friend. This is one of the most difficult aspects of medical practice—the fact that your patients become your friends and you therefore become doubly worried about them. I remember, for example, the case of another close friend with whom I had gone to school and who later became a brilliant lawyer. I correctly diagnosed appendicitis, but during the operation he went bad under the anesthesia. I was terribly frightened, and I stood there at the operating table thinking about his wife and three children as I watched him sink. Fortunately, he recovered but the experience made me very sensitive about recommending surgery. If a patient had a clear-cut cancer of the stomach, or something of that kind, you had no choice. You went in and did your best, hoping you could give the individual a chance to live. But elective surgery was what drove me wild. In that era, gynecologists would routinely recommend hysterectomies and pelvic repairs for very minor pathology. I saw the young daughter of one of my older colleagues die while undergoing a pelvic repair for a situation she could have lived with to a ripe old age. But all this is a long way from my research on hives.

As it happened, I had a patient, a wealthy but rather eccentric widow, then in her seventies. She liked me and I liked her. When I told her I wanted to do research on hives, she gave me five thousand dollars, the first research money I had ever had. Then three other patients each gave me a thousand dollars or so, and I put together a team at the Jewish Hospital of St. Louis, where I was a member of the staff. We worked on the problem and began getting reasonably good results by putting patients on a high potassium, low sodium diet. *The Journal of the American Medical Association* published an article on our study, and a few weeks later one of the editors of the *Journal* sent his wife to me for the treatment, which was a thrill for a young doctor. As I look back on that whole experiment today, however, I am quite sure the potassium was not an actual specific for the hives. The therapy was the magic of patient-doctor relationship. Those patients improved because they believed—for the first time—that someone was interested in their problem and trying to help them. I was a young doctor then, and maybe I knew more about science than I did about people, but I learned rapidly. There is no substitute for tender loving care.

The depression came along just as my practice started to build and some 20 percent of my cases were "no charge"—nurses, doctors, ministers and people who simply couldn't pay. Another 20 percent paid part. Forty percent paid the usual fee, which was three dollars for an office call, and five dollars for a house call, and the other 20 percent were people of substance; they paid five dollars or ten dollars for an office call. Then when the serious depression set in, around 1931, '32 and '33, a lot of people were out of work, out of money and just living from hand to mouth. We sent them bills, which they weren't able to pay, although they were honest people and wanted to pay, and I began to notice that they weren't even coming in for anything. Apparently they were embarrassed. So I dictated a little note which we called Note D., for Depression, which said, "Dear ——: I know things must be difficult for you now as they are for everyone else. But I don't want you to neglect your health for that reason. I want you to know you're welcome to come in here any time you have the need. I'll send you no bill. When times get better, I know you'll pay." They continued their treatments, and after the depression practically all of them met their obligations and remained steadfast friends.

The years went by and I did more and more research. The projects weren't earthshaking, but they were interesting, and I got great satisfaction out of seeing my articles published in medical journals. I was interested in obesity and think I was one of the first to recommend a high-protein, low-carbohydrate diet with limited salt and added potassium. I was by this time a member of the staff at Barnes Hospital, chairman of the Intern Committee at St. Luke's Hospital, which was my first love because I had interned there, and a teacher at Washington University Medical School. My practice had grown so much that I had taken on three associates—a very bright doctor named Harold Newman, whose wife was an anesthetist at St. Luke's; a young expert in gastroenterology named Bruce Kenamore, who went into the Air Force about the same time as myself; and an excellent cardiologist named Julius Jensen, a scholarly Dane, who has since written a number of fine books on his specialty. On what we called our long days, we would see as many as seventy-five patients among us, maybe more, since there were also house calls and hospital rounds afterward. I can't understand doctors who refuse to make house calls. If you have accepted the responsibility for a patient and he becomes acutely ill at home, you must go see him. You can't dodge it, unless you have an assistant who is qualified to go in your place. Another thing, your patients become your friends, and if your friend needs you, then you simply have to go.

All of this meant that I was very busy. But a doctor can't complain about that. On a typical morning, I would get up early and ride for three quarters of an hour. Then I would jump in and out of the shower, gobble my breakfast the way I advised my patients not to do, and make my first house call a little before 8 A.M. After four or five calls, I would get to the university for my teaching stint about 10 A.M., and at noon I usually had to be downtown to examine insurance patients—this was my bread and butter—so I took no lunch hour. My office hours began at one and lasted on some days until four, on other days till six. Then I would have three or four more house calls, followed by hospital rounds. With good luck, I'd get home around eight or nine o'clock.

A few years earlier, Glad and I had bought five beautiful acres in a lovely section just outside St. Louis that was ideal for keeping horses. We built our house there, in which we planned to raise our family (three children) and live forever. We had ample bedrooms, a paneled study, a play room for the kids, woods all around and, of course, a stable. Riding was our favorite hobby, and besides our horses we had two ponies for the children.

We were living comfortably in those days, yet I was still restless and vaguely dissatisfied with what I was doing. Maybe it isn't fair to call it dissatisfaction, however, for in the late thirties all of us were restless. It took only a glance in the direction of Europe to realize that we were heading for a terrible conflict. So on that fateful December 7, 1941, I knew the war would be long and tough, and that I had a place in it. I could have stayed out of it if I'd wanted to; I was too old to be drafted. But sometimes a person does things because he feels that he has to do them. Thus I began making contacts with the Army, Navy and the Air Force, beginning my military experience and facing challenges that were bewildering and frightening, but which stirred my blood.

CHAPTER

· ·

IV

· ·

THE NEED TO DEVELOP A PROGRAM of complete rehabilitation for war-damaged men did not dawn on me suddenly. My basic concept of it probably began without my realizing it while I was a doctor in St. Louis, and it was my Air Force experience that made me concentrate on such problems.

I remember one very tough sergeant at the Jefferson Barracks hospital who had a leg off and a badly burned face. He frightened me because he was so bitter, so bewildered and so helpless when it came to working out for himself some kind of plan for the rest of his life. His symptoms were as easy to diagnose as a measles rash. He was full of anxiety about being accepted as a man, accepted by his family, accepted as a worker and a dignified human being. Something had to be done for this boy. The country owed him more than just an artificial leg, a discharge and the Purple Heart.

Before I left Jefferson Barracks I met some other boys like him, back from combat, shot up and hurt deep down inside. They were different from any patients I had treated before. When you talked to them you were talking to men who had really been through combat, who had really had it. When they looked at you their eyes seemed to be saying: You're not a member of our fraternity. You and your silly convalescent program, how much do you know about the real world out there, and what we need when we come back here. You haven't been to war; you have to see it and be in it to know it.

The Army Air Forces had already begun air evacuation of the wounded from Europe and Africa. The planes that took supplies to Europe had primitive stretchers strapped into them and seats for the walking wounded. They were attended by flight surgeons, air evacuation nurses and specially trained corpsmen. They were usually landed at Mitchel Field in New York, and anyone who ever saw a planeload of them come in would never forget it—or want to see another. Boys with burns, and half their faces blown away, without arms or legs, boys with broken backs.

We didn't know much about rehabilitating broken backs in those days. I always felt a terrible inadequacy and insecurity when I looked at those kids. They needed something far beyond the ordinary type of medical care we were providing.

I recall someone asking me how paraplegics had lived up to that time. The answer was, except in extremely rare cases, they usually died—their life expectancy in those days was often less than a year. They got terrible bedsores, developed kidney and bladder problems, and simply lay in bed, waiting for death. It was almost the same with strokes. The old wives' tale was that you had one stroke, and then you sat around waiting for a second one, or a third one, or however many it took to kill you. If you had any kind of brain injury affecting your locomotive functions, everyone assumed your life was finished.

I should say almost everyone felt that way. I was not, of course, the first person ever to be concerned with rehabilitation. There was no organized movement at the time, but for many years there had been people who worried about the fate of the disabled and who tried to do something about it. Their work was not well known, and like most doctors, I was virtually ignorant of their efforts.

Later, a patient of mine and a good friend, Orin Lehman, prepared a graduate thesis in which he studied the origins of the rehabilitation concept. He found that one of the prime movers in this country had been Dr. Simon Baruch, whose son, Bernard Baruch, will figure very prominently in this story as it progresses. Dr. Baruch, in 1885, when he was chairman of the attending staff at Montefiore Hospital in New York, spoke of a goal at which we are still aiming today: "It will be a proud achievement when our records will tell that a goodly proportion of those who have entered our gates only to die in peace have again issued from them entirely or partially restored and enabled again to enter upon the battle of life from which they had regarded themselves as permanently banished."

The elder Baruch was not completely alone. In Cleveland a group called the Sunbeam Circle had founded a school to train crippled children in various crafts. My alma mater, the University of Pennsylvania medical school, early in the century appointed one of the first American professors of physical medicine. But I'm afraid this didn't make much of a dent in established medical thinking at the time. As years passed, various private philanthropies did what they could for disabled people. In Europe, during World War I, thanks to the inspiration of two Belgians, Paul Pastur and Azer Basque, the French founded a school to retrain disabled soldiers.

Here in America, in 1917, the Red Cross founded the Institute for Crippled and Disabled Men. Several states, as well as the federal government, passed laws from time to time with the aim of helping the disabled, but few techniques were developed and nothing was ever done on a wide scale, either in the armed forces or in civilian life. One of our most immediate frustrations in early 1943 was that if we discharged these wounded and disabled veterans from the service—which we had to do since they could no longer function as soldiers—we were turning them over to the Veterans Administration, which at that time was like sending them into limbo. The V.A. had no program for them. They would simply lie around getting custodial care, with nothing to do, bored to distraction, helpless, hopeless, waiting for some kind of infection or disease to carry them off. Gradually the concept of rehabilitation came to me as I found out how much really could be done for these men. In the beginning, I knew only that everything possible should be done to return them to physical and mental health. This meant finding ways for them to function despite their disabilities. First, I had to remember that this was the Air Force, that we were fighting a desperate war, and that we needed all the manpower we could find. It was immediately important, then, to make these men in some way able again. Our initial aim had to be to send them back to duty in the best possible condition and in the shortest time. If they could no longer do their previous jobs, we should help them choose jobs they could do, and then retrain them. This approach would be beneficial to the Air Force and it seemed the best for the boys themselves, too, because it would make them feel that despite their disabilities they could still function usefully. The next question was how to bring severely injured men back to mental as well as physical health. I knew we couldn't do it in our Air Force regional hospitals. We didn't have the room, the facilities or the personnel. It seemed also that such a program should not be attempted in a hospital atmosphere. If we wanted to convince these boys that they were not as disabled as they appeared to be, we ought to get them out of the hospitals and into pleasant surroundings which would improve their outlook. I began thinking about the possibility of opening special Air Force rehabilitation centers. By this time we already had special hospitals for treatment of specific illnesses. At Davis-Monthan Field in Tucson, Arizona, for example, we had a facility for rheumatic-fever patients which my friend Dr. Paul Holbrook helped conceive and organize. Rheumatic fever was a plague in those days. There was so much of it among the younger men, and we didn't yet know that penicillin would stop or prevent it. Our rheumatic-fever patients were hospitalized for weeks and weeks. Many of them were also suffering from rheumatic heart disease and all kinds of other complications, so we had set up this center in Tucson because of the hot, dry climate there.

As it happened, one of our first patients at Davis-Monthan was Lowell Thomas, Jr., son of the famous news commentator. Young Thomas made a perfect recovery. He was our first rheumatic-fever and rheumatic-carditis patient to return to full duty. He was able to complete his pilot training with no residual aftereffects. Because of his son's experience, Lowell Thomas, Sr., became interested in our convalescent program and came to see me in Washington. Our meeting soon passed the subject of convalescence and I began telling him of my newly developing dreams of rehabilitation.

He sparked to it immediately. "You know," he said, "up in Pawling, New York, where I live, there's a wonderful school that's been closed. And next to it there's also a fine recreation area, which the Consolidated Edison company developed for its employees. I think you might be able to put both of them together. If you did, you'd have an ideal situation. Besides that, we've got a wonderful community in Pawling, with very interesting people. I know they'll get in and pitch like fury if there's anything they can do to help you."

The upshot of this was that General Grant and I went to Pawling and looked the place over. General Grant was behind the idea all the way, and we both agreed that everything Lowell Thomas had said about the Pawling facilities was true. The community was very helpful; we were soon at work, enlarging and refurbishing the school.

General Arnold did something that same summer of 1943 that helped the program enormously. It also showed what kind of man he was. When the Army Air Forces began getting the first amputees back from battle, most of them had to go to an Army general hospital first (since the Air Force was still part of the Army), and we didn't get them until weeks or months later, after they had been fitted by the Army for artificial limbs. General Arnold and General Grant were both unhappy about this. These were our boys and we wanted them right away because we thought we could do more for them than the Army could. There was a continuing fight about it, but we seemed to be losing.

At the Walter Reed Hospital, which was then starting a comprehensive amputee program combined with a convalescent unit at adjacent Forest Glen, there was a remarkable man named Henry Viscardi, Jr., working for the Red Cross. He had been born with only rudimentary legs and didn't walk until after surgery when he was twenty-six. He learned to walk beautifully with specially designed limbs, and he took this job with the Red Cross. He was supposed to teach the amputees at Walter Reed to walk. But for some reason he didn't get along with the physiotherapists there, so he would get the boys out behind the bushes on the hospital lawn and give them secret lessons. Imagine the irony: boys who had lost their legs for their country having to sneak out of a service hospital and go behind the bushes to get their walking lessons! And the reason they did it was that Viscardi had great empathy for them. After all, he was in the same situation. If anyone could understand what they needed, he could.

One day he walked into my office in the Pentagon with the three angriest young men I had ever seen. All three were Air Force pilots who had lost legs, and they were sizzling.

"Is this what you get when you give your leg to your country?" one of them asked. "A goddamn papier-mâché replacement?"

"Look here," the second one said, rolling up his pant-leg. "I fell down getting on a bus and almost got run over because one of the rivets came out."

Difficult as it may be to believe, these boys actually did have papier-mâché legs—the cheapest, most unreliable kind you can imagine. The Army policy at that time was to give amputees temporary limbs, and after discharging them from service, to send them to the Veterans Administration, where they would presumably be fitted with good, permanent limbs. But this was a questionable policy because the Veterans Administration had no program for providing first-class limbs.

When I saw these three boys with their temporary legs, I knew it was time to strike. We all went to General Grant's office, and as I began unfolding their story to him I could see his face get redder and redder. Finally, without even hearing me through, he picked up the "squawk-box" and asked for General Arnold. Two minutes later, the air surgeon was marching us all down the hall to the commanding general's office. When General Arnold heard these boys' stories and took a look at their legs, he got so mad I thought he was about to have a stroke. He reached over and pushed down every button on his squawk-box. In ran Robert Lovett, the Assistant Secretary of War for Air, along with a flood of three- and four-star generals.

By this time, General Arnold was on his feet, pacing back and forth behind his desk. "This is the goddamnedest outrage I ever saw!" he cried. "I'm too old to fly these airplanes, and so are all of you. These boys are doing it for us. They're fighting for our lives. I spend all my time trying to get them the best airplanes, the best gasoline, the best clothes, the best food, the best of everything. By God, they're going to have the best legs." With that, he grabbed his telephone, called the Army surgeon general, and began dressing him up one side and down the other. "Not only are we going to get these boys the best legs available," he said, "we're also going to do research to develop some better legs. And if you don't get started on it within thirty days, I'll go directly to the President."

General Arnold was a formidable man when he became aroused and in a few weeks we had much more than just an Army research project. We had a new law, passed by Congress, setting up the prosthetic research program with an adequate budget that still operates today, providing the best possible artificial arms and legs for our wounded veterans.

When we took possession of the Pawling school and our

rehabilitation program was almost a reality, we had to do something quickly about getting doctors trained to run it. So we began scrounging for qualified people and searching for places to get them trained. I noticed that Columbia University was offering a summer course in care for the disabled, and General Grant gave permission for one of our bright young officers to go to New York and sit in on it.

The day this young officer returned to Washington, sometime in late July, I called him into my office to report.

"Everything I learned of any practical value," he said, "I learned in about half a day from a doctor named George G. Deaver. He's the medical director at a place called the Institute for the Crippled and Disabled at Twenty-third Street and First Avenue, and it seems to me he's one man who knows what he's doing."

Some checking of the situation showed that the Institute for the Crippled and Disabled in New York had been founded during World War I with funds from a philanthropist named Jeremiah Milbank; its primary aim was to provide vocational training for disabled people. I came to New York, met Dr. Deaver and liked him immediately. We talked at length with Colonel John Smith, the administrator, about the kind of training rehabilitation personnel needed, and then I asked, "Do you think you could set up such a program?"

Deaver smiled at me and said, "We've already offered a program like that to the Army. We've also offered it to the Veterans Administration. They both said they didn't need it."

"We need it in the Air Force," I said.

"We'll be glad to do it for you," he replied. "It shouldn't take more than six months to set up."

"Impossible," I said. "It can't take six months. We want to send you the first group in three weeks."

Dr. Deaver shrugged and smiled. "In that case, three weeks it'll be."

I recall another incident that day. When I was waiting for the elevator to go up to Dr. Deaver's office, a little girl with cerebral palsy came struggling along on her crutches. Following her was a girl in a sparkling new wheelchair. The girl on crutches glared at the girl in the wheelchair and said, "You're such a rich bitch I guess you don't have to struggle to walk. You can ride around in your fancy wheelchair, but I've got to work every step of the way."

The girl in the wheelchair didn't answer, but I could see how angry she was. I soon learned that she was Betsy Barton, daughter of Bruce Barton, the advertising executive. She had broken her back in an accident and the other girl's remark had a tremendous effect on her. She was so mad, she decided she had to learn to walk.

I happened to be there later when she began her training. Four young Air Force doctors were on hand to encourage her, but she was fearful at first. I told her, "Go ahead, Betsy, walk. You've got a doctor in front of you, a doctor behind you and one on each side. They're all handsome, and none of them will let you fall."

She smiled and started to take her first step since her accident. Within a short time she walked like a dream, and after that she was helping the Air Force people who came to New York to study Dr. Deaver's methods. We sent doctors, physical educators, therapists—all types of personnel—and the school grew so rapidly, we soon had to move it from the Institute for the Crippled and Disabled quarters in New York City to Mitchel Field on Long Island.

By then Dr. Deaver was training as many as two hundred Air Force people at a time. We all looked upon him with tremendous respect because he was the man who actually proved that paraplegics could walk. It was his idea that if it was possible to walk on stilts, then it was possible to walk on paralyzed legs, provided they were properly braced. The first patient to prove it for him was a man named "Hod" Mansur, who had been a paraplegic for many years but who had a great motivation to walk and did. Betsy Barton was the second, and both of them were very helpful to us, demonstrating to our paraplegics that walking was possible.

By this time I had met General Arnold's wife (Bea to her friends), who was head of a ladies' organization called the Air Force Emergency League. When I told her what we were hoping to do, she was so enthusiastic she made an appointment for us to have lunch with Mrs. Eleanor Roosevelt at the White House. I'll never forget that lunch—it was almost the worst I ever ate. Mrs. Roosevelt was such a sincere person she had decided that if other people in the country had to suffer from rationing, then the White House should also suffer. So we ate boiled eggs with some kind of cream sauce, a little wisp of salad with a gelatin for dessert, and that was all. Of course, the food was incidental. The important result of the lunch was that Mrs. Roosevelt became a supporter of the program, and as I learned later, she interested President Roosevelt in it as well.

Shortly thereafter, Mrs. Arnold invited Glad and me to dinner with the general so I'd have a chance to give him a complete picture of what we were doing. It was a pleasant evening, but I remember feeling somewhat frustrated. Here I was, still a lieutenant colonel, thinking I would have the ear of the Air Force Commanding General for a whole evening.

When we arrived, however, he was upstairs trying to help his son with his algebra homework. At dinner I was seated next to him, and I was talking a mile a minute, making what seemed to me excellent points when suddenly there was a knock on the front door and in came General C. R. Smith. In civilian life he had been the president of American Airlines, and he entered the Air Force to serve as an assistant to General Arnold. He had just flown in from England and had with him the first copy of a film about a flying fortress called the *Memphis Belle* that he thought General Arnold would be eager to see. His arrival ended the discussion of rehabilitation. From then on, we all watched the film. It's amusing in retrospect—I was so annoyed when the film started I was determined not to like it, but this saga of a bomber in combat was so good, I couldn't help enjoying it, and that annoyed me even more. I needn't have worried, though. General Arnold was a man who caught on fast. He had understood everything I was trying to tell him, and became a driving force behind both the convalescent and rehabilitation programs.

By the end of 1943, the Pawling center was almost ready to receive its first patients. The training program for rehabilitation personnel in New York under Dr. Deaver had created so much interest we had people fighting to get into it. One such person was a fellow named Eugene J. "Jack" Taylor, a sergeant in Miami Beach who had been the first instructor in the convalescent program there. He felt he had exhausted the possibilities in Florida, and having heard about Dr. Deaver's course he was determined to take it.

Alfred Fleishman, who had become a major, was then in charge of inspecting our convalescent centers around the country. One day, when he arrived in Miami Beach, he was confronted by a very determined Sergeant Jack Taylor.

"Each time you send us a list of men to transfer to New York," Taylor said, "I look for my name. How come you haven't sent me?"

"Because they need you here," Major Fleishman explained.

"They do not need me here," Taylor insisted. "This program is running like a clock. And if you're getting ready to start something new, I want to be part of it. I'll tell you frankly, sir, unless you give me a chance to be a part of it, to hell with you. I know what you can do to me for talking that way. You can put me on kitchen police. You can penalize me in a lot of ways. But I've done a good job for you down here and there's no more challenge in it. I want to go someplace where there's a challenge."

Fleishman knew that you can't penalize a man when he has an attitude like that. Jack Taylor's name was on the list for the next shipment of men to New York. But that didn't quite satisfy him either. He asked for a three-day delay en route, which was fairly easy to get in those days, and he came to Washington asking to see me. We had met once when I was in Miami Beach on an inspection trip, and I had praised his work, which was easy to do. In civilian life he had been a teacher, and he had worked out the details of the whole program down there.

As it happened, I was pretty busy that day, and while the sergeant was waiting to see me, Fleishman said to him, "Listen, Taylor, you know the educational field. Colonel Rusk has to make a speech in New York to the American Association for Health, Physical Education and Recreation. I've done a draft of it but he doesn't like it. Why don't you take a crack at it for me?"

By the time I could see Taylor, he was already at work on the speech—my first major speech before a nonmedical audience—and it was so well received that *The New York Times* printed a three-quarter-column story on it. More important, it was the beginning of a lasting relationship. Jack Taylor is still associated with me at the Institute of Rehabilitation Medicine in New York as an adjunct professor on the New York University faculty, and as secretary-treasurer of the World Rehabilitation Fund.

We officially opened the first Air Force rehabilitation center at Pawling on a bitter cold day in early 1944. Glad and I flew up from Washington with General and Mrs. Arnold and Mrs. Helen Reid, the publisher of the New York *Herald Tribune*. It was an exciting experience. When we arrived at Pawling, a large number of reporters were waiting for us, but if they were expecting the usual kind of military ceremony they must have been surprised. There were no brass bands, nor men standing at attention. Pawling just wasn't that kind of institution. At the time of the opening we had about ninety men already there, but some of them didn't even bother to show up for the ceremony. I guess you might describe the Pawling center as a combination of a hospital, a country club, a school, a farm, a vocational training center, a resort and a little bit of home as well. The discipline was minimal and the program informal. Old regular Army people would have shuddered, but fortunately General Arnold didn't have the traditional Army man's outlook. He made a nice short speech reaffirming his full support of the program and his conviction that it would prove its worth, not only by returning men to healthy lives, but by returning many of them to duty.

After the speech, we went on a tour of the place, and when we reached the farm that was part of the property we found a half-dozen airmen in one of the buildings, butchering hogs.

The hogs were hung up by their hind feet and the place was steaming from the scalding water used for eviscerating and scraping. The first thing that struck you about these fellows was that they had butchered hogs before. They were so absorbed in their work, they didn't even stop and come to attention when the commanding general of the Air Force appeared. They simply went on with their butchering while I stood there wondering if I shouldn't call them to attention.

But after watching them for two or three minutes, General Arnold edged around to where he was sure they could see him. "Hello, boys," he said.

They said, "Hello, General." They were scraping like mad and they didn't stop for a moment.

"What are you doing?" the general asked.

"Butchering hogs."

"Why?" It was a reasonable question. Even in a hospital like this you would hardly expect to find the patients butchering hogs.

"We're doing it because we want to," one of them said. "We all came from farms and we like to butcher hogs."

General Arnold shrugged. "Well, don't let me stop you."

"We can't stop, General," another of them said. "We've got to keep going while the hogs are still hot."

One of them spat some tobacco juice on the floor and said, "This is the best time we've had since we've been back from combat."

General Arnold said, "Fine, do a good job." Then, with a smile on his face, he turned and walked out.

Pawling was the first of twelve such centers the Air Force opened during World War II. Some of the boys there had physical disabilities; others had psychological disabilities. Many had a combination of the two. A lot of them had simply flown too many missions and had become what we call hostile aggressives. They wanted to go out and punch some civilian in the nose. They were not easy to manage, but that was exactly why we felt they should be in a center like Pawling, where they could be away from the atmosphere of a hospital or the Army, and in a community with understanding and sensitivity.

It has often been said that anyone who tells you he is not afraid in battle is either a fool or a liar. I'm convinced it is also true that everyone, no matter how brave he might be, has a breaking point, an end point beyond which he can't go either physically or emotionally. If we were to put fifty-pound weights on a dozen people and tell them they had to run around the block until they dropped, they would all drop at different places. When you talk about a person's being normal, you're only saying he's comfortable and functional in a particular environment which he has found for himself. We published a study in the early days of the program in which we defined a "normal" person as one who is self-supporting, or capable of self-support, and who is oriented in his environment. We used three examples to illustrate this:

The first was a street sweeper in New York, a good man with an excellent job record but rather strange in other ways. He almost never spoke to anyone. He lived in an old hut down near the East River where he kept six or eight cats and a couple of dogs. He was living a comfortable enough life when he was drafted into the Air Force. Within three or four hours he was brought to the hospital in a complete state of panic. What do you do with this man? The only thing you can do: you discharge him from the service. He returns to his hut, his pets and his broom, and he's "normal" again.

Example two was a teacher of Shakespeare, a very bright

man. The Air Force doesn't need many Shakespeare teachers, so he's sent to school to become a tail-gunner on a bomber. He does all right in training. He becomes a tail-gunner and shows no sign of stress until he gets to the staging area for combat. Then he passes his end point and he develops a bleeding ulcer—just like the boys I used to meet at Jefferson Barracks who got ulcers just from the experience of being in the Army and undergoing basic training. You could treat that man's ulcer until doomsday to no avail. You could give him antacids or milk, or put him on a strict diet. You could even operate and remove the ulcer, but he would get new ones. As long as he remained in a combat environment he could not endure, his ulcer would just not heal.

The third example was the type of person who could endure combat—a type of which there are many gradations. We found that among those men who went on missions some could fly five without a rest period, others could fly fifty. But whatever their endurance, they all had end points, and a flight surgeon could read the signs as they approached that point. They lost their appetite, slept poorly, had bad dreams and would wake up screaming. If a flight surgeon read these signs correctly and pulled a man off duty for a two- or three-week rest, usually the man could fly combat again.

This was only one of the many areas in which the flight surgeons did outstanding work in preventive medicine. They lived with their men, watched them closely, and learned to pick up these symptoms early. They were doctors in the true sense.

In spite of this care, a lot of men in combat did reach the breaking point and needed a place like Pawling. Eventually, we had between four and five hundred patients there, beat-up boys from battlefronts all over the world. About one third of these boys had purely psychological problems from flying fatigue, while the other two thirds had severe physical disabilities, which, of course, were often coupled with psychological problems. During the formal opening, Quentin Reynolds, the great war correspondent and author, had come up from New York City with the press contingent. There was an unusual boy there named Gordon Manuel, whom Lowell Thomas had already met, and whom he introduced to Reynolds. The boy was so fascinating Reynolds decided to write a book about him

Gordon Manuel had been a tail-gunner on B-24 bombers in the Pacific, flying out of New Britain Island, near the huge Japanese air base at Rabaul. Before going into service, he had been a Maine woods guide, so he was most resourceful. On one mission, his plane was shot down by the Japanese, and he and another member of the crew parachuted into the sea. It didn't do the second boy much good, because the Japanese planes came around again and riddled him with bullets. But Manuel's parachute had only opened halfway, so that when he hit the water the impact was great enough to break one of his legs. While that seemed to be disastrous at the moment, it turned out for the best. Because his chute opened only partially, he had descended faster, and when the enemy planes came around to strafe him, he was able to duck underwater out of sight. He floated until dark, and then crawled onto the beach of the nearest island and dragged himself into the jungle. The next morning he set his own leg, bound it with a splint made of sticks and vines, and began searching for food. It was dangerous to eat jungle vegetation unless you knew what it was, so he would wait until dark, then crawl back down to the beach and catch shellfish or whatever happened along. Once he killed a snake, and he feasted for two or three days on the meat.

After about three weeks, his leg began to heal and he could move around better. One day a native found him and indicated he would go get help for him, but Manuel, for some reason, suspected that the man intended to turn him in to the Japanese. Instead of waiting for the man to return, he plunged deep into the jungle and eventually was discovered by other natives, who seemed to him more friendly and trustworthy. His instincts were apparently good, because these people brought him to a group of fifteen or twenty other American Air Force boys who had come down in the jungle and were also hiding. After scrounging around awhile, Manuel and his new friends took a radio from a crashed plane, eventually made it work, and contacted the nearest American base. Their elation was short-lived, however, because the Americans they reached didn't believe their story. It sounded like a plot by English-speaking Japanese to lure an American force onto the strongly held island. Finally, Manuel figured out how to make it abundantly clear they were Americans. He reviled the radio operators at the other end with every profane word he knew. It must have been effective, for the next day American planes dropped guns and equipment to them, and they began their own private war against the Japanese. Manuel said they killed more than one hundred enemy soldiers in the jungle before an American submarine was able to come in one night and pick them up. Manuel, who had been a sergeant, was commissioned immediately, but he was not yet well, so he was returned to the States and sent to Pawling.

When Quentin Reynolds heard the bare outline of his story, he got Manuel to take a week's leave. The two of them locked themselves up in Reynolds' New York apartment while Manuel told all the details, and Reynolds recorded them for a book entitled *70,000 to 1*. I wish I could say the saga of Gordon Manuel ended on this happy note, but his combat fatigue was so severe that treatment was ineffective and he died shortly after the war—a real hero.

The commanding officer at the Pawling center was Major Hobart M. Todd. He was ideal for the job, not only because he had been a flight surgeon in combat, but because before we had fully developed the Air Force convalescent program, he had been badly wounded and had lain for six months in one hospital after another, staring at the walls while he waited for his recovery. No one had to explain to him the importance of the rehabilitation program. He had an immediate feeling for what we were trying to do. He made sure the food was superb; he kept close contact with the men and encouraged their families to keep coming to see them. And without laying down a lot of rules, he maintained discipline through persuasion and friendliness. He was helped in this by the fact that Pawling was a nice place to be and most of the boys appreciated it. But their problems were often too great for their environment to overcome.

We had a special problem, for instance, with some of the married men. Many of them had been married only a few days or weeks before being shipped out to combat. Husbands and wives didn't really know each other. This, added to the problems and disabilities the boys had developed in battle, created severe tensions both for them and their wives. It was a bad situation, and we were trying to think of what to do about it when General Jimmie Doolittle's wife, Jo, came to visit us. She and my wife, Glad, were talking about the problem, and Glad said, "Those girls seem to need rehabilitation as much as their husbands." She turned to me and said, "Why don't you set up some kind of program for them?"

I said, "Maybe we could, if Jo would like to run it for us."

Jo Doolittle carried the ball from there. She went up to Pawling, gathered the patients' wives together for a meeting, told them what she had in mind and gave them a questionnaire to fill out about the subjects in which they were most interested. They included such things as child care, interior decoration, charm, golf, cooking, etc., and the winner by several lengths was "charm"—which was not surprising. The girls obviously felt that if they were more attractive, their husbands would be happier and their marriages would be sounder. So that was the first course Jo set up for them. We contacted Helena Rubinstein and Du Barry's, and when they heard about our predicament they sent lots of samples and some of their top beauty operators and hairdressers to Pawling, and simply took over the course. It's not hard to imagine how well received it was. Then Jo Doolittle, working without portfolio, went all over the country, establishing the same kind of program for the wives at other rehabilitation centers as we opened them, and every place she went she was a great success.

I don't want to give the impression that Pawling was just a country club for the boys and a beauty parlor for their wives. Besides the fun, there was a lot of hard work. We gave courses in French, Spanish, accounting, civil and military law, photography, astronomy, graphic arts, instrument flying, journalism, navigation, physics, radio mechanics, radio production, shorthand, typing, woodwork, salesmanship, and many other subjects. When a boy arrived at Pawling, it was impossible to know whether we were training him for a return to duty in the Air Force, or a return to civilian life. If he was severely disabled, of course, we would have to assume we were getting him ready for civilian life. And by offering the widest possible variety of courses, we were usually able to get the boy himself to choose the direction in which he should go.

There were some boys, though, who had become so withdrawn as a result of their battle experience that it was difficult to get through to them. I remember one in particular. He wasn't hostile or aggressive. He just wouldn't talk to anybody—not to the doctors, the nurses or his fellow patients. It seemed as if no one up there could get through to him. One day, a Red Cross Gray Lady, who had a very nice way about her, decided she would give him a try.

"Hello," she said.

"Hello," he said.

"How are you?" she said.

He shrugged and turned away.

The next day she tried again, and the next day and the next day, until she began to get as discouraged as everyone else who had tried.

Finally one day, in exasperation, she said to him, "Isn't there anything in the world you want?"

He looked up at her and said, "Why should I tell you? I can't have it anyway."

"You can at least tell me what it is."

"All right. There's only one thing I want. A dog."

"A dog!" she said. "In a place like this? Why?"

"Because I've always liked dogs. I like to work with them and train them. I could take a dog for a walk in the woods and he wouldn't ask me a lot of silly questions."

The poor woman may have been somewhat bewildered, and she may have felt unwanted, but the one additional question she asked him went straight to the heart of the matter. "What kind of a dog do you want?"

"I'd take any kind," he said, "but I'd prefer a cocker spaniel about two or three months old."

Before nightfall the boy had his dog, and it was the key to his whole rehabilitation. He trained it, and all the other boys became interested in it. He began to talk and to open up in general. Soon he was just one of the boys.

This created an amusing complication. Before long everyone wanted a dog, and we had to make a decision. We did a bit of agonizing over it until someone asked, "Why not?"

Major Todd, the commanding officer, called the boys together and said, "All right, anyone who wants a dog can have one. We'll even get it for you, provided you're responsible for it. You've got to train it and housebreak it, and make sure it doesn't become a nuisance."

From then on, we had almost as many dogs as people. Outside the mess hall at noon there was always an absolute pack of dogs, from Great Danes to fox terriers, but all tied up to trees or chairs or benches, waiting for their masters to come out. And before long we had added one more course to our curriculum: dog training.

There were times when I began to think Pawling was too successful. Some of the boys didn't want to leave. I remember one fellow named Palmer. He was a private first class who had gone through his rehabilitation program so well he was able to go back to duty when he was discharged from the center. But before returning to duty, he had a thirty-day furlough coming. When he left, everyone gave him a big send-off, and that was the last anyone at Pawling expected to see of him.

Three weeks later, a sergeant on the hospital staff was walking down the hall and there was Palmer, coming toward him.

"What are you doing here?" the sergeant asked. "I thought you were discharged. You're supposed to be on furlough."

"I am on furlough," Palmer said.

"Well, didn't you go home?"

"Sure, I spent almost three weeks at home."

"What brought you back here? Did you get readmitted?"

"No."

"What the hell are you doing here, then?"

"I've still got ten days left of my furlough," Palmer said. "But it's so nice here, I thought I'd come and stay until I have to report for duty."

Pleasant as it was at Pawling, however, it was not just the environment that made the rehabilitation concept work. If there was any one factor that made it—and all the other centers we eventually established—successful, it was the practice of assigning each man to a personal physician, or, as we called him, a family doctor, usually a junior medical officer. He had his office in the barracks and he knew his patients well because he actually lived with them. When he met a new arrival he would say, "I'm your doctor, just like your doctor at home. If you have any problems at any time, come to me. It's my job to help you solve them."

The value of the family doctor concept is best illustrated by the story about a boy who had come in from the Pacific in rather bad shape. His condition wasn't critical. He was ambulatory, although just barely. He had a severe back injury and he was suffering from chronic malaria. The day he arrived, the young doctor to whom he was assigned gave him the usual talk about being his doctor and told him to speak right up if he had any problems.

About an hour later, the boy came into the doctor's office and said, "Sir, I need a forty-eight-hour pass."

The medical officer looked at him as if he were mad. "A forty-eight-hour pass!" he said. "You've only been here an hour."

"I know but I have to have it."

"I can't give it to you."

The boy looked at him cynically and said, "I thought you told me if I needed help I should come to you."

"I did, but . . ."

"Well, take a look at this." He handed the doctor a letter which said, "This is to tell you I have never loved you. I never even really liked you and I hope I never see you again. I'm going out with any man that asks me to. Yours truly," and it was signed by his wife.

The young soldier said, "That's all right with me as far as it goes. She's never been any good anyway. But we've got a three-year-old son, and I don't think she gives a damn about him either. I've got to know he's being taken care of, and that's why I need the pass."

He got the pass, of course, and two days later, when the medical officer made his morning rounds, he was back. But the medical officer did a double take as he passed his bed because there were two heads on the pillow. The soldier had brought his three-year-old son back with him.

The soldier peered up at the doctor and said, "Did you really mean it when you told me I should bring my problems to you, Doc? Because if you did, here's my problem."

Fortunately the medical officer was a real doctor. He told the man, "You did exactly right."

He contacted the Red Cross immediately and they found a foster home for the child right across the street from the base. He also called the judge advocate general who helped the man start divorce proceedings. By the time he was ready to leave the hospital, his sister had offered to take care of the little boy, and that young man went back to duty in perfect health. They could have treated his back and his malaria and anything else wrong with him, but if they hadn't solved the most important of all his problems, he would never have been rehabilitated.

AMERICA'S WAR CASUALTIES INCREASED as the year progressed, and both the convalescent and the rehabilitation
programs in the Air Force grew to keep pace with the
needs. We now had a sizable staff in Washington and
plenty of funds, as well as people to manage the more
than two hundred and fifty centers around the country—
which was amazing when you stop to think that during
our first year of operation we had run the whole program
by begging, borrowing or stealing everything we needed.
We had so little official authorization we bluffed our way
along half the time. The original two-paragraph directive
from General Grant and General Arnold in early 1943
covering the convalescent program was vague, since no
one had any conception of its scope, and as for the
rehabilitation program, there simply wasn't any official
authorization for it. All we could show was the short
speech General Arnold had made at the formal opening
of the Pawling center in which he had praised the idea of
rehabilitation and promised to back us up with any help
we needed. That speech was our salvation. I couldn't

count the number of times we pulled it out to wave at people who were refusing us things.

For example, Donald Covalt, a member of our Washington headquarters staff, was a champion at using General Arnold's speech to get us whatever we wanted, and he had Air Force Supply believing we were authorized to get absolutely any kind of equipment they had in stock. This led to a ludicrous incident when one day somebody brought Covalt a list of brand-new items that supply had just received. Since many of these items were listed only by number, Covalt put in an order for one of everything with the idea that he could then decide what we might need and send the rest back.

The supply department apparently did its best, but when the order was filled, there were six numbered items we didn't get. Covalt immediately called the supply officer.

"What do you mean, holding those things back?" he demanded. "You know General Arnold says we're to get anything we want."

"Yes, but I don't think you really want any of the six items you didn't get," the supply officer said.

"How do you know?"

"Because those are our six latest experimental airplanes."

Meanwhile Dr. George Deaver's training school for rehabilitation personnel at the Institute for the Crippled and Disabled in New York had outgrown its quarters, and Sergeant Eugene J. Taylor took charge of the job of moving it from the city to Mitchel Field on Long Island where there was more room. Jack was now a staff sergeant, but he was doing the work of an officer, and since he was constantly dealing with officers on what should have been equal terms, it was important to get him a commission. But we didn't want to let him go long enough to take the officers' training school course. Jack himself came up with the solution. He had a friend in personnel (he is the kind of fellow that has a friend everyplace), who suggested we write an order for twelve officers, to be commissioned directly from civilian life or from the enlisted ranks. He then enumerated the job qualifications these men would have to have, and strangely enough, those job qualifications were an exact description of Jack Taylor. I think everything was there except his weight, height, and the fact that he wore glasses. Needless to say, he was the only person we could find who qualified for any of the twelve commissions.

He did an excellent job at Mitchel Field, and we had a bang-up program there, for which we also had to thank the commanding officer at the field, Colonel O. K. Neiss, a bright, progressive young man who was very sympathetic to us, and who later became surgeon general of the Air Force. Dr. Deaver, who was still the medical director of the Institute for the Crippled and Disabled in New York, came out regularly to Mitchel, where many of the Air Force people he had trained were instructors, teaching physical rehabilitation subjects under his guidance. We were bringing in trainees from all over the Air Force to get their indoctrination there.

Mitchel Field was also our patient-distribution center on the East Coast, where the Air Force flew in wounded boys by the planeload, especially after D-Day in Normandy in the summer of 1944. Some of those boys hadn't been out of combat more than seventy-two hours when they got here. (Some of them hadn't been in combat more than a few minutes before they were wounded.) On arrival, the thing most of them asked for first was milk, and I often saw them drink two or three quarts without stopping. We had an arrangement that each man, as soon as he arrived, could make a long-distance call to his wife or girl friend or family. After that, if he was quite ill, he stayed at Mitchel until he was able to travel. Those who could travel were sent out, according to their needs, to the various hospitals around the country.

Because Mitchel Field was so close to New York, many New Yorkers volunteered money and services, especially the theater people. One was a producer named Dan Melnick, who was our angel. The casts of Broadway shows were constantly coming out to give performances, and I remember one afternoon when Dan appeared with the whole cast of *Oklahoma*. About two hours before the performance, four or five planeloads of boys arrived, almost all of them amputees, and we wheeled them right in, so they filled one whole side of the theater.

The first act was so good that at intermission I went backstage to speak to the cast. "I don't believe you know it," I said, "but there are at least fifty boys out there who have lost their legs, some of them just within the last week or two. During this last hour they've forgotten about their lost legs. You ought to see how excited and happy they are, getting a chance to see a show as wonderful as this. I just want to tell you what you're doing for those kids."

Well, if the first act was good, we hadn't seen anything yet. Throughout the rest of the show, every actor performed as if he were floating on a cloud. Later we discovered an ironic circumstance. He hadn't known it at the time, but one of the members of the troupe had a son sitting out there in a wheelchair—minus a leg.

I suppose it would be fair to say that the men who lost their legs were not as badly off as those who lost arms, because there have been crutches of one kind or another from time immemorial. On a tombstone which scientists have dated at

2380 B.C., there is a drawing of a man leaning on a shoulder-high stick with a crosspiece. But even as recently as World War II, and for some time after 1943, when Congress passed its prosthetic research bill at General Arnold's instigation, we didn't have really scientific, workable artificial arms. If a man lost his arms any place above the elbows, he was almost helpless.

With time, our concept of rehabilitation had grown, and we realized it was not enough just to treat a man's physical needs. We had to worry about his emotional, social, educational and occupational needs as well. We had to treat the whole man. And we also had to teach his friends and family how to accept him and help him in his new condition. There was a pilot whose face had been badly mangled and burned in combat. He had been a handsome man who had been married only a short time before he went overseas, and now his face looked so terrible that he didn't want his wife to see him, at least not until after he had completed his plastic surgery. But it was going to take a score of operations before he would be even halfway presentable. Meanwhile his young wife kept insisting that he see her; one day she came to the hospital and simply would not leave until he saw her. The doctor, Colonel James Barrett Brown, head of the Army Plastic Surgery Center at Valley Forge General Hospital, where the patient was having his surgery, talked to her and tried to reason with her. But he couldn't budge her, so he finally let her in, even though he was full of trepidation as he watched the scene.

When she came into the room her husband's back was turned. He was looking out the window, shaking with fear. But she walked directly to him, turned him toward her and kissed him, saying, "You never needed to worry about me, honey. I married a man, not a face."

The doctor left the room knowing he would never have to worry about that marriage.

Unfortunately, the split between the Army and the Air Force medical services was growing wider over the question of what should be done with Air Force battle victims, and over the whole concept of rehabilitation, especially for men with mental or emotional problems. The men who were returned to the Air Force directly from the battle zone went right into our regular rehabilitation program with all kinds of other patients. We didn't want to isolate them. We felt that in addition to psychiatric care they needed activities, schooling and retraining just as did men who had lost arms, legs or eyesight. But many Air Force battle casualties did not come back to us directly. The Army (which still controlled the Air Force, even though the Air Force, in many respects, acted independently) put thousands of them into its own hospitals. We wanted our boys turned over to us immediately because we didn't think the Army hospitals were giving them the total care they needed.

I was only a lieutenant colonel, so I was on the sidelines in this dispute, but it became so bitter at one point that President Roosevelt decided to send General Grant, the air surgeon, and General Magee, the Army surgeon general, around the world on an "inspection" trip in the hope that being together for such a period they would work out the problem. They were "chaperoned" by the distinguished senior consultant for the Army in psychiatry, Dr. Edward Strecker of Philadelphia. I wish I could say they settled the matter on that trip, but they did not.

About this time I was invited to speak at the *Herald*

Tribune Forum by the paper's publisher, Mrs. Helen Reid, and Bernard Baruch was scheduled to appear on the same program. I knew of his interest in the handicapped (an interest he had no doubt inherited from his father), because I was a member of the Baruch Committee on Physical Medicine.

I had never met Mr. Baruch, but when I got to New York for the speech, I called his secretary, and said I would like to have a short talk with him. She said if I came at two thirty in the afternoon I could have twenty minutes with him but no more.

When I arrived, he was just up from his after-lunch nap. As fast as I could, I told him the story of what we were doing in the Air Force and mentioned my connection with his committee.

He listened attentively, and when I was through he said, "That interests me very much. Now, young man, what is it that you want from me?"

I shook my head and said, "I don't want anything from you. I just wanted you to know about the program. The Air Force is solidly behind the rehabilitation concept, and we've got everything we need."

He looked at me skeptically and said, "Come on, now, everybody who comes to see me wants something."

I smiled sheepishly and said, "Well, maybe there is something I want from you at that. Only the Air Force has this program, you see. And I believe in it so much I think the Army and Navy should also have it. But I'm afraid they don't see it the way I do. I'd like to have the boys in the Army and Navy get the same breaks the Air Force boys are getting."

Baruch said, "That sounds reasonable," then looked at his watch. "I have to go down and get my throat sprayed," he said. "I'm speaking at the *Herald Tribune Forum* tonight. Do you want to ride along?"

I said I was also speaking, and would be delighted to ride along. In the car he asked me more questions, very pointed and precise questions about the Air Force rehabilitation setup. Finally, he said to me, "Do you think you can explain this whole program on one typewritten page?"

The idea startled me. I wasn't sure I had explained it to him adequately even in two hours of conversation, and I could not understand why he wanted it explained on just one page. Later, I learned that all his life he had a fetish about boiling things down and explaining even the most complicated matters on a single page. But in this instance, as I was to learn, he had another reason for it. I said I didn't know whether I could do it but I would try.

I went back to my hotel room that night and began trying to boil down my thoughts. I don't know how many times I rewrote that document. I single-spaced it on the typewriter, cut it, rewrote it, and deleted every adjective, but in spite of my efforts I couldn't get it any shorter than a page and a quarter, which seemed to me close enough.

I had an appointment with Mr. Baruch for ten o'clock the next morning, and when I showed him my page and a quarter he said, "It's fine except that it's too long. We've got to get it on one page."

I couldn't understand why it was so important, but if he said so, I guessed he knew what he was doing. The two of us then sat down and worked on it together for two hours. Finally, by starting at the very top of the page and using almost no margin, we were able to squeeze it onto one page.

"Now, son," he said, "I'm going to teach you a lesson. I'll show you what we're going to do with this. We're going to send it to the President, and here's how we'll do it."

He took a piece of his own stationery and wrote in substance: "My dear Mr. President, I am attaching a summary of a program that has deeply impressed me. I think it would do great good for our casualties returning from overseas. If you feel as I do, I suggest you sign the attached letter."

Then he wrote an attachment, which was to be a letter from President Roosevelt to the Secretary of War, Henry L. Stimson. It said: "My dear Mr. Secretary, I'm deeply concerned about our casualties returning from overseas, as I know you are. I would like you to see that no one is discharged from service until he has had the full benefit of hospitalization, which will include not only medical care but resocialization, psychological adjustment and rehabilitation. I would like you to see that this is put in operation as soon as possible."

If the President approved and signed it, this letter, along with our one-page summary of the Air Force rehabilitation program, would soon be on the desk of Secretary of War Stimson.

"Now, the lesson I want you to learn is this," Mr. Baruch said to me. "The President is a busy man. If we hadn't sent him the idea in the most concise possible form, and if we hadn't made it easy for him to send the word on to Secretary Stimson, there's a good chance he wouldn't have had time to go over it and it would have gotten lost in the pile of papers on his desk. But this way he's got the whole package in three sheets of paper, and all he has to do is sign his name to one of them."

When I returned to Washington two days later, I quickly understood how clever a man Baruch was. All hell had broken loose. The Secretary of War had already ordered the Army to start a rehabilitation program. The Joint Chiefs of Staff had appointed a special committee, and the surgeon general was rushing off in nine directions trying to find old camps that could be converted into rehabilitation centers. And soon after that, at a cocktail party, I overheard a general say, "We know this is the work of that so-and-so Rusk. We recognized his wording. But what we can't figure out is how the hell he did it."

The Army scrambled like crazy. They brought consultants in to develop a program and they put a lot of effort into it, but it never worked. The reason was simple. Instead of doing it informally, and in a relaxed atmosphere, with personal physicians for every patient, they did it the Army way, by the numbers. If you were in Class I-A you were to play basketball 10:15 to 11:10; you were to take three laps around the track from 11:15 to 11:35; and so forth. They made a sincere effort, but the war was over before they actually got it off the ground.

There's one postscript to this story. About ten days after the Army announced its rehabilitation program, I was in New York again and I went to thank Bernard Baruch for what he had done. After accepting my thanks graciously, he pulled out a copy of a letter he had just written to the President and said, "Now, take a look at this."

"Dear Boss," the letter said. "You really hit a home run when you made that decision on the rehabilitation of the returning veterans. Congratulations. It was great."

When I finished reading it, Mr. Baruch said, "You know, he's human too."

As everyone knows, President Roosevelt died in April 1945, shortly before the war came to an end, and my fellow Missourian, Harry Truman, replaced him in the White House. The Germans surrendered in May 1945, and in July Mr. Truman had to go to Potsdam, where, for the first time, he was to meet Winston Churchill and Joseph Stalin.

With Japan's surrender in sight, there was already much talk about reorganizing the Veterans Administration, which most people agreed should be done as soon as peace came. I had known Mr. Truman for a good many years and he apparently had confidence in me, because he called me in and told me he'd like me to have a hand in whatever was done with the V.A. He thought it would be a good idea for me to go to the Potsdam Conference with his entourage, and though his real purpose was to have me talk to General Omar Bradley, who had been chosen to take charge of the V.A., he suggested that to minimize speculation about why I was there, I should go as General Arnold's doctor. The general had suffered four or five coronaries, and though he was still vigorous, he did need a doctor with him on a mission as important as the Potsdam conference.

We were to leave Washington on July 10, but before we left, it seems to me I got advice from everyone in the Air Force about how to take care of General Arnold. The people around that man really loved him. Especially Brigadier General Charles R. Glenn, a tough old regular who had known him, I guess, as long as anybody. Charlie got hold of me one day and said, "Now listen, Howard, you've got a hell of a responsibility. Hap has got to come back here as healthy as he leaves because we need him. You've got to save him, which may mean you'll have to save him from himself. I know what can happen to him. He gets into those meetings and his temper flares and his blood pressure goes up and he beats on the table and gets red in the face. When he reaches that point, you've got to get him out of there. But if I know him he won't want to leave. He'll call you every name in the book. The thing to do is stand right up and talk back to him. With good luck you'll wear him down."

I gulped uncomfortably and said, "Thank you for the advice."

We took off from Washington just before midnight on July 10 in a converted C-54. It was an enormous thrill for me. In our party, besides General Arnold, were General of the Army George Marshall, Lieutenant General John Hull, Major General Lauris Norstad and six other Army and Air Force officers, including myself. I was in awe of General Marshall, of course, as was almost everyone who ever met him. He was a very dignified, private sort of person, and there are stories that even President Roosevelt didn't call him by his first name. That may have been true, but I noticed that Hap Arnold called him George, and they got along like a couple of old pals.

It was a typically hot July night in Washington when we left, but when we reached Mingan, Quebec, a thousand miles distant, on the first leg of our journey, it was cold and rainy. We got off the plane at 5 A.M., and as we walked toward the mess hall, General Arnold said to General Marshall, "I want to tell you a story about this mess, George. I landed here the second of January 1942 on my way to London. It was about this time of morning, and when we went into the mess, do you know what they offered us? Cold boiled potatoes, Brussels sprouts, mutton covered with fat, and tea. I screamed, 'What the hell kind of food is this for an American Air Force base?' To which the commanding officer said, 'We're sorry, General, but we can't make much fuss about it because we have a contract with the Canadians and they run the mess.' I said to him, 'I'll be damned if they're going to run a mess like this. If our boys have to sit up here in this God-awful hole, with no recreation, and in a terrible climate, at least they're going to have good food.' I got right on the phone to

Barney Giles (an Air Force general and General Arnold's executive officer in Washington) and I got him out of bed and I told him what I had for breakfast here. I said, 'Damn it, Barney, first thing in the morning I want a plane to take off from Bolling Field loaded with pancakes, fresh eggs, sausages, oranges, beef, everything. I'll be back through here in five days and if this isn't the best mess in the Air Force, you're in trouble.' When I came back here five days later, the food was great. But that was three years ago. Now let's see how it is this morning."

Apparently the people at Mingan hadn't forgotten General Arnold's last trip through here. The breakfast they gave us was a memorable feast. Afterward, Generals Arnold and Marshall went salmon fishing for a while (I think they really wanted to talk quietly), and when they returned, we took off again, at about 8 P.M. for a nonstop flight to Paris. Bunks were made up for us and the plane was quite comfortable, but I was too excited to sleep very well. I got up early in the morning while we were still over the Atlantic, and I noticed that the only other person already up was General Arnold. So I sat down in the seat next to him. I wanted to clear up something that was bothering me.

"General, I feel a tremendous responsibility looking after you on this mission," I said, "and I've had more advice than you can put in your hat about how to manage you. Everyone tells me how tough you are and how you pound on the table, and how I should speak right up to you and all that, but I just don't operate that way. If I see you getting too excited and your blood pressure going up, I'll stand where you can't fail to see me and begin tightening my tie. If you don't leave, I'll keep tightening it until everyone in the room thinks I'm about to choke to death, and that ought to break up the meeting."

He laughed and said, "That's the best idea I've heard yet for breaking up a hot meeting. I'll go along with your method if you'll go along with mine. Any time I see you tightening your tie, I'll get up and leave. Any time you see me tightening my tie, that means I want to get out of there and you should tell me I have to leave. I expect there'll be a lot of meetings I'll want to get out of."

We stayed at the Ritz in Paris, where I got the impression that many Frenchmen had already begun to resent the presence of American troops because of the very scarce food supply. When we got to Germany we took a look at Hitler's eagle's nest in Berchtesgaden, and then we went on to Berlin, where people were picking up the rubble that was left after our bombers finished their job on the city. Potsdam, where the three-power conference was held, is a suburb southwest of Berlin, but we stayed in lovely houses in another suburb, Babelsberg, which is a movie colony between Potsdam and the city. The Russians had come in two or three weeks before and commandeered all the houses. The story was told that in the house where we were quartered, when they came, the elderly lady who lived there said, "This is my home and I want to stay here." It was reported that the officer pulled out a gun, shot her and said, "If you want to stay, stay." The lake in front of the house still bubbled from the corpses that apparently had not yet disintegrated.

It would be pointless to go into all the details of our crowded days—so many writers have done so—but I remember being impressed by the swarms of soldiers everywhere, especially the Russians, and the constant bargaining between Russians and Americans for watches, pistols, cameras, cigarettes and chocolate or whatever else anyone could find.

On the 20th of July (according to the notes I made at the time) President Truman called me to the Potsdam "White House," where I was introduced to General Bradley, who seemed from the first to be the salt of the earth. A very plain straightforward man, he was from Moberly, Missouri, not too far from Brookfield. I liked him immediately. We talked about rehabilitation of soldiers who would need such care before separation from the service, and he told me he was planning to bring General Paul Hawley, his chief medical officer, back to Washington with him as medical director when he took charge of the Veterans Administration.

"Rehabilitation will evidently be one of our biggest jobs," General Bradley said. "I don't know much about it, so I'll have to feel my way along."

I assured him I was ready to help in any way I possibly could. Just then, the President came into the room with General Eisenhower, and lunch was announced. It was a real American meal—ham, peas, corn, salad.

After lunch we went to a flag-raising ceremony, which Secretary of War Stimson attended, as well as nearly all the generals. Among them was George Patton, and I recall a remark General Arnold made about him to General Marshall. He said, "You know, George, you've got five stars and I've got five stars, but old Georgie Patton has twice as many stars as the two of us together. He's got 'em on his swagger stick, his boots and he's even got 'em on his cuff links. He looks like the Milky Way walking down the street." The American flag that was raised that day was the same one which had flown over the White House in Washington on December 7, 1941.

Each time I saw Winston Churchill he was wearing a summer tan British naval uniform. I wonder if he chose military dress to match Stalin, who would arrive at meetings in a huge black armored car wearing an impeccable white Russian army tunic with just one medal on his chest. As it turned out, I myself didn't have much to do, but I enjoyed every minute of the trip, and especially the victory review of British troops on the Unter den Linden, at which I rode in a car with General Marshall and General Arnold. It was very colorful, with Churchill standing proudly in his car, saluting in every direction, but the most interesting thing about it to me was the fewness of the Germans there to see it. Though the Unter den Linden is a busy street, there weren't many Germans on it that day, and those I did see, in the background, stared at us with blank faces.

I also saw something that convinced me that the legendary Russian reputation for eating and drinking is no myth. I was in the dining room at the conference site when two Russian generals came in for a midafternoon snack. They started with three glasses of vodka, then they had two servings of suckling pig with horseradish and cream sauce, fresh caviar, several glasses of brandy, a main course of cutlets, fried potatoes, tomatoes, more brandy and for dessert, coffee glacé made of ice cream, coffee, whipped cream and almonds. They each had two of these with some white Georgian wine. Then they noticed me and another man in American uniform, and began drinking toasts to us.

I was astounded by their capacity to absorb vodka, and I was reminded of another incident. A new Air Force captain, who had been a general practitioner in the Missouri Ozarks prior to the war, was assigned to the first shuttle Air Force base on the Black Sea in the lend-lease days. I saw him about a year after his assignment and he told me about his experiences:

"The first six weeks were the most miserable ones I can

remember in my life. I was drunk every night and sometimes found myself undressed and put to bed in my quarters. All of the Russian officers played a game of drinking toasts. I had to respond to each one, so that I found I was drinking six to eight toasts to their one. Otherwise they would have been insulted. I knew I had to do something or die of delirium tremens or cirrhosis of the liver. So I bought a 'drinking outfit'—a dark-green shirt and a dark-green tie that I tucked in under the second button. Under this I wore a heavy sweat shirt. Then I practiced before a mirror so I could take a small vodka glass and with a slight twist of my wrist I would pour it down my necktie where it would be filtered by the absorbent sweat shirt. As soon as I perfected my technique I drank all the Russians under the table and we became best friends."

On July 30, we flew back home, and two weeks after my return, the atomic bombs fell on Hiroshima and Nagasaki and the Japanese finally surrendered. The war was over, and we began to take a tally of the effectiveness of our programs. We discovered we had saved at least forty million man-hours of duty time, and that we had gotten more sick or injured men back on duty than any branch of service had done during any war in history. More important, we had prepared thousands of boys for useful roles in civilian life after the war who might otherwise have wasted away for years in veterans hospitals. And by proving the value of rehabilitation, we had made certain that the Veterans Administration, after this war, would actually rehabilitate its disabled men rather than letting them languish in bed, or die for lack of understanding and a program. It is worth noting that of the four hundred men who became paraplegics in World War I, a third died in France, another third died within six weeks thereafter, and of the remaining third, 90 percent were dead within a year.

In World War II there were 2,500 American service-connected combat paraplegics, and three fourths of them were alive twenty years later. I might add parenthetically that of these survivors, 1,400 were holding down jobs.

It was truly providence that Glad was with me on V-J day. We were in Kansas City, and late in the afternoon the news came that Japan had surrendered. I can remember standing with her on a little porch at the Muehlebach Hotel with tears streaming down our cheeks as we watched the parades and the frenzied people. We walked down the street a block or so, dodging the celebrants and ducked into a little church. There were a lot of people in that church, saying private prayers, and we did likewise. It was also a moment of recognition, not just that the war was over, but that now I was going to have to make some hard choices about my future.

A short time later, in Washington, General Hawley, representing General Bradley, called and asked me if I would act as his consultant in organizing the rehabilitation program for the Veterans Administration. I accepted, with the understanding that I would remain only long enough to get the job started, as I wanted to return to civilian life. Fortunately, I was able to interest Dr. Donald Covalt in directing the veterans rehabilitation service, so I was soon free of my last military obligation.

One question remained, however. To what kind of civilian medical practice would I devote myself? Would I go back to St. Louis, where a very comfortable established practice as an internist still awaited me? Or would I follow the uncharted course of rehabilitation medicine in civilian life, where the concept of rehabilitation for the disabled was virtually unknown or unaccepted, even by the medical profession?

The question took many sleepless nights to resolve. In March 1945, Dr. Donal Sheehan, who was then acting dean of the New York University medical school, having heard and read about our Air Force programs, came to Washington to see me and asked me what I was planning to do after the war. Sheehan was a man of great imagination. Though he was a Ph.D., not an M.D., he had collaborated in writing a book called *Mission of a Medical School,* which was like a bible to New York University in its plans for the future, and later to other medical schools as well. He told me he thought rehabilitation was one of the great new fields in medicine. The university had received a small grant from the Baruch committee, and Sheehan thought this money ought to be spent organizing a department of physical medicine and rehabilitation at NYU. It wasn't much money—just enough to get started—but Dr. Sheehan asked me if I would at least consider coming to New York to help launch it.

I had already begun thinking about establishing a rehabilitation institute for civilians. I knew that for every veteran who needed such help there were a dozen more civilians who needed it. The veterans were going to get it, through the Veterans Administration, but very little was being done for civilians with disabilities, and there were then an estimated twenty million of them in this country.

My first thought had been to open such an institute in St. Louis. I went and talked to my old friends and colleagues there, especially at Washington University, where I had taught. I can't say the idea was well received. The orthopedists, in particular, said, "We're doing all that anyway," and it was true that they had adopted some good methods of therapy. But they failed to see my point: the whole person needed rehabilitation, not just the part of him that had been damaged. They had no concept of the emotional problems which follow disability, or the problems of job placement, or the other fundamentals behind our philosophy. These weren't strangers to whom I was talking. These were my old friends and colleagues, fine men and excellent doctors, but the kind of rehabilitation I wanted to do had never been done. And they didn't see any need to start it.

Dr. Evarts Graham, a great professor of surgery at Washington University, was one former colleague who understood what I was interested in doing. Dr. Graham had great prestige because he was the first in medical history to remove a cancerous lung and have the patient survive. But even he was unable to sell rehabilitation to the rest of the faculty. They seemed to think I was trying to push some kind of "social service boondoggle." It got back to me later that some of them even referred to the idea as Rusk's Folly.

Had I gone out and bought a building and set up a private rehabilitation program, starting with my own prewar patients, it would have been a worthwhile venture, and, I am sure, a financial success. But it would hardly have been noticed, and it would have done very little to advance the cause of rehabilitation. If I was going to enter the field, I wanted to do something which would help make the whole country —indeed the whole world—accept the idea and appreciate its value. That meant I would need a connection with some large institution or university through which there would be opportunities for scientific research and development.

I also had to decide what to do about my prewar practice in St. Louis. Two of my assistants, Dr. Harold Newman and Dr. George Ittner, had kept up the practice throughout the war. Another, Dr. Bruce Kenamore, had gone into the Air Force like myself, but had now returned to St. Louis. So I talked to them at great length about what I should do. I also discussed it with many of my old patients, two of whom had had a very deep effect upon me.

One was a beautiful woman named Vera Kennard, a friend of Glad's and mine, who was just a few years older than we. About three years before I went into the service she had suffered a stroke, which paralyzed her left side. Her family was adoring and solicitous, but she felt so helpless, so useless that she was miserable. I kept thinking that if only I had known more about retraining stroke victims, this wonderful woman would not have to be an invalid.

The other was a friend named Harry James, a real estate broker who also had suffered a stroke and was partially paralyzed, but whose mind was as clear as ever. I was his doctor when he had his stroke, before the war, and as I talked to him in 1945 I couldn't escape the feeling that I had made him an invalid. There was so little you could do to help a stroke victim in those days that, like many other doctors, I had developed a technique in dealing with them that did no more than pacify them. I had scores of them in my practice, people who were partially paralyzed, and who, therefore, sat home all day, no longer considered fit to work, and with nothing to do but think about their condition. They would want to see me periodically for checkups, but I wanted to see them as seldom as possible. I didn't realize it at the time, but in front of such patients I was overcome by a feeling of insecurity. Deep down inside I felt guilty because I didn't know how to help them.

Whenever they came into the office they wanted to talk. They would talk for an hour if you let them, while thirty other people sat in the waiting room. So I would go through the routine of taking their blood pressure, then I'd let the blood-pressure machine run down and tell them they were about the same as before, or whatever, and immediately they would begin to ramble on about this or that symptom that troubled them. I would interrupt and say, "Just a minute, let me check the blood pressure again." I would go through the process once more, repeat what I had said before, and prescribe a little meaningless change in their medication that would make them feel that at least something was being done. Then I'd hurry out of the room while the nurse came in to dismiss them. I didn't want to talk to them because I really didn't know what to say, and I'm sure that's always been true of most doctors everyplace. If a patient came in with a brain tumor you might not know how to remove it yourself, but you would at least know of a neurosurgeon to whom you could send him. If he was paralyzed, however, or disabled in some other way, there was virtually no one to whom you could send him. You could get him maybe a "nickel's worth" of physical therapy, and that was about all.

Such reminiscences reinforced my determination to throw my energies into rehabilitation. At the same time, I had to think about my family, and I must say Glad was wonderful about it. She knew what I wanted to do and she wanted me to do it. She did not want to go back to St. Louis, preferring an uncertain future in New York as long as it gave me a chance to do what I wanted to do. It was going to mean a severe financial sacrifice and it might be hard on the children for a while. Martha was then thirteen, Howard eleven, and John nine. But we had a long talk with them and they felt the same way as their mother. I know, of course, that it was she who made them feel that way.

She said to me one day, "Are you convinced you're the only person who can do the job you want to do?"

And I said, "I don't know anyone else who's about to stick his neck out to do it."

"Then, by all means you should go ahead and do it," she said.

While I received encouragement from my wife and children, the reaction from my mother, and from Glad's mother, was somewhat different. My mother thought the idea was terrible. I had started with nothing in St. Louis. I had built up an excellent practice. I was respected in the profession and the community. We had a good life and financial security. I think Glad's mother had the same reservations, especially about financial security, because both of our families had suffered severely from depressions in the past, and one of the nice things about my success in St. Louis was that it enabled us to help relieve any money worries they might have had. Both of our mothers had small legacies, but not enough to make them self-sufficient, and they didn't want to see me do something which might leave my family in difficult circumstances. I couldn't convince my mother at the time; I simply told her I had to do it. I felt this so deeply, there was no other decision I could make. And I must say that when it became apparent that I was going to come to New York, however uncertain the prospects were, she wrote me a most moving letter:

> The way ahead, if you choose the institute, is like a pathless forest through which you must walk very cautiously in order to keep the briars (of criticism) from clutching at you and your high aim for humanity . . . A rehabilitation institute, I take it, would more nearly meet your heart's dear desire than anything else . . . But please remember, I am ignorance speaking, for I know nothing of the details of the work.

If you should or could return to St. Louis and do what you wish to do without having to raise your own funds by solicitation, I would like it. I would be opposed to your going about, soliciting.

Having been frank, I am glad the end of suspense is near for you. Whatever it be, let us never forget, God is on the side of right and that is our side. "If He be for us, who can be against us?" . . . Each hour you are in my thoughts, my dear, and I am petitioning for guidance. . . .

Yours, longing to serve you to greater purpose
MOTHER

She was a very strong, intelligent, wonderful woman, and she was quite right when she warned me of the dangers of my decision. I'm happy to say that after we came to New York, she also came to live with us, and long before she died, at the age of ninety-five, she told me she thought I had made a wise decision. Glad's mother felt the same way.

My future in New York did not look too promising. I would be reducing my income to one third of what it had been. And as for starting a rehabilitation institute, I had nothing but an idea, plus the friendship and support of Dr. Sheehan and Dr. George Deaver, who had been such a help to us in the Air Force, and who was still the medical director of the Institute for the Crippled and Disabled.

I also had other friends in New York and one of them was most important: Arthur Hays Sulzberger, the publisher of *The New York Times.* He had become so interested in our military program, he had visited some of our centers and came to Washington to learn more about it. At one point he even tried to get the Red Cross to agree to take over rehabilitation as a national peacetime program for civilians, but the

Red Cross decided it was too big a project. Just before peace came, he said to me, "What are you going to do when the war is over?"

"I don't know," I said, "but I'd like to go someplace where I can teach people about this thing."

He wanted to know where I might go. I mentioned St. Louis, as well as a couple of other places which offered possible opportunities.

Sulzberger said, "You're forgetting the greatest university in the United States—*The New York Times.* I feel that if there's anything good about war, it's taking new ideas developed in wartime and making them available for people in peacetime. Rehabilitation is just such an idea. If you could do a public education job on it through the *Times,* and at the same time educate the professionals, without getting kicked out of the union [the American Medical Association], you could save ten years in bringing about a general acceptance of what you're trying to do."

"But I'm not a writer," I said. "I'm a doctor. I've never written much and I don't like to write. It's hard for me."

He said, "Think it over." That was the end of the discussion, but every week after that, I got a letter from him. Usually it was just one line and it would say something like, "You'll never sleep well if you don't take a crack at this."

So when I decided to come to New York, I got in touch with Mr. Sulzberger and said to him, "All right, I'll do a weekly column for you on a six-month trial basis."

He not only accepted me on that condition, he also sent me uptown to Columbia University, where he was a trustee, to talk to the medical faculty about starting a rehabilitation institute there. They had an ideal building for it on Fifty-ninth Street, the old New York Orthopedic Hospital, which had just merged with Columbia. For a few dollars, that building could have been made into an operating rehabilitation center within a couple of weeks. But I could see that the Columbia faculty was reluctant, even though Mr. Sulzberger held their feet to the fire, and they simply wouldn't take on such a new idea.

Meanwhile I had talked to Dr. Alan Gregg, who was one of the great medical statesmen of our time. He was vice president in charge of health affairs for the Rockefeller Foundation, and was a leader in starting the Peking Union Medical College. I asked him what he thought I should do, and he said without hesitation that I should take the New York University offer.

"There's a lot of change going on there," he said. "They've got younger people. Dr. Sheehan is a man of great ideas and I don't believe you would have as many roadblocks there as you might have at an older, more circumspect university."

So it was finally decided. I came to New York City in December 1945 under rather impecunious circumstances, as a weekly medical columnist for the *Times,* and as chairman of the New York University medical school's Department of Rehabilitation and Physical Medicine, a department which, at that time, was all in my head. Shortly after my arrival, a very blunt friend of mine, a St. Louis orthopedic surgeon, came to visit me and said, "Howard, when are you going to get rid of this damned crazy notion of yours and come back to practice medicine among your own people, where you belong?"

I replied, "I'm not coming."

He said, "You're the biggest fool I ever met."

There were times during those first days in New York when I almost agreed with him. I had visited the city often enough but never before undertaken to live in it, and I quickly found that there would be surprises. Because of the postwar housing shortage, for instance, we had a terrible time locating a place to live, and when we did come upon an old house, for which we were able to get only a six-month lease at what seemed an exorbitant rent, we discovered there was a stipulation that if, at the end of six months, we weren't willing to buy the house at the owner's price, we would have to forfeit $2,000. Since we had no choice, we took it, but together with the awesomeness of the city, the crowds, the pace and the excitement, this incident reminded me forcefully that I was embarking on a new life in an America quite different from the Midwestern America that I knew and loved.

CHAPTER

· ·

· ·

DURING THOSE FIRST MONTHS IN NEW YORK, I had to do more than settle down and get used to the city. To sell my program I spoke to any crowd that would stand still at breakfast, lunch, tea, cocktails, dinner or later in the evening. Whenever more than twenty people gathered in one place, they weren't safe from me. I would have spoken at bus queues or in subway cars if people would have listened. I made my speech so often I could almost do it in my sleep. Sometimes I almost did. I remember one dinner at the Hotel Astor. It was the fifth meeting at which I had spoken that day, and I was so tired that after filling myself with the usual chicken, mashed potatoes and peas, I could barely stand up when I was supposed to speak. The minute I started, the room began going black and I felt myself breaking out in a cold sweat. I thought, Oh my God, I'm going to pass out and they're all going to gather around me, and they're going to say, "Who is he to tell us about health when he's a sick man himself?" I clutched the speaker's stand with all my strength, and I told myself, No, no, no, I must not pass out. Gradually my eyes began to focus again, and I realized I was still on my feet, still talking.

When I finished, I sat down and asked the man next to me, "I got awful sick up there for a while. Did you notice anything? Did I act strange?"

He looked surprised. "Sick?" he said. "You didn't look sick. You just kept right on talking."

That's what I did, day after day. Much of my message came not only from my experience in the Air Force, but from the findings in a report I had helped prepare for the Baruch Committee on Physical Medicine, of which I was still a member. The statistics were shocking. We learned that in the United States of 1945 there were about twenty-three million people handicapped because of disease, injury, maladjustment or disabilities resulting from wars previous to the one that had just ended. And while the three-and-a-half-year time span of World War II had produced about seventeen thousand amputees among servicemen, it had also created a hundred and twenty thousand amputees among our civilian population. Meanwhile the federal government's Office of Vocational Rehabilitation had proven that the civilian handicapped could be retrained for new jobs, just as we had done in the Air Force. More important, the industrial accident rate for handicapped workers was lower than the rate for able-bodied workers. Of those workers the Office of Vocational Rehabilitation had trained in 1944 the average annual income before training had been $148. After training, the average annual income of the group increased to $1,768, a sum which was, of course, more significant in 1945 than it is today. In those days a person could live on that much money—without having to go on welfare.

I kept reiterating these facts in speeches, in my weekly Times column, and in several articles I did for the Sunday New York Times Magazine. To convince the public it was worthwhile to salvage these millions of handicapped people

I had to prove it was profitable and socially useful. One example I used was a man named Edward Levy, a former president of several large corporations, who retired and started a smoking-pipe company in Paterson, New Jersey. "The reason I started this business," Mr. Levy had told me, "was that I always wondered what happened to the people industry didn't hire—people turned down because they were over forty-five, or because they had a bad heart and couldn't do any heavy work, or because they had an artificial leg or an amputated arm. What became of them when they left the employment office? And what could they do if they were given a chance?

"I had an idea they'd be able to do just as good a job as anyone else if their special problems received a little consideration. But I couldn't convince anyone else of that and I couldn't use the stockholders' money in the corporations I ran to experiment with my own theory. So after I retired, I invested some of my own money to prove it. The result was fantastic."

The result of which he spoke was a very profitable factory, Smoking Pipes Inc., which employed a hundred and fifteen people up to the age of eighty who had endured every conceivable handicap. "But it's not only the money they earn here that's important to them," Mr. Levy continued, "it's the fact that they're working. They're not wasting away from sheer boredom. They're making their own way."

I told also about a firm called G. Barr & Co. of Chicago, which manufactured pharmaceuticals and cosmetics. It was started in 1935 by two men, George Barr, a University of Wisconsin chemistry graduate who had lost a leg in a car accident, and Mitchell Echikovitz, a deaf-mute. Ten years later, they had 148 employees, of whom 128 were handicapped, and their business was grossing $1,500,000 a year. George Barr now was completely sold on the policy of hiring handicapped workers. Not because he wanted to do them a favor, but because he had learned that in jobs where handicapped workers were doing the same work as able-bodied men, the handicapped were producing up to 22 percent more per man-hour.

To me these seemed excellent arguments, but they did not prevail in the marketplace. Only a few companies had enlightened policies about hiring the handicapped. Some companies didn't hire them at all. Others that had hired handicapped people during the war—when able-bodied labor was in short supply, and had capitalized on the public relations value of this wartime policy—were now firing them and replacing them with more able-bodied returning servicemen.

What I was hoping was that American businessmen would start putting the handicapped to work on a nation-wide basis. I was certain that if this idea were accepted as practical and profitable, we would eventually have rehabilitation centers for the handicapped all over the country. But this was still a dream at a time when there wasn't a single such center in the country. What had to be done then was to start one in New York. Toward that end I had going for me not only the friendship and encouragement of people like Arthur Hays Sulzberger, Bernard Baruch, Dr. Donald Sheehan of NYU, and Bernard and Alva Gimbel, but also the help of a man whom I can only describe as one of the great champions for the cause of the handicapped—Dr. George Deaver.

Dr. Deaver, as I have explained, had continued his work as medical director of the Institute for the Crippled and Disabled in New York City. When the possibility arose of my coming to New York, he expressed a desire to work with me because he felt, as I did, that we could complement each other. He knew what a terrible job it was to raise funds and sell ideas to the public. He hated it. What he loved most was working in the hospital, among disabled people, and especially children. When he walked down the corridor, kids came popping out of their rooms, in wheelchairs, on crutches, any way they could move to grab hold of him, to hug him and kiss him. He realized as well as I did that we would need a university connection if we wanted our work to develop, so he accepted Dr. Sheehan's offer that he become acting head of the NYU Department of Physical Medicine until I arrived, and thereafter we worked closely together.

Dr. Deaver had done some magnificent work in rehabilitation. I've mentioned that it was he who first taught paraplegics to walk. He also developed the concept that the first part of rehabilitation should be to train the individual to meet all the manipulative needs of his daily living. He and his therapists worked out a check list of forty-five daily activities which the average healthy person does without giving them any thought. Things like brushing your teeth, combing your hair, going to the bathroom, putting on your shirt or tying your shoes. That check list is still the starting point in rehabilitation, although there are now a hundred and fifty checkouts, divided into segments such as eating, grooming and dressing. But it was Dr. Deaver's concept originally, and the first person on whom he practiced it was a paraplegic Navy veteran named Tom Miley.

This was still during the war, when the Navy, like the Air Force, was getting tragic cases which just couldn't be handled properly. Tom Miley was a tall, red-haired, very pleasant boy, who was wasting away in the Navy hospital on Long Island. When his father, Thomas Jefferson Miley, who was head of the Commerce and Industry Association in New York, went to see him the first time, Tom weighed only seventy-four pounds, though he was six feet, three inches tall, and he had a number of large ugly bedsores.

After talking to the boy, Mr. Miley was so distressed, he went immediately to consult the doctor in charge of the case and asked him, "If this were your boy, what would you do?"

The doctor said, "I'd get on my knees and pray to God that he'd die tonight."

The doctor talked that way because he had no idea what to do to help the boy. He wasn't as cynical as he sounded, but Mr. Miley was horrified. Fortunately, he heard about Dr. Deaver's work and came to see him. I happened to be there at the time.

"That kind of attitude doesn't satisfy me," he said. "I'm taking the boy out of the Navy hospital. Would you be able to accept him here?"

The Institute for the Crippled and Disabled was on Twenty-third Street, but there were no beds, so Tom was put in a private hospital and they would bring him over by ambulance. I can remember him during his first days of training, feebly trying to pull himself up off the ground. But before he was through, he finished the whole check list. He learned to walk on braces and crutches and take care of himself. And eventually he fell in love with a wonderful girl named Alice, a patient at the Institute for the Crippled and Disabled, who was partially paralyzed in both arms and legs from polio, and they were married. They built a house in Dutchess County where they did everything for themselves, even putting up and taking down the storm windows, and they started a telephone answering service that was very successful. They adopted two children. He became head of the Boy Scouts and she did community work. Meanwhile Tom's father became an absolute Trojan in the fight for rehabilitation, and he was a great help to us through the years. Unfortunately, the senior Mr. Miley died in 1970, and about six months later, Tom died, after a useful and wonderful life. But his wife, Alice Miley, is still alive, and his mother, Mrs. Thomas Jefferson Miley, is now a dedicated member of our job-placement committee.

Another boy, a New Yorker named Herb Klinefeld, who had been a junior at Harvard with top grades before he went into the service, came to Dr. Deaver during the early months of 1945, but in even worse condition. He had broken his back by falling out of a tree during maneuvers in Oregon, and had then been discharged from the service into a Veterans Administration hospital, where he got no help because the doctors there had no idea how to meet this problem. In trying to do something about his bladder, over which he had no control, they had messed him up to the point where he was lucky to be alive at all. When he finally got into the hands of Dr. Deaver and an experienced urologist here in New York, he was desperately sick. By the time I got to New York and began to work with Dr. Deaver, he was in excellent condition and ready to return to college.

That set the stage for one of the first battles I had to wage for patients who fought to get back into everyday life. Herb wanted to go back to Harvard, and though he had been a fine student there, they didn't want to readmit him. They were convinced that a paraplegic simply couldn't do the work.

The top doctor in the health service at Harvard, Dr. Arlie Bock, was a friend of mine, and I got into a scrap with him over whether this boy could keep up with the able-bodied students there. I pointed out that the boy could go up and down stairs on his crutches, he could drive his car, and most important, he had already proved himself to be a good student and he was determined to finish college in spite of his handicap. Though Dr. Bock was unconvinced, he admitted the boy. Herb Klinefeld not only graduated from Harvard College with honors, he stayed on to earn his Ph.D. He was still a graduate student when my own son Howard went to Harvard. He was the house leader where Howard lived, and the two became great friends. However, his struggle didn't end when he won his doctorate. He wanted to be a teacher, but because of his handicap he had a terrible time finding a job. He finally did get placed, and he's teaching now in a college in Brooklyn. He's happily married and still comes in to see me periodically. But the teaching profession, I'm afraid, is not yet sensitized to the concept of rehabilitation. It's one profession in which it is still difficult for a handicapped person to find work.

While I was making speeches and settling in at the university, I was also working every angle I could think of to create a true rehabilitation center. Through Dr. Edward Bernecker, the New York City Commissioner of Hospitals, I met Mayor William O'Dwyer. I kept pestering these two men with the idea that New York municipal hospitals needed a rehabilitation program, that this could be the first city hospital system in the world with such a program, and that Bellevue could be the first municipal hospital in the world to take such a forward step. They were very understanding. They also must have gotten tired of listening to me. Anyway, they gave me two wards at Bellevue and told me to go ahead and see what I could do. They also assigned me a small sum of money for a staff. Just a few thousand dollars, but it was all they could afford from the city's budget, and I was grateful for it.

We had already received a modest grant from Bernard Baruch to set up a pilot rehabilitation program, so with this money, plus the two Bellevue wards and the small budget from the city, we were ready to go. But day after day, then week after week passed and nothing happened. Though the two wards had been assigned to us, we couldn't use them because there were people in them and nobody seemed interested in moving these people to other wards. When they finally did move them, we were still stymied because we couldn't get any equipment.

One day I became so frustrated I went to see Dr. William Jacobs, the Bellevue administrator, who was surely one of the busiest hospital administrators in the world, since Bellevue is one of the largest hospitals in existence.

"I'm terribly distressed," I said. "I just can't seem to get our rehabilitation program off the ground. The wards have been open for some time now, but the equipment hasn't come and nothing seems to happen."

Dr. Jacobs frowned and said, "What program are you talking about?"

I said, "The rehabilitation program."

"I don't know a thing about it," he said. "You've never talked to me about it."

I said, "I sent you a memorandum."

"I get hundreds of memoranda every day," he said. "Look at this stack." He pointed at a huge pile of papers on the corner of his desk. "They're all memoranda. Maybe yours is in there someplace. If I read all the memoranda I get, I'd have time for nothing else. Why didn't you come to see me about it in person?"

I was feeling so sheepish by that time I wished I could forget the whole thing. "I thought you'd get word of it from downtown, from City Hall," I said. "But I see I've made a grievous mistake. I should have come to talk to you about it before I talked to anyone. All I can do now is throw myself on your mercy, tell you about the program, what we're trying to do, and ask for your help."

When I finished he said, "I believe in that. I'd like to help. I just didn't know about it. I'll have a crew up there tomorrow to get those wards cleaned up. Tell me what you want and we'll have it in ten days or so."

From that moment on we were friends. Chagrined as I was, I realized afterward what a valuable lesson Dr. Jacobs had taught me about getting along in a giant organization. You'll never go very far by ignoring the man responsible at the operating level.

We soon had the program started in those two drab, bare Bellevue wards with Dr. Deaver, two therapists, a few "spade workers" and me standing by, ready for action. For a while there wasn't much to do, and perhaps that was fortunate, because it gave us time to teach our tiny staff what we were trying to accomplish. Up to that time, there had been masseur and masseuse types of therapists at Bellevue. But all they knew was the old conventional therapy using heat, light, water and massage methods, which we thought had only limited importance in the total program. A qualified physical therapist could be paid only $2,370 a year by the city in those days (now the starting salary is $9,600) and as a result we had no good ones. In an effort to get qualified therapists we supplemented these salaries with some of Mr. Baruch's money. The first two girls we hired are still at Bellevue. One of them, Margaret Fortmann, is the chief physical therapist there; the other, Terese Anastasia, is now co-ordinator of the Bellevue Rehabilitation Program.

Meanwhile we let the word out that these wards were available for rehabilitation patients, and we circulated among the doctors at Bellevue and on the NYU faculty, trying to explain to them what rehabilitation was. But they were busy men and it wasn't always easy to get them to stand still and listen. We told them we were trying to practice the third phase of medicine. The first phase, of course, is prevention of illness. The second phase is definitive care leading to cure. The third phase, what we were trying to create, was what should come after the stitches were out and the fever down, a training program for people with disabilities to get them out of bed and back on the job, or back into the mainstream of life.

I used to corner these doctors at lunch, if you could call it lunch. Everybody put a quarter in a basket and we had the same kind of cold sandwiches, day after day, with bitter coffee, while I would harangue them. "If you have any patients for whom you can't do anything more," I would say to them, "patients you think might possibly respond to training, send them to us the same way you might send them to any other specialists."

Their first response, unfortunately, was to send us what doctors sometimes refer to as "old crocks." I like Dr. John Romano's definition of a crock. Romano was a very dynamic and broad-thinking but also amusing professor of psychiatry at the University of Rochester. "A crock," he once said, "is a patient from whom the diagnostic sheen has been worn" —in other words, a patient for whom the doctors have run out of theories and prescriptions.

One of the very first of these patients was a man in his eighties, blind, suffering so severely from Parkinson's disease he almost shook himself out of bed, and plagued also by aphasia as a result of a stroke, so that he couldn't talk. In addition, he had brain damage. Dr. Deaver and I stood sadly at the foot of his bed, shaking our heads. Here, indeed, was an old crock. There was nothing we could do for him except to get him placed in a nursing home.

Dr. Deaver said, "We've got to develop some ground rules for this thing and do it fast, or we'll become a depot for hopeless cases."

We set up feasibility standards and began passing on patients before accepting them. Then Dr. Deaver, with two or three residents and faculty members who had begun to help us part-time, went through the other Bellevue wards looking for likely patients, and explaining to the doctors there what kinds of patients we thought we could help. After that, our two wards began to fill up with patients who had good potential. We were soon so short of space we had to use the sun room between the wards for beds. Then we were given some adjoining rooms which had been offices but which we converted into a gymnasium and classrooms. Within a very few months, we were operating nicely, but I was still distressed by the drabness of the place. The colors were dull and the paint was badly chipped. It had been on those walls, I would guess, since long before World War II.

Despite the strong displeasure my mother had once expressed to me in a letter at the idea of soliciting funds, I had already realized there was no alternative. So I had begun scrounging from my friends, and I now had a little money, about $1,500, to spend on whatever seemed necessary. The Junior League of New York gave me some of that money (they had become interested in rehabilitation very early and began sending bright young girls to us as volunteers), and I went to my old friend William Pahlmann, who had helped me before.

"Bill," I said, "I've got fifteen hundred dollars and I've got two awful-looking wards at Bellevue. I want as much done for those two wards as you and the fifteen hundred dollars can do."

He did wonders. He painted the ladies' ward a pale pink and the men's ward a pale blue, and he got us some cheap but attractive furniture to put at one end so we had a lounge area. Then a friend of his painted twenty-four big, splashy, colorful pictures, which they framed in plain wood and hung all over the place. When they were through, our area was so bright and cheery, people used to break out in spontaneous smiles the minute they saw it. That didn't mean, however, that everyone thought the decorating job had been a good idea.

One doctor took a look at it and said, "Howard, you're out of your mind. You don't know Bellevue. In thirty days, this place will look like a pigpen."

He was wrong. It was ten years before those wards were repainted, or redecorated, and except for the dirt in the air, there was not a mark on them after those ten years. The patients would have attacked anyone who defaced the walls, because they took pride in them. They were the only colorful walls in the whole hospital.

One of our greatest problems in those days was red tape. If a patient had lost a leg and needed an artificial one, the rule was that you had to have three different limb makers bid on the job, and you always had to take the lowest bid, even if it wasn't the best leg for the patient. The question then arose as to whether the leg would be for immediate delivery, which took thirty days, or delayed delivery, which meant up to ninety days. If you took delayed delivery, they gave you a 10 percent discount, so there was always pressure to accept the ninety-day delay. It apparently had never occurred to anyone that while the patient sat in the hospital for an extra two months, saving the City of New York $15 in discount on a $150 leg, he was costing the city the expense of keeping him at Bellevue, which was in those days $25 a day. In other words, to save $15, the city was spending $1,500. The same thing used to happen with patients who needed orthopedic shoes. We would apply for them through the Social Service Department and the Welfare Department. But by the time we got the shoes fitted, the patient had wasted an extra month in the hospital. I'm happy to say such matters have been improved somewhat, but the red tape is still a great problem there, as it is in all municipal hospitals.

While we were having trouble convincing many people we had anything good to offer, there were two men we never had trouble convincing—Drs. Warren Draper and Royd Sayers, the medical directors of the miners' Welfare and Retirement Fund. They sold John L. Lewis, president of the United Mine Workers and a very controversial figure in his day, on the idea that rehabilitation was good business. Lewis was a man who always spoke his mind and always made great demands for his union members, and often did great things for them. The union welfare fund was a case in point. Every time he negotiated a new contract, he would bludgeon the mine owners into kicking in what would seem like astronomical sums for the union welfare fund. People used to say, "What's he doing with that money?"

I had occasion to find out and was impressed. I remember that during one month in 1946 the death toll of American miners was forty-five men, and the injuries were many, many times that number. One of the common injuries was a broken back. Walls would collapse, or timbers would fall, and the men would spend the rest of their lives as paraplegics. So the mine workers' union was interested in our work, and we were interested in their problems. Through their welfare fund, they were willing to do everything possible to rehabilitate their disabled men, and they began sending paraplegics to our program in New York for treatment.

One of the first to come was not a miner but a miner's wife who had broken her back in an automobile accident. She trained very well, and while she was being rehabilitated we brought three of her children to New York to see her. I was there when they came into the women's ward and you could see from the expressions on their faces how amazed they were when they looked at her.

I walked out of the ward with them and in the hall I said to one of them, "Are you having a nice time in New York?"

He was the oldest, a boy about eight. He looked up at me with wonder in his eyes and said, "Oh yes, sir. It's so nice to see my mother look like my mother again."

By now we were beginning to get some public attention. Looking back, I just can't say too much for Mr. Sulzberger's contribution in allowing me to use my column in the *Times* that way, even though I was finding it more difficult to write newspaper articles than to take care of patients. I thought of myself as a doctor rather than a writer, and if the column had any success it was largely because of Jack Taylor, who passionately believed in the cause and kept me from writing fancy technical language that was over people's heads.

I had had my first lesson in verbal communication years before in August of 1928, when I was a young doctor in St. Louis and was invited to present my first scientific paper before the annual meeting of the Ozark Tri-County Medical Association. Several months before that, I had seen a patient who I decided had a very rare and exotic malady called Concato's disease, which causes the pleural cavities to fill up with fluid. I studied all the literature and read all the fine print of excerpts from international medical journals; I discovered that in France they were using a substance called Gomenol in an oil suspension on certain tuberculous patients with recurring pleural effusion. I tried it on guinea pigs and it worked, so I decided this should be the subject of my report to the Ozark Tri-County doctors.

The meeting was held in an old country hotel. The temperature was 104 degrees and the scientific session was preceded by several surreptitious slugs of corn whisky served to the entire audience, twelve country doctors, behind a grape arbor. After these "cocktails," everybody ate a real country dinner of fried chicken, Missouri ham, mashed potatoes, six kinds of vegetables, ice cream, cake and four kinds of pie. At the conclusion of this feast, the doctors gathered to hear me read my paper.

For fear I might forget some important scientific detail, I had included everything even remotely pertinent, pointing out with numbered references what Dieulafoy had said, what André had observed, and what every other erudite authority thought about the matter. All this in my most impeccable medical prose.

Shortly after I began my full-hour presentation, the chairman fell sound asleep. He was quickly joined by eight of his colleagues, some of whom snored quite richly. When I finished reading, the three members still awake clapped politely, thus waking the chairman, who reeled to his feet and said, "Gentlemen, this young doctor from St. Louis has read us a mighty fancy paper, and I want to hear a good discussion on it. I'll open the discussion by saying I didn't understand a damned word of it. Now let's adjourn to the lawn and drink a little home brew."

As a result of this fiasco, I tried to make sure the readers of my articles understood every word I said. I pointed out that each year in this country, 350,000 people were being permanently disabled by accidents. And while eleven thousand soldiers had been wounded on the beaches at Normandy during the first ten days after D-Day, twice that many civilians were injured by automobile accidents on our highways during the same ten-day period. At that time eight million working-age males were disabled to such an extent that only after physical, vocational and emotional rehabilitation could they ever again become gainfully employed. Most important, I kept pointing out that these men could be salvaged, instead of being a drain on their families and on welfare, and they could be contributing tax revenue rather than using it. Rehabilitation was not, of course, the only subject of my *Times* articles, but it was the subject to which I kept returning.

We were helped along at this time by a young paraplegic veteran named John Crown, who was not even one of our patients. For months he had lain, staring at the ceiling, in a bed at the Veterans Administration's Halloran General Hospital on Staten Island. Some days, as he later explained, he simply wished he would die. Other days, he would put his pillow over his head and weep for hours. He could not learn to accept the fact that he would never again have the use of his legs.

One day he said to a Red Cross lady who stopped to talk to him, "You know, I've been thinking, if I were a writer, being paralyzed wouldn't be so bad. I could think up things and put them on paper."

Thanks to the Red Cross lady, Henrietta Bruce Sharon came to visit John Crown. She had founded a group called the Writers' Workshop, and she invited him to join it. Suddenly, he had something to live for. After learning a few fundamentals, he began to write. Then he began to eat better and to do the exercises which had been prescribed. He began moving around the hospital in his wheelchair, and eventually learned to walk with the aid of braces and crutches. His writing progressed to the point where he had something he wanted people to see, and having read my column in the *Times,* he sent me what he had written. It was so moving that instead of writing a column that week, I published his letter. Here is what he wrote:

My name is John Crown. I am a paraplegic at Halloran General Hospital. My physical wounds are very small in comparison with my spiritual wounds. I have come back from death to a world that I no longer care for. I, who have been engaged in the great struggle to save the world from tyranny and having seen my comrades die for this cause, can now find no peace in the world or in my country.

Having lived close to death for two years, the reasons why there is no peace seem infinitesimally flimsy. Russia wants the Dardanelles, Yugoslavia wants Trieste, the Moslems want India, labor wants more wages, capital wants more profit, Smith wants to pass the car in front of him, Junior wants more spending money. To these I say, is it necessary to kill and cripple human beings for these petty gains?

Anyone who thinks a human body is so cheap that it can be traded for a tract of land, a piece of silver, or a few minutes of time should be forced to listen to the moans of the dying, night and day, for the rest of his life.

All the troubles of the world originate in the common man. The selfish and the greedy ways of nations are just the wars of each individual man multiplied a hundredfold. When the morals of the common man drop, so do the morals of the nation and of the world.

As long as our individual morals remain at a low ebb, so will be the world. Until each of us stops "hogging the road" with his car, stops fighting over a seat on the bus, stops arguing over who is going to cut the grass, there will be no peace in the world. If man wishes peace again, he must return to the great Commandment, Love thy neighbor as thyself for the love of God.

That letter, and the story of its author, produced a flood of interest in the disabled. Letters arrived by the thousands. I think almost every newspaper in the country printed John Crown's story and several syndicated columnists wrote about him. He was soon able to leave the hospital and return to his home in Brooklyn, where he happily continued his writing. I'm sorry to say John Crown did not have a long life; he died of complications four years later. But he had left behind him an eloquent plea for reason and understanding at a time when the world was showing its need of both.

At the American Medical Association convention held in San Francisco, in the summer of 1946, I began to see progress in achieving our goals. The federal government's Committee on Prosthetic Devices, which had been formed in 1944 partly as a result of pressure applied by General Arnold, had now been in operation for two years. With the help of American

industry, the committee had developed some greatly improved artificial arms and legs.

I went to look at these new devices with a colleague of
mine in rehabilitation, Dr. Henry Kessler, who has been
one of the great pioneers in the field. He had been an orthopedic surgeon and had served in the Army during
World War I; he had recognized the need for rehabilitation medicine before World War II, long before I did. He
became a leader of the movement in New Jersey and also
became involved very early in the international movement. I know of no one who traveled more or did more
for rehabilitation around the world than Henry Kessler.

While Dr. Kessler and I were watching a demonstration of new prosthetic devices, we were approached by a
man who introduced himself as Charles McGonegal. He
had lost both arms in World War I when a grenade exploded, and he was then working for Northrop Aircraft,
where many of the new devices had been invented. He
was wearing hooks which were developed at Northrop.

As he approached, he addressed himself to Kessler.
"Say, you were my doctor thirty years ago, in the First
World War." Sure enough, it was true. As soon as they
reintroduced themselves, McGonegal began to reminisce.

"Do you remember the first appliance you tried on
me?" he said, raising his sleek, new artificial arm. "It was
a safety pin that you sealed into the plaster-of-Paris cast
on my right stump. The nurse would light a cigarette and
close the pin over it so I could smoke. I'll never forget
the thrill of independence at being able to smoke almost
by myself."

"But what about the second hand we gave you?" Dr.
Kessler said. "That's the one I remember best. We sub-

stituted a clothespin for the safety pin and you even learned to pick things up with it."

For 1918 that was a remarkable accomplishment, but to McGonegal it was only a beginning. Because he had terrific drive and determination, he gradually became master of what we call "hooks," those pincerlike hand substitutes which are operated by shrugging the opposite shoulder. With these, he learned to live an independent, productive life, ran a business and raised a family. When World War II came, he realized he had something special to offer, so he became a full-time employee of the American Legion's rehabilitation committee. Going from one amputation center to another, he showed men what they could do despite their handicaps. Then he heard that Northrop Aircraft, thanks to its president, Jack Northrop, was at work on new prosthetic devices, so he volunteered to become the project's guinea pig and chief tester.

"It was my job," he said, "to help get the bugs out of the blueprint models. And here is the result." He glanced down at his new arms. "These things can almost talk."

Later at the convention, I met another man who worked for Northrop in the prosthetic division. His name was Lonnie Carberry; he was a stocky dark-haired Texan who had been a gunner in a tank during the North African campaign of 1942. He was in the open turret of his tank when an exploding shell severed both of his arms above the elbow. This is the toughest kind of amputation to cope with, and if you don't think so, just hold your own elbows absolutely straight for a while and see what a limitation that puts even on able-bodied hands. You can imagine how much more difficult it makes the rehabilitation of someone with artificial hands. But it didn't stop Lonnie Carberry. He was wearing a new elbow clutch lock perfected by Northrop, and during a dinner at which I met him he proved he could do anything the rest of us were doing. He held his own glass, cut his meat, fed himself, drank his coffee, and when the meal was over he brought a package of cigarettes out of his pocket, extracted one and lit it for himself. His clutch lock enabled him to bend his "elbows" and hold them in position while he operated his "hands" independently.

This was a great step forward for arm amputees, and I returned to Bellevue after that convention more enthusiastic than ever. Our greatest need still was trained people rather than mechanical devices or equipment. I've always felt that the most necessary ingredients of successful rehabilitation, besides the patient's determination, are the trained hands and the dedicated hearts of the therapists and doctors and nurses. If you have these ingredients, you can do a good job with a minimum of equipment. At Bellevue, we made our own parallel bars and our own flights of steps on which patients could learn to go up or down. We got hold of an old city bus and they cut it in half for us so we could put it up in the training room, where patients learned how to get on and off, as well as make change for the fare. Our equipment might have been primitive, but that was not a problem. What was really difficult was to find and train qualified personnel, and then find the money to pay them. Bernard Baruch and a small list of other contributors came to our rescue in solving the money problem. As for the training of doctors and therapists, we embarked on that ourselves.

We had trouble interesting older doctors in our work unless they or some member of their families had suffered a disability. Most older doctors had their own specialties, of course, but when someone close needed rehabilitation, they very quickly were sold on it. We had much better luck with younger doctors, perhaps partly because we kept hounding so many of them. Some of the residents at Bellevue were afraid to come near us. They used to say, "Don't let Rusk see you wearing a white coat; he'll put you in that damned program of his."

We were able to lasso quite a few, however, and good ones too. Take the first three men we trained, for instance. Dr. Bruce Grynbaum is today the Chief of Service at Bellevue. Dr. Sam Sverdlik is today the Chief of Service at St. Vincent's Hospital in New York. And Dr. Harold Dinken is now heading the General Rose rehabilitation program in Denver. Dr. Deaver deserves the major credit for the training they received. He was highly respected and well loved as a teacher. He said exactly what he thought and sometimes this would get people's backs up, but I can remember very few times when he spoke that he wasn't absolutely right.

Among the young doctors was one that I met one day in the spring of 1946 when I was in my office at the *Times* and my secretary came in to say a handsome officer was outside to see me. She ushered him in and he was indeed handsome —a blond, blue-eyed Dutchman who introduced himself as Dr. Klaas Schmidt. His uniform was that of a Dutch ship's surgeon. He told me that before the war he had been a physical therapist in Holland, and that he had emigrated to Java in the Dutch East Indies, where he decided to study medicine. He graduated from a medical school in Java, married a young lady whose father was a Dutch planter in Java, and had been practicing medicine for a year or two when the war came and both he and his wife were captured by the invading Japanese. They were put into separate prison camps and in the three and a half years of their captivity, they saw each other only once, when she was being marched past, from one compound to another, in a group of prisoners. After seeing her that one time at a distance, and without being able to say a word to her, he had spent the rest of his captivity deeply distressed at how thin she had looked. As he later learned, in addition to starvation rations, she had undergone serious surgery in prison, and was apparently just recovering from it when he saw her. In the spring of 1945, he was chosen with a group of other prisoners to be shipped to Japan in a labor battalion. En route, their ship was torpedoed by an American submarine and two thirds of the men drowned. Being a strong swimmer, Schmidt stayed afloat until he was picked up by another Japanese ship and taken to Hiroshima, where he was assigned to work on the construction of air-raid shelters near the outskirts of the city. On the morning of August 6, when the atomic bomb fell on Hiroshima, he was already underground, helping to dig a new shelter.

"We heard this great explosion," he said, "and the ground rumbled and earth fell down around us. We rushed topside to see what was happening and here was this enormous cloud billowing out above the city obliterating the bright sunshine. The whole city was on fire, and our fellow workers who had been above ground looked as if they had been burned all over, even though the explosion had taken place only a couple of minutes earlier. People were running in all directions. Our Japanese guards were nowhere to be seen, so I got hold of some Red Cross packages and we set up a first-aid station for people with burns. Some of them were in very bad condition, even though we were on the edge of the city and the explosion had taken place near the center."

Ten days later, the war was over. The Americans arrived

to free all prisoners, and before long Dr. Schmidt was reunited with his wife on the Swedish ship *Gripsholm*. They returned to Holland, where he had begun a general medical practice, but he wasn't happy in it. Having read in a magazine about the rehabilitation work we were trying to do in New York, he had taken a job as a ship's doctor and worked his way over here to see if he could join us. Though I was very much impressed by him, we had no money to spare, so I told him to apply for a grant at the usual places—the Rockefeller Foundation, the World Health Organization, etc. His chances for a fellowship were slim, and my fears were justified. Unable to obtain any promises, he got back on his ship and I was afraid I'd never see him again.

Six months later, however, he showed up again at my *Times* office wearing the same uniform.

He said, "I haven't even heard from the people to whom I applied for grants, but I desperately want to come here, so I signed on to the ship again to work my way back. Isn't there any way you can find a place for me?"

He was so earnest and appealing I replied, "Go back and get your wife. We'll have something for you when you return."

They arrived with twenty dollars between them. We found them an apartment over a small store and gave both of them jobs, she teaching activities of daily living and he working as a medical trainee. He wanted to get a license to practice physical medicine in the United States, and that meant passing the State board exams, so he put himself on a work-and-study routine of sixteen hours a day. One night his wife, Phene, invited us to a Javanese *rijstafel* dinner; he came to the table just long enough to eat, then excused himself to go back to the bedroom to study. He passed his examinations, got his license, and built up a very successful practice in physical medicine in New York, rehabilitating private patients. Later, he took the message of rehabilitation back to Holland and for several years traveled between here and there.

Two of the first foreign doctors who went through our rehabilitation training at Bellevue came from Czechoslovakia on State Department fellowships. One was a man in his early forties whose special interest centered on spa treatment and hydrology. He had published a few papers and his credentials looked good, so we took him, even though his interests did not exactly coincide with ours. The other was a twenty-three-year-old man named Otokar Machek, a recent medical school graduate. During the war he had been a foot soldier in the British army for two years and then had flown Spitfire planes. His father, who was a doctor in Czechoslovakia, had motivated him to come here and go through our training program. Young Dr. Machek had been married only a few weeks, to a very lovely girl named Mirka, the daughter of a Czech industrialist. Her father had not been able to give her the usual dowry; instead he gave her two hundred beautiful wool dresses, knowing she would be able to sell them on this side of the Atlantic—which she did in Canada, earning enough to supplement the meager salary her husband received as a trainee.

Both of these men did well with us. They had been here less than a year when the Communists took over Czechoslovakia. When I saw them the next day, I was startled. I had never before thought of them in political terms, but now I noticed that the older man looked like the cat who swallowed the canary, while the younger man, Dr. Machek, looked as if someone had hit him over the head with an ax.

I soon suggested to the older doctor that he had had enough training with us and he happily returned home to Communist Czechoslovakia. Dr. Machek, on the other hand, could not return home after the Communists took over unless he wanted to land in a prison camp, so he and his wife sought our help in becoming American citizens. It wasn't easy. When their visas expired, the immigration people insisted on deporting them. For several years we used every argument and legal procedure, but to no avail. They were about to send the Macheks back to what they knew was a dismal fate when I finally remembered that an old friend of mine named Watson Miller had become the Chief of Immigration Services in Washington. I went to see him and told him about the Macheks' predicament.

"I'm sorry," he said somberly, "the law is the law and there's nothing I can do about it." Then he broke out in a big smile. "However, I can tell you this," he continued. "They will not be deported until I sign the final papers, and you see this great pile of papers on my desk. I'm far behind in my work."

Thereupon, he took the Macheks' deportation papers and put them at the very bottom of the pile. A few weeks later the Displaced Persons Act was passed and the Macheks were on their way to becoming American citizens. They went to Missouri, where he passed the licensing boards and took a teaching position at St. Louis University. He and his family are still there. They have raised four fine children and he has made a strong contribution to rehabilitation, not only nationally but also internationally.

One of the most remarkable patients we had during those early days at Bellevue was a Tennessee girl, a paraplegic who sent me a letter after reading about our program in a Memphis newspaper.

Dear Dr. Rusk:

I am a 23-year-old paraplegic. I do believe that if I could get the right treatment and care, I could walk again, somehow, some way.

Since I was in a hospital in 1941, nothing has been done for me. I was only left with that eternal word, "Time." Now I have learned to my stark horror that the longer I go without walking, the less likely it will be that I shall ever walk again.

I am aware of the fact that paralyzed patients do not recover by sheer magic, and that it is a long, hard struggle at best. I am aware how presumptuous it is to write to you like this, but Doctor Rusk, when it comes to walking or not walking, pride and reserve fly out of the window.

Is there not some possible way I could come to Bellevue Hospital? If I could drag about any old way on crutches, I could work to pay back everything I owe. My parents know nothing about my writing to you, or how frantic and desperate I have become. I'm that "little crippled girl who is so cheerful even though she is handicapped." That's because I can smile while everything inside of me is freezing and dying.

I am sure you receive thousands of letters similar to mine, so I don't expect you to read this. I suppose that is the reason I could write it so frankly.

Yours truly,
JAMIE COFFMAN

I was indeed beginning to get a sizable volume of mail from people all over the country. But Jamie Coffman needn't have worried about whether I would read her letter. I wrote her immediately and told her that if she could get herself to New York, we would find a way to get her admitted to Bellevue. This was illegal, of course, because Bellevue is primarily for indigent New York City residents. But some things are more important than rules.

I took her letter to Mr. Sulzberger and I could see he was very much moved by it. "I'm going to put her in Bellevue," I said, "but I don't know how I'll manage it."

He said, "Don't tell me that. I can see by the glint in your eye that you're going to manage it. Let me know when she arrives."

When Jamie arrived, I gave her a fictitious address in New York and signed the papers admitting her. When she was wheeled to her bed, there was a big bouquet of flowers on the table beside it from "A friend." The friend, of course, was Arthur Hays Sulzberger. Jamie came with her sister, Ellen, who had just graduated from a nursing school in Memphis; so she went to work for us right away. Their father was a country doctor, eking out a living in the small town of Whiteville, Tennessee. Jamie's paraplegia was the result of an automobile accident in 1941, when she was a very pretty, popular high school girl. She and a date were coming home from a dance, and their car swerved off the road and crashed, fracturing her spine. The best doctors available in Memphis at that time were unable to do anything for her. So she had been sent home to spend the rest of her life in bed, which is what she had done for four years. But only seven months after she entered the hospital she was walking on her braces and crutches like a dancer. She was one of the greatest crutch-walkers I have ever seen.

Shortly after Jamie's discharge, I had a chance to go to Paris to read a paper before a French medical society on this very subject, the rehabilitation of paraplegics. I didn't have to be very smart to realize that to a group of Frenchmen a girl as pretty as Jamie could sell my ideas much better than I could, so I took her and her sister, Ellen, along to demonstrate, and I must admit we resorted to a shameless bit of show business. While I read my paper, describing all the things that could be done for paraplegics, Jamie lay on the stage behind me on a stretcher putting on her braces. When I was through, she sat up, reached for her crutches, got to her feet and went racing back and forth across the stage. After that, "Mademoiselle Jamie" was the toast of Paris. All the French newspapers printed her story, and people would stop to congratulate her as she walked along the Champs Elysées.

She said to me, "I suddenly realize I'm part of the picture again. I don't have to live a life of retreat any more. I've found my own world."

She had indeed found her world, and I'm happy to say her world is our world. Jamie Coffman is now the head of the A.D.L. (Activities of Daily Living) Department here at the institute, and in my opinion, she knows more about the complex subject of training for the handicapped than anyone else in the world. Her sister, Ellen, is also still with us as our Chief Nurse.

Our program began to grow at Bellevue, and our vision expanded. We began accepting cases which earlier we would not have had the courage to consider. I suppose in a way we were eager to see how high we could fly. Anyway, I was walking through the wards at Bellevue one day when I found someone who was destined to give us a real challenge.

His name was Johnny. He was three years old, and he had been born with what we call "a sack on his back." In other words, he was a *spina bifida* case. He had a congenital defect in the vertebra from which an undeveloped spinal cord protruded in a sack filled with spinal fluid. Sometimes in such cases, pressure develops in the brain from the excess amount of cerebral spinal fluid, and the patient's head becomes en-

larged—he becomes what we call hydrocephalic. Little
Johnny had a tiny, emaciated body with a sack the size of a
grapefruit attached to it, and he had a head too big for the
rest of him. He looked definitely hydrocephalic. He was in
the last bed of the children's ward. It was pointless to put him
where he would get more intensive care. He was not acutely
ill, and there was nothing they could do for him there. He
had a beautiful face but he was very pale. He didn't talk. He
only whimpered softly as he stared out at the world around
him from a bed that was constantly wet. *Spina bifida* cases
usually have no control over their bowels or bladders or any
of their lower extremities.

I was there the day one of our therapists rolled Johnny into
our clinic for evaluation. His skin was as white as paper. He
was wearing diapers. He didn't say a word. He just gazed
into space. He was such a forlorn creature his own parents
had become despondent looking at him and rarely came to
the hospital to see him. We brought him down for evaluation,
and as the therapist lifted him off the stretcher onto the
examining table, he put his arms around her neck and gave
her a pathetic little squeeze. It was the most fortunate thing
little Johnny had ever done. From that moment on, he owned
the therapist. She insisted we keep him, even though his
situation looked hopeless, and she lavished her love and care
upon him. She gave him the first real understanding love he
ever had.

Within a month, he could say about thirty words. In two
months, his bladder came under control. He had been emaciated when he came to us because he was eating poorly, but
now he was eating like a little pig and we began to realize he
was not a hydrocephalic. His head had looked big only because his body was so small. He grew now almost as fast as

he ate. He stopped whimpering and began to smile. He even laughed a little. When we put him on the floor he began to crawl toward us and pull himself up. We wanted to strengthen his arms but we didn't have any parallel bars for children, so we built some, two feet high. We also had braces made for him, the first time, to my knowledge, that had ever been tried on this type of *spina bifida* patient. Dr. Deaver got him special braces with a band around the pelvis, and both knee and hip locks, so he could sit down.

We started training him on the bars, then taught him to use crutches, and within three months or so, he began walking on his crutches away from the bars. By this time, his family eagerly followed his progress and when he finished his training, they took him home.

Although Johnny came back periodically for checkups, I didn't see him again for six or seven years, and then accidentally. One day I went to a meeting at a public school in Brooklyn. It was recess time and the kids were running up and down the halls screaming at each other. Among them was this fine-looking boy who came stumping along at a great rate on his crutches, yelling at the top of his voice. Since I have more than a passing interest in people on crutches, I took a good look at him and suddenly I realized it was Johnny. He didn't remember me, of course, but I remembered him. So I went to see his teacher.

"There's a little boy named Johnny out in the hall," I said, "a paraplegic. I understand he's one of your pupils. Could you tell me how he's doing?"

"Johnny?" the teacher smiled. "He's at the top of the class."

Johnny was our first *spina bifida* case. We now have between four and five hundred such cases under our care, and they all should be thankful to Johnny because he proved to us that even such a disability can be managed. It is worth noting that about thirty years ago a distinguished neurosurgeon used to advocate calculated neglect for such cases to encourage their death. Today, almost 90 percent of our *spina bifida* cases are living at home with their families, and about 80 percent are in school.

We got a good start at Bellevue, and I still have a warm feeling for that hospital for the chance it gave us. But in those first couple of years, when we were limited to Bellevue, we ran up against a growing problem. We kept getting inquiries from patients who, like Jamie Coffman, were not eligible for Bellevue. The pressure was on us to take these patients, and we wanted them, yet while we might sneak in one Jamie Coffman, we couldn't make it a practice. Besides, Bellevue itself was supplying us with as many patients as we could handle in those two wards. We knew the eventual answer. We had to start raising funds to build a full-sized institute. Meanwhile we had to take care of all the patients knocking at our door.

AS THE PRESSURE TO OPEN A REHABILITATION CENTER for private patients increased, all kinds of ideas occurred to me, including one which was more spectacular than it was practical. We suggested to Bernard Baruch, who seemed always ready to help us, that as a temporary expedient we secure a Navy hospital ship that had been decommissioned, moor her in the East River just across the street from Bellevue, and convert her into an interim rehabilitation center which would be open to the public. Willing as he was to help, he couldn't do us any good on this project. It was unbelievably expensive, so we looked around for another solution.

One day, when I was visiting Mr. Samuel Milbank and Dr. Frank Boudreau of The Milbank Memorial Fund in an effort to get financial support for our permanent institute, I told them about our desperate desire to take care of the growing list of people who needed treatment but who were not eligible for Bellevue. Mr. Milbank turned to Dr. Boudreau, the fund's director, and said, "What about that old building we've got on East Thirty-eighth Street?"

Milbank was a wealthy financier who had long been active

in public health projects, and whose foundation has supported many good health causes, nationally and internationally. The building to which he referred was a run-down five-story structure, and he had loaned it to the city for a dollar a year rather than let it sit vacant. But the city wasn't using it for anything important and he had the right to take it back on sixty days' notice. Though it was ill-suited architecturally for our purposes (its one small elevator was barely large enough to accommodate a stretcher), we had some architects make an estimate of the cost of refurbishing it. They told me it would come to sixty thousand dollars.

Sixty thousand dollars in those days looked as big as the national debt, so I went to New York University Chancellor Harry Woodburn Chase and asked if he would advance the money. He was a kind man and he liked our program, but he didn't have any money to spare.

"I'll tell you what I'll do," he said. "I'll loan you the sixty thousand from university funds, but I've got to get it back pretty fast. How soon do you think you could have your institute operating in the black?"

"Six weeks," I said.

He looked at me as if I should consult a psychiatrist, but he gave me the money. Actually I was not as crazy as I sounded. We already had quite a list of people who wanted treatment, and we had also developed our relationship with John L. Lewis and his United Mine Workers welfare fund, which promised to send us as many disabled miners as we could handle. They had no doctors trained in rehabilitation, no adequate hospitals, no facilities for rehabilitation treatment in the coal-mining areas of Kentucky, West Virginia, Pennsylvania and Ohio. Lewis wanted to do something for his men that would be both useful and visible, so he had sent the medical directors of the fund, Drs. Warren Draper and Royd Sayers, to see me.

The story they told was shattering. Up to the end of the war, nearly two thousand miners a year were being killed in mine accidents, and well over thirty thousand a year were injured. "Our union now has fifty thousand men who are totally incapacitated because of injury or disease," Dr. Draper said. "And we've got an enormous number of men with broken backs. Walls of coal fall on them, or heavy wooden beams, and after they've had the routine hospital treatment, nothing is done for them. They lie around in their dingy little homes, rotting away with bedsores and kidney complications. It's perfectly awful. Nobody has ever made an attempt to rehabilitate men like these. We'd like to try it but we have no place to send them."

I had assured Dr. Draper that as quickly as I could manage it, he'd have a place to start sending them. Now that we had the building on Thirty-eighth Street and the sixty thousand with which to refurbish it, I sent him word that he should start getting his first group ready. But as often happens, rising costs made the sixty thousand inadequate, and we found ourselves about twenty-five thousand short. Once again I had to thank Bernard Baruch. He was not as wealthy as people thought he was, but he didn't hesitate to dip into his own pocket and come up with the twenty-five thousand for us. This was in addition to the $250,000 he had already given New York University to help launch the Department of Physical Medicine.

So when we opened our small forty-bed temporary institute on Thirty-eighth Street on March 1, 1948, we opened with a full house. The United Mine Workers sent us twenty-seven men; the rest of our patients came from private sources. Though the facilities were makeshift, the care was not. Dr. Donald Covalt was now our clinical director and he is still with us today as the associate director of the Institute. Dr. Edward Lowman joined our staff at this time and today is director of professional services. We were able to offer physical therapy, occupational therapy, physical rehabilitation, social service, vocational guidance and testing, plus prosthetic services. We even had the first model kitchen designed by Dr. Lillian Gilbreth, the subject of *Cheaper by the Dozen,* to teach disabled housewives how to keep house from a wheelchair.

One of the first miners sent to us was a man with a broken back who had been in bed for nineteen years. They found him when the union sent a team into the mountain coal communities looking for people who needed care—he was one of many men they found that nobody knew existed. He lived on a mountainside in one of the Kentucky counties near the Harlan area. They couldn't even get a wagon up to his house. They had to carry him down piggyback. He had never had any real medical care. His wife looked after him, using old bed sheets for bandages; she boiled those bandages day after day for all those years to keep him clean—and alive. They had never heard a radio, never seen a movie. But after being told about our institute, he wanted to come.

When he arrived in New York, his legs were so contracted it took four surgical procedures to straighten them out. He had eleven bed sores that required twenty-six plastic surgical skin flaps to close. And he had a stone in each kidney that had to be removed. It was nine months before we could even start training him. But he was a man of great courage and was determined to get back home and look after his wife and children. Soon he was on his feet and within six months he was walking beautifully with crutches, taking care of himself as if he had no handicap. But the question remained, what would he do when he got home? Then one day he got an idea. He decided to run for sheriff of his county. It was not a very popular job around the Harlan, Kentucky, area. A number of previous sheriffs had died of "lead poisoning," so the competition for the office wasn't great. When he went home and announced his plans, he got the nomination on both the Democratic and Republican tickets, and for several years after that, he was the sheriff. He had won so much respect he survived in a job which had been fatal to a series of able-bodied men.

Another of our first miner patients was a black man in his early thirties named Wesley Smith, from Birmingham, Alabama. He was born tongue-tied, had a harelip, and his education stopped at second grade. He went to work in the coal mines when he was in his early teens and a piece of rock fell on him, breaking his back. At one of those mining-town hospitals where the care was less than adequate, they tried a bone graft, but infection set in and they had to amputate a leg. So here he was with one leg, a partially healed broken back, and no education. The only thing he had going for him was a warm, winning smile, and everyone in the institute came to love him. We fitted him with an artificial leg and he quickly learned to walk. His back problem straightened out. We untied his tongue so he could talk quite well, and pretty soon he was ready to go home.

One day he came to me and said, "Doctor, I don't want to go back to work in no coal mine no more. I want to be a hospital man. Couldn't you give me a job as a porter?"

I said, "I don't know, Wes, but we'll see. We'll give you on-the-job training while you're still a patient, and if it works out, maybe we can manage it."

He turned out to be one of the best men we had, and excellent with patients. The day we discharged him, he went to work for us and he was with us for ten years before he died.

Altogether we trained more than five hundred paralyzed miners through the years, and 80 percent of them went back to work in some capacity with mining companies or in their communities after going to vocational schools to learn new trades. One man went into business for himself, making fishing flies and repairing fishing gear. Several went to work in filling stations. They stayed with us an average of three months each, and the very day one of them was discharged, another arrived in New York to take his place.

At the same time, we had as many private patients as we could take. And within six weeks, as I had forecast, we were paying our way. The only thing I regretted was that we had to do so, because our need to remain solvent made us turn down many patients who needed help.

Nowadays, 90 percent of our patients at the institute are what we call third-party cases. Some or all of their costs are paid by insurance, labor unions, organizational funds, Medicare or Medicaid. If that doesn't cover them, we're able to help out through a fund of our own. But in those days, we didn't have a dime to spare, and we were out begging for money to build the permanent institute building.

It wasn't easy for me to go out and ask for money. Because of my Midwestern pioneer tradition of self-reliance, I was deeply embarrassed whenever I asked people for money. Then one day I looked in the mirror and told myself, "You silly fool, if you go on this way you'll always be miserable.

You're not raising this money for yourself. You're raising it for something in which you believe, and if that embarrasses you, you're in the wrong business. If you feel that way you'd better go back to private practice and forget rehabilitation." And suddenly I remembered an expression I had heard often from our minister, Walter McNeely. He used to say in his sermons, "The most important thing in life is to first get yourself off your hands." That's how I got myself off my hands in those early days of fund-raising.

Still, I was never what you'd call a "hard sell" man. I let the facts stand for themselves. I talked about our need, and if people wanted to give, they gave. In the early days of our fund-raising, besides all those speeches I made, we developed a technique which was better than a million words. We already had several patients who had been trained to a level where their performance was a little short of miraculous. There was Jamie Coffman, for instance, and Tommy Miley and his wife, Alice, all of whom I've mentioned, and Tom Francis, a young lawyer who had suffered polio. All of them enjoyed demonstrating their skill at these meetings whenever we could arrange to take them. They liked to feel a part of the team. Alice Miley had a wonderful demonstration; she would throw away her crutches and fall flat on her face, breaking her fall with her hands. Then, by a technique she had carefully developed, she'd get up and walk away. She always stopped the show. Further words were not needed.

Tom Francis, incidentally, was an interesting and unusual case. He was a young lawyer from Oklahoma. I was introduced to him by a mutual friend because we had something in common. We both had gone to the University of Missouri. But on his first vacation after becoming an attorney, Tom had contracted polio during a trip to Mexico, and he was completely paralyzed in both his arms and his legs. He could turn one hand outside and one hand inside, and he could move his fingers just slightly. After his attack he had spent six years in hospitals, including two in a polio rehabilitation center, all to no avail. When I met him he was in the process of using all that remained of his savings to buy his way into a home for incurables.

He said to me, "What do you think of the idea?"

"I think you're an absolute fool."

He was taken aback, and I guess, rather startled and hurt to have a stranger talk to him this way.

"I didn't realize you practiced law with your hands and feet," I continued. "I thought you used your mind, your knowledge, your training, your personality, your eyes, ears and voice. You've got all those things."

"Yes, but what can I do with them?"

"You can come down to us at Bellevue and learn how to take care of yourself," I said. "Then you can go back to practicing law. That's what you can do."

He looked incredulous for a minute, then he smiled and said, "All right, when can I start? I'll be there tomorrow if you want me."

As soon as we had a bed for him he checked in and we went to work on every bit of muscle power he had left. We got him a special electric typewriter which had just been invented by IBM, thanks to Mrs. Thomas Watson, Sr., who had seen the need for it when she visited a veterans hospital two years earlier. She had gone home and asked her husband, the president of IBM, to put his brilliant research and development staff to work on a feather-touch keyboard for handicapped people. The electric typewriter was the result. The day it arrived Tom Francis wrote a full-page single-spaced

letter on it to his mother, the first personal correspondence
he had been able to accomplish in seven years. He was soon
rattling along on it at a merry pace and in the meantime we
taught him how to handle other things. The placement of his
legs when he went to sleep, for instance. That may not sound
like much, but it was very important to him because if his
legs weren't properly arranged, he couldn't turn over in bed.

Before long, another wonderful thing happened to him. He
fell in love with one of our pretty nurses, a mature girl about
his age, and she fell in love with him. Suddenly I found
myself in the advice-to-the-lovelorn business.

Tom would say to me, "Do you think I really ought to
marry her?"

I would say, "Not if you're marrying her for security. Not
if it's just to be mothered. That'll be more trouble than you're
in now."

The next day, she would say to me, "Do you think I ought
to marry him?"

And I'd say to her, "Not if you just feel sorry for him and
want to mother him."

Her family came to talk to me and I told them the same
thing. Finally, the lovers made up their own minds and they
were married. My friend William Zeckendorf helped them
get a little apartment at Forty-eighth Street and Third Avenue. The company for which Tom had done oil briefs in
Oklahoma before his illness gave him some work he could do
at home on his electric typewriter. Then P.C. Spencer, the
president of Sinclair Oil Company, to whom I had spoken
about Tom, gave him a few trial assignments and he was so
good they put him on a retainer to do oil briefs for them. He
and his wife had a very happy life for twenty years. He
became a member of the vestry in his church. He worked in

the Boy Scouts. He mastered all the techniques of self-help so well the two of them used to travel by air to the oil fields together, even though he was confined to his wheelchair. Unfortunately, on one of his working trips to Colorado a few years ago, he contracted pneumonia, which, combined with his severe disability and the high altitude, proved fatal. But during the twenty years they were together, I knew of no happier, more loving, and self-reliant couple than Tom Francis and his wife.

By the latter part of 1947, we had some very efficient fund-raising groups organized. We developed committees, took ads in the local newspapers, spoke on radio and television and continued our demonstrations.

At the same time I was cultivating some potential sources of large contributions. When I first came to New York, I had spoken to Mr. Sulzberger at the *Times* about my dream of building an institute. He was a sensitive man and especially concerned about rehabilitation problems because he was having a most difficult and painful time himself with arthritis of the hands. He could endure pain, but he was very much bothered by a recurring dream in which he was a pianist. His hands would suddenly become disabled and he could no longer play the piano and earn a living. He would awaken from this dream night after night in a cold sweat and full of anguish. Though he was a man of substance, he developed as a result of this dream a great empathy for those whose handicaps might deprive them of their means of livelihood, and he was therefore always eager to help us fulfill our aims.

One day I asked how he felt about asking Mrs. Bernard Gimbel, wife of the great department-store owner, to help. He replied, "If you can get her, there would be none better." I had met Mrs. Gimbel once before, and when I called her she was most gracious about seeing me. She had been very active during the war in the American Women's Volunteer Service, and I suggested to her now that it would be a great thing if this organization were to continue its work in the field of rehabilitation. She was so enthusiastic about the idea that she called all her New York friends who had been part of the group and set up a meeting at which I could speak to them.

Though I did speak to these ladies, with every nickel's worth of salesmanship I could muster, it didn't work. Mrs. Gimbel told me later, "They just won't buy it. They think it's too big. Some of them don't even believe in it. One lady who is interested in New York Hospital pointed out to me that they have no such program there, so it can't be much good. But I believe in it, so let's see what we can do."

From that moment on, Mrs. Gimbel was totally dedicated to our program. She wrote letters to her friends, and she set up meeting after meeting where I could talk to people. Then one cold winter Sunday, she invited Glad and me to their home near Greenwich, Connecticut, for lunch. Besides the Gimbels, Mr. and Mrs. John La Gorce were there (he was the editor of *National Geographic* magazine), Mr. and Mrs. Gene Tunney, and Mr. and Mrs. Sidney Rheinstein (he was a stockbroker, one of Bernard Gimbel's closest friends and his number one gin-rummy partner).

After a splendid lunch, Mr. Gimbel cocked his head toward me and said, "Alva has been telling me a lot about this program of yours. It interests me. She also tells me you had a big practice in St. Louis and you made considerable sacrifice to come here and try this thing. But I want you to know I don't take anything for granted. I've had you looked up one side and down the other. I've had you investigated in St.

Louis, in Washington, and in New York, and I find that everything Alva told me is true. So we're going to support you. We're going to give you a hundred thousand dollars."

I nearly fell off my chair. This was the first big contribution we had ever been offered, aside from what Mr. Baruch had given to New York University, and I thought surely I had misunderstood him.

Sidney Rheinstein then spoke up and said, "If you give a hundred, Bernard, I'll give fifteen."

Mr. Gimbel said, "Excellent, Sidney. You can afford fifteen."

Gene Tunney said, "I'll also give fifteen."

Mr. Gimbel said, "No, Gene, you can't afford that much. You can give five."

Then Jack La Gorce, who was not in the same financial league with these other gentlemen, also gave a generous contribution, and we had our fund-raising venture off the ground. As our campaign progressed, several other large contributions came from a score of foundations, many business firms and labor unions, totaling more than five hundred thousand dollars. Meanwhile, countless numbers of smaller contributions from individuals added another two hundred thousand.

About two or three weeks after that memorable lunch, Mrs. Gimbel again invited me to lunch and introduced me to Mr. Louis Horowitz, the great contractor who build the first Gimbel store, the Waldorf Astoria, the Union Station in Washington and many other famous structures. He had been on the board of directors of Gimbel Stores for years, and Bernard Gimbel was like a younger brother to him. After lunch I began giving Mr. Horowitz my pitch about the need for a rehabilitation center, but I could see that as he listened he was embarrassed.

Finally, he said, "It sounds like a wonderful idea, but I'm a man who likes to do only one thing at a time, and the bulk of my foundation funds are going to another program in which I am deeply interested. I can see the need for your program but I just can't do anything for you."

I thanked him and assured him I understood. Then one day months later in the summer of 1948, after our temporary institute was in operation on Thirty-eighth Street, he called and said he wanted to come down and see me.

He came into my office and said, "All right, tell me about this program again."

I went over what I had told him before, but in addition, I was able to show him something of our work. Jamie Coffman, who was by then working for us, put on a demonstration for him, and they soon became fast friends. Then we took Mr. Horowitz through the building and let him meet our patients.

When we got back to my office, he said, "I may make a change in what I'm doing with my money. I'm looking into a number of programs. I'll think about yours, and if I am interested I'll get in touch with you."

A month passed. I didn't hear a word from him and was getting itchy, but I fought off the temptation to call him.

Finally, he came back to see me. "I've made my decision," he said. "This is what I'm going to do. I'm giving you a hundred thousand dollars now and I'll give you more two years from now."

Had he stopped right there it would have been enough to make me jump with joy. But he wasn't finished.

"I've also decided something else," he continued. "I'm going to make your institute the beneficiary in my will so you'll get my entire residual estate. I've taken care of my wife and everyone for whom I want to provide. I've talked to

Bernard Baruch, whom I've known for years, and John D. Rockefeller, Jr., and my family doctor, and they all agree about the great future need for what you are doing. So you'll get the rest of what I leave. Right now it amounts to about six million dollars. How do you want it?"

It was a day I'll never forget. When I recovered my voice, I thanked him and said, "If possible, I'd like one third for training, one third for research, and one third to help take care of patients who can't afford to pay for it."

Eventually it worked out not quite that way. Mr. Horowitz decided to leave one million for training, a half a million to endow a chair in physical medicine and rehabilitation here at the New York University, and the rest for patient care at the institute. And in the meantime, Mr. Horowitz's resources continued to grow, so that when he died in 1956 it was not just six million, but eleven million dollars that he left to us.

Before leaving the subject of gifts to the institute, I must mention another one, a $450,000 contribution from a source which will surprise no one. It came in 1949 from Bernard Baruch.

By this time the need for research and training in the rehabilitation field was so pressing, we were seeking money for this purpose at the same time we were soliciting for our building fund. I went to Alan Gregg at the Rockefeller Foundation and told him about all of our various needs. When we got onto the subject of research projects he said, "Here's what I want to do. Don't come to us with something easy to sell, something you could get somebody else to finance. Wait till you get a fundamental project, something colorless and difficult to sell. Bring that to me and let me take a look at it."

As it happened, we felt the great need for a project that

would define the role of neurology and psychiatry in rehabilitation. An important research but not a very glamorous one. I took it to Alan Gregg and sure enough, the Rockefeller Foundation gave us the money for a five-year program which taught us how best to use these two important specialties in total rehabilitation.

Shortly after moving into the Thirty-eighth Street building, by overcrowding ourselves a bit, we were able to increase our capacity to fifty-one in-patients and about one hundred daily out-patients. The place was dark and a bit dingy, but the spirit was great because we felt we were getting someplace. We were still short of staff (our entire budget for that first year was less than sixty thousand), but we got a lot of outside volunteer help, especially from the Junior League of New York, which sent us a number of lovely, talented young ladies who pitched in to do any kind of work they could manage.

One of our patients at that time was a New York girl who had been a commercial artist until she broke her neck in a Colorado car accident. When she came to us, she had the use of her arms but not her hands. A brilliant girl, she trained beautifully, and with the aid of special handles on combs, brushes, toothbrushes, powder puffs and so on, she learned to take care of her daily toilet. She also learned to feed herself, to turn over in bed, and to get around in a special wheelchair we had designed for her. But one thing that still worried us was what we could do for her vocationally. She couldn't go back to being a commercial artist. Or could she? We were then learning that you don't tell handicapped people what they can't do, because you're never sure they aren't able to do it until you see them try. We made a special leather mitten for her with a thong clasp so she could put it on herself or take it off and fasten or unfasten it with her teeth. At the finger end of the mitten were sockets for paint brushes. An artist paints by moving his arm, not his fingers. This girl was soon painting almost as well as she had before she was hurt. And when she was ready, it took us only three days to find her a job. Instead of becoming a lifelong drain on her parents, or on the City of New York, she was soon earning her own way again.

We also had a wonderful middle-aged Jewish lady from the Lower East Side of New York whose children were grown and had left home, and who lived with her husband, a day laborer, in a two-room, walk-up cold-water flat. Because she was completely helpless and they had almost no resources, she and her husband had come to the tearful conclusion that she would have to be put away for the rest of her life—which might be many years—in a city institution. When we heard of her case we took her as an experiment, not knowing what we could do. She had been in bed about four months, and was a flaccid type of hemiplegic, with absolutely no control on one side. It took us a month to get her so she could sit up four hours a day in a wheelchair. Then we fitted her with a long leg brace and she started to walk. She soon went back to their little cold-water flat and resumed keeping house, and I remember her husband bragging about her one day about two years after she had finished training.

"She cleans, she dusts, she cooks, she does everything," he said, "and she still makes the best gefüllte fish in New York. You should taste it."

Around that time I received a letter from my old friend Dr. Frank Lahey, a distinguished surgeon and head of the Lahey Clinic, that gave me a certain amount of satisfaction. Frank had been one of the doctors who said to me when I came to New York at the end of the war, "When are you going to stop this departure from internal medicine and get back into the practice of medicine where you belong?" But the letter he sent me in 1948 went something like this:

Dear Howard,

I just returned from a meeting of the Western Surgical Society out in Utah and I saw one of my classmates, a brilliant, distinguished surgeon who has suffered a stroke. He's paralyzed on one side of his body and he can't speak a word. I've been asking around, trying to figure out what can be done for him, and I keep hearing from other doctors that you've got the only place where he might be helped. Will you please take him in? He's a wonderful man and he badly needs help. I'll deeply appreciate anything you can do.

Sincerely,
FRANK

P.S. I think I gave you bad advice two years ago.

Needless to say, we did take in his friend and helped him considerably. Dr. Frank Lahey's conversion to our viewpoint meant a lot to me, not only because he was a friend, but because it represented the beginning of a change in the attitudes of many doctors around the country. The change was painfully slow, however, even though the need was great. The Yale University Department of Public Health did a survey in New Haven about this time and discovered that 121 people out of every 1,000 in that community suffered medically from a chronic disease or a physical disability. Forty percent of that number, or 4 percent of the population, were so severely disabled that they were housebound, and of these helpless people, almost half were under the age of twenty-five. If New Haven is a typical community, you would have to conclude from this that 12 percent of the American population had some type of demonstrable disability which called for the application of special training devices and help in emotional adjustment as well as occupational training in order to make them useful citizens. We were proving in case after case that such rehabilitation would pay off both to the handicapped themselves and to the taxpayers, but our findings had barely made a dent in the thinking of most Americans, including doctors.

I remember, for example, the case of a medical student in the Loma Linda Medical School in California, who had been in an automobile accident during his second year and had broken his neck. He was a quadriplegic with a high cervical lesion which meant that he was paralyzed from the neck down, but had the power to clench his fists partway, although he couldn't close them. He could bend his elbows, and gravity would straighten them; he could extend his wrists, and gravity would relax them; and he could shrug his shoulders. That was all. One of the reasons we took him was that the medical school out there pressured us to do so. I said, All right, we'll rehabilitate him if you promise to readmit him as a medical student when he's ready. They agreed to this, so he came and trained with us. It took about eleven months, and among the things we did toward the end of that period was to service-test him on microscopes and various laboratory equipment to make sure he could do the lab work he would have to do. By now he was self-sufficient in a wheelchair, and when we were satisfied he was ready to go back to school, I wrote the dean and told him so.

Two weeks later we got a letter from the dean saying he

was very sorry but they couldn't readmit the boy because he would never be able to qualify for the California licensing board. In order to qualify for practice in California he would have to deliver six babies. In their view, that eliminated him.

Generally speaking, a qualification like that makes sense. One would ordinarily expect a doctor to be able to deliver a baby. But this boy had no intention of being an obstetrician, and it was ridiculous that limitations of his ability in that direction should bar him from the use of his abilities in other medical fields which might be just as important. So I called the dean and asked, "Is that the only problem about readmitting him?"

The dean said, "If he could overcome that, we'd be glad to welcome him back."

"Then here's what you do," I said. "When he comes up for the obstetrical service, arrange for him to live in the hospital for two or three weeks. You pick out the first multipara that comes in [a woman who has had several children] with a history of easy deliveries, put him in his wheelchair in a gown and gloves, drape him with sterile sheets, roll him up into position under the stirrups and give him something with which to catch the baby. I don't care what. A trout net, maybe. I'll guarantee he won't let the baby fall. He has enough strength and skill to tie the umbilical cord, and I'm sure he'll be able to deliver six babies that way as well as the next doctor."

I guess they saw the absurdity of the situation. They readmitted the boy, he finished school, took his examinations, got his license and went into teaching. He is now an assistant professor of neuropathology in one of California's top medical schools. And his story is not unique. I know of three quadriplegics who have gone through medical school, earned their licenses, and are now practicing medicine and doing a first-rate job.

People like that illustrate one of the most important rules in rehabilitation. When you work with a handicapped person, you've got to think of his abilities more than his disabilities. You've got to remember that our society doesn't pay for physical strength. We now have machines to do the heavy labor. Our society really pays for just two things, the skill of your hands and what you have in your head. You could be the fastest runner or highest jumper in town and still be too stupid to make a living. The average person uses only about 25 percent of his physical capacity in daily life. A blind man has to learn to use a hundred percent-plus of his abilities in at least two areas—his senses of hearing and touch—to compensate for his loss of sight. He taps his white cane. Why? Because he can hear the echo coming back and tell from the sound whether it has bounced off a wall, a tree, a hedge or an open space. The rest of us can't hear that echo at all. Such abilities don't even show themselves until they are needed.

It has been said no one has been able to learn Braille accurately and rapidly until his sight was gone. Many people, discovering that they would be blind in six months or a year, have tried to learn Braille. They can get a little head start, but nobody can really master it until he is actually sightless and his untapped ability comes into play. A deaf man hears with his eyes when he reads lips. Put him in a job where eyesight is the ultimate essential, make him a typesetter or an inspector on an assembly line for instance, and he'll be better than the so-called normal worker. In the same way, if you put a paraplegic on a bench job requiring hand skill and upper-arm strength, he'll outstrip the production output records of the ordinary workers beside him because he has developed muscles they don't even know they have. You don't need physical wholeness to be the best at a particular occupation, whether it be lawyer, doctor, elevator operator, teacher, researcher, potato peeler or even President of the United States.

I've mentioned our continuing campaign to find doctors interested in training for rehabilitation careers. We had already begun to attract some very fine young American doctors when, in 1948, the United Nations gave us a break which made me begin to see the tremendous need for programs like ours in foreign countries, and the great impact it could have on international understanding. The U.N. that year sent us two doctors on fellowships. One of them was a general practitioner from Guatemala, Dr. Miguel Aguilera, who had become interested in what we were doing after reading about the program in a magazine. He was a short, rotund man with a quiet smile, a good student and a hard worker. At the end of a year with us, he knew he wasn't yet ready to go back and launch a rehabilitation project in Guatemala, so with the help of friends we got him a fellowship for a second year. As that time drew to a close, he said to me one day, "I still don't know how to get such a program started in my country. There's nothing there. What should I do?"

I said, "I'm sure you have many paraplegics in the Guatemala City municipal hospital. Go down there and pick out two or three of the most likely ones, fit them with braces, teach them to walk and try to get jobs for them. When you've got them ready, present them before the staff at one of their meetings."

He did this and his colleagues were overwhelmed by it. Nothing like it had ever happened there. The government welfare and social security officials were especially impressed because they had so many disabled people on the relief roles. They practically mobbed him when they saw his patients perform. He was the answer to their prayers. One of them said, "We'll send you a hundred patients tomorrow."

Dr. Aguilera was bewildered. He wrote me and said, "What can I do? I'm only one man."

He began sending us more people to train. Fifteen Guatemalans took our courses—doctors, nurses, therapists —and when they returned home they established a school of their own. The social security program in Guatemala provided an excellent building in which Dr. Aguilera set up a 200-bed program. Later, the government became even more interested, as did the people of Guatemala, and they built another facility, the Franklin Delano Roosevelt Hospital and Rehabilitation Center for Crippled Children, in Guatemala City. Now, thanks to Dr. Aguilera, they have the finest such program in all of Latin America. If the Guatemalans have reason to thank him, so have we: he helped prove the value of our foreign-fellowship program. Through the years we have trained more than a thousand doctors from eighty-five different countries, and 95 percent of those doctors are now back in their countries looking after their own people.

A year after we began training doctors from other countries, a surprising thing happened. The Communist government of Poland, through the United Nations, invited me to go there and see what could be done to help with the problems of the disabled. As I later learned, there were more amputees in the city of Warsaw (a result of the Russian–German battles for the city) than our Army, Navy or Air Force had during World War II. An estimated two hundred thousand citizens of Warsaw were disabled by the war. They also had forty thousand polio cases and forty thousand children with cerebral palsy, plus other congenital disabilities.

Fortunately, I was able to take my wife with me. We landed in Warsaw at the height of a great windstorm in October 1949; fifteen minutes after we arrived, we were taken to a large hall, where about three hundred people had assembled—doctors, health workers, government officials. I could see they were expecting an immediate speech, which was all right, except that I soon realized my audience might not be as friendly as I was assuming it to be.

The young man who introduced me had black hair and the blackest eyes I had ever seen and showed more challenge than friendship when he looked at me. His introduction was curt.

"Dr. Rusk, we greet you in Poland," he said, "but we are a little surprised that a person like you would deign to come behind the Iron Curtain."

I was tired, a bit apprehensive, and also a bit angry. I decided I might as well make or break the mission right then, especially when I sensed that the audience was as cold as the man who had presented me.

"Mrs. Rusk and I are in Poland as guests of your government," I said. "We've come here for only one reason, to try to help you with your disabled people, of whom I understand you have many. If a man's legs are off, his difficulties are the same, whether he's a Pole, a Russian, a Chinese or an American, and if we are to proceed, we'll proceed in that frame of reference."

I began to talk and I showed some films, and the ice gradually broke. After the speech we went to dinner with a small group, and as the evening progressed, our escorts became friendlier. By the next day, doors began opening for us and eventually we were allowed to travel all over the country, visiting places our embassy's staff had never been.

The aftereffects of the war were evident throughout the

country. When we reached Poznan, we met Professor Wiktor Dega, a truly great physician, who later was given a cherished Lasker Award. He was doing what he could to cope with the problems of the disabled. It was a cold day in October and his office was freezing. There was no heat because the coal supply, not the weather, dictated when the furnaces would be started. Hanging on the office wall was a picture of a very handsome young man, obviously a doctor, with a stethoscope sticking out of the pocket of his white coat. It was apparent that this man meant something to the professor, so I said, in an effort to begin the conversation on a friendly note, "What a wonderful-looking man. I hope we'll meet him."

"Unfortunately, you can't meet him," the professor said. "He was in the Warsaw underground during the war. He got an emergency call to the ghetto one night after curfew, and while he was operating on a desperately sick Jewish child, the Nazis burst in upon them. They killed him, the child and everyone else in the room."

Dr. Dega also told me that between 65 and 70 percent of the faculty at the University of Poznan had been wiped out by the Germans. When the survivors returned they found the head of the Dean of Faculty pickled in a bottle of alcohol in the basement of one of the buildings. Dr. Dega and his wife, though both eminent physicians, were still having a hard time getting anything done in their area, but they did arrange for me to see a wonderful children's rehabilitation center in Swiebodzin about sixty miles from Poznan.

This institution was run by a man who had lost both of his legs, and you could sense what a fine place it was because you could feel throughout it the deep love everyone had for these children. It was like a summer camp. The kids themselves had helped dredge a part of a reed-filled lake to make it into a swimming pool. Someone had a camera and had taken a picture of a one-legged boy on a diving board, with his hands up, ready to go into the water. The caption under it said in Polish, "I have fulfilled my life's ambition. I can swim."

The staff at this institution had built special equipment for these kids, but it was pathetically inadequate, as was the equipment we saw throughout Poland. In Piekary Slaskie the only equipment available was a set of German physiotherapy machines already about forty years old, operated by an elderly physical culturist, who had been trained in Germany and considered these machines the world's most modern. Actually what he had was a torture unit. One item was an iron contraption that looked like a horse. When you got on, it would shake you in all directions. I tried it and it buffeted me about so hard I was stiff and sore for days.

Just before our departure from Poland, I went in to see a man named Zygmunt Lancmansky, chief of the Invalid Foundation in the Ministry of Labor and Social Welfare, a good-looking man about forty years old with snow-white hair as the result of spending three years in a number of German concentration camps. I thanked him for his many courtesies, and he thanked me.

Then he said, "This has been a good mission. We have learned much to help us with our disabled, but more than that, we have learned that Poland and the United States have many common problems. If we could just work on these problems together, maybe someday we could learn to know each other well enough to live peaceably together in this world. If we don't learn this, we're all wasting our time."

"Those words are worth the whole mission to me," I replied. I was deeply moved and felt this passionately.

When we returned home, we began sending paper, pencils, paints and other supplies to the children's center in Swiebodzin. The first two letters that came back were very gracious and friendly. But after the third shipment, we got a formal card which said, "Thank you so much, but don't send any more. We don't need anything, we have all we need."

The political climate on both sides of the Iron Curtain was becoming colder at that time. Later, the situation eased, and in 1957 I was invited back to Poland. I found that the country had made remarkable progress in developing rehabilitation services. A college-level school of physical therapy had been launched. There were six hundred rehabilitation officers throughout the country, as opposed to thirty in 1949. Five vocational training centers were graduating twelve hundred physically handicapped workers each year, and more than ninety-five thousand disabled workers were employed in cooperative workshops. Dr. Wiktor Dega had been a strong factor in this progress, as had the man who was my interpreter on my first trip, Dr. Alexander Hulek. The latter eventually became head of the whole program in Poland and then served as director of the Rehabilitation Office of the United Nations and has been a leader in all international rehabilitation activities. The U.S. government, responding to this kind of initiative among the Poles, has supported a number of research projects there, including a very interesting one directed by Dr. Marion Weiss at a center called Constantin, just outside Warsaw.

About ten years ago, Dr. Weiss found that patients having their legs amputated could be fitted—right on the operating table—with plaster-of-Paris casts from which peg legs could be attached. If everything was done properly, these people could walk with little discomfort the day after the operation.

He put a crude kind of shoe on the end of this temporary leg to lessen the psychological impact of having lost a limb, and he found that such patients felt less discomfort and got out of the hospital several weeks earlier than those who stayed in bed the conventional period of time. Dr. Weiss's findings were soon reported at an international medical meeting in Copenhagen. His methods are now in general use throughout the world, especially here in America where it has become standard procedure to ambulate the amputee very early and, when possible, fit him for his limb on the operating table.

In 1949, thanks to our success at Bellevue, our institute assumed an additional responsibility for the City of New York. At Goldwater Memorial Hospital, a municipal institution on Welfare Island in the East River, we were given a hundred beds in two wards, and some additional basement space, where we set up a rehabilitation service for older people. Dr. Michael Dasco took charge of the project. He was a Hungarian physician who had come to the United States as a refugee in 1939, a splendid doctor with great feeling for his patients. Later we were given an additional hundred beds, but Dr. Dasco and his co-workers found that of the new beds assigned to us, ninety already had patients in them, and it would take a long time to get them placed somewhere else. So he and his staff decided to begin their work by finding out something about these patients.

He discovered that these ninety people had been in the hospital an average of five hundred days, and that some of them had been there since the place opened twelve years before. But only seven of them were now in need of continuing hospital care. They were there because they had no money, no families, and no place else to go. They had been there so long, they were permanent fixtures. They had fallen between the slats of memory, which was not only sad for them but expensive for the City of New York. This discovery led to another project, sponsored by a great medical philanthropist, David M. Heyman, president of the New York Foundation and the American Hospital Association. We did a carefully planned study encompassing ten thousand patients in all the New York City hospitals and learned that at least a third of them did not need hospital care, but were there for the same reason as those poor people at Goldwater. They had no money and no place to go. And while the per diem cost at Goldwater was nineteen dollars, in the city's general hospitals even then it was more than forty-five dollars a day. It was a terrible waste, both in money and lives.

When you studied these patients, there were great similarities among them. It seemed that whenever I went into a ward in a municipal hospital anywhere in the country, the patients in the back beds were always the same. They were older people who had suffered a fractured hip or a stroke, or Parkinson's disease or some chronic vascular disease. On the bedside table there would be an old candy box (usually a box of chocolate-covered cherries), in which, if you opened it, you would find two or three last-year's Christmas cards, maybe one letter, a comb, sometimes a hairbrush or a little box of face powder, and often a preparation to keep false teeth from falling out. If they were lucky they had a little bedside radio. Instinctively you knew that, though they had disabilities, they weren't actually sick and they didn't need day-to-day hospital care. Yet here they lay, bored to death, day after day, year after year, in an atmosphere of acute sickness. In the middle of their favorite radio soap opera— the one thing to which they looked forward—they would be told to turn it off because there were sick people in the ward.

Because of our findings, we started an experiment called Homestead. We fixed up special wards at Goldwater, painted them with bright colors and began moving in people like those I've described. There were no doctors regularly assigned to it, but doctors did come in daily to hold office hours, just as they would in a community. We helped these people set up a system of self-government and they elected their own officers, including a Homestead "city" council, which worked very effectively. One of the first items of business the council took up was the fact that these people got only two dollars a month in spending money. (On admission, they had signed over all of their welfare and pension rights.) With that they could get a suit cleaned every two months, a tube of toothpaste or a package of razor blades every three months, one Coca-Cola a month, one hamburger a month. It was awful the way they had to budget themselves, so I took this up with the Board of Hospitals, of which I was a member, and they raised the allowance to $4.50. Far from adequate, but to the Homesteaders, a bonanza. And I am happy that today the allowance has been substantially increased.

These old people were now beginning to recover their self-esteem and show signs of new vitality. They organized their own clubs. The diabetes club would invite doctors to give lectures; the drama club put on little plays; the art club encouraged people to paint. One day, while making the rounds, I learned that some of these people hadn't been off Welfare Island for ten years or more. I mentioned this to Dr. and Mrs. James Seamans, and before I knew it, their foundation had given the Homestead a bus in which the people could go on tours to the Statue of Liberty or the Aquarium, or Radio City Music Hall, or the most favored place of all —Aqueduct Race Track. They loved the races, and though they didn't have enough money even to go to the $2 window, they would do their own handicapping and bet pennies or nickels with each other.

Since that time, the Homestead at Goldwater has developed wonderfully. They now have their own flower gardens and a beautiful new pavilion that will accommodate a hundred wheelchairs and several hundred seats for ambulatory patients. In the daytime, the pavilion is used as a rehabilitation training gymnasium, and in the evenings they have movies and all kinds of entertainment. Best of all, they have a community in which they can take pride.

As our work at Goldwater and on Thirty-eighth Street developed, we continued to direct the rehabilitation program at Bellevue. Dr. Deaver had come to the conclusion that too many polio cripples were housebound when they should be in school or at work. He did a survey of five hundred such people, and found seventy-five whom he felt could be freed from their helplessness if they were properly retrained, so he began bringing these people into Bellevue to see what rehabilitation would do for them.

The first patient he brought in was a twenty-eight-year-old girl named Helen Rynack who had suffered polio when she was a year and a half old. She was partially paralyzed in her arms, totally paralyzed in her legs, suffered some paralysis in her abdominal and back muscles, and had undergone twenty-six surgical procedures. She had learned to drag herself across the floor with crutches, and by studying at home, had graduated from high school with honors. She had even learned to type sixty words a minute with her crippled hands. When she earned her high school diploma, the principal and a few other people came with a potted palm and an American flag, and he gave a little speech about what a wonderful girl

Helen was. Then, after she received the diploma, everyone left and there she was, still housebound because, while she could drag herself from room to room, she still could not manage steps or curbs.

Thus for twenty-six years, Helen Rynack had stayed inside her home because she couldn't manage steps. She couldn't even get up or down an eight-inch curb. In a city, if you can't do that, you're housebound. You can't cross a street, you can't get in or out of a car or bus. You're helpless, and that's the way Helen Rynack was when Dr. Deaver brought her into Bellevue. He put her on a full program to redevelop every muscle trace she had left. He gave her special exercises to strengthen her arms and legs. He taught her how to make gravity work for her. Everyone tried to help her, but in fact she did more for herself than any of us did for her.

After working constantly for eleven weeks, she accomplished the key move. Luckily I was there in the gymnasium to see it. We had a simulated section of street curb, and she was standing in the gutter, on her bad leg, with her back to the "sidewalk." With great effort, she flung her good foot backward and the tip of her heel caught on the top of the curb. Putting pressure on her good leg, she gave a push and a little twist, and she was up.

It was a great moment, but Helen didn't stop for any applause. She stepped back down into that gutter and stepped out again. She did it ten times that morning, and the next day, Thursday, she did it until she could no longer stand. Friday morning, she must have done it a hundred times, and Friday afternoon, we discharged her. The following Monday morning she came to work for us on the switchboard. She worked for us for many years, never missed a day and was never late. When she left us, it was only because she had been offered a better job in a hospital on Long Island near her home. She's a very capable woman, but for twenty-six years she had been a prisoner in her own house because there was an eight-inch wall around it.

One day about this time I encountered another girl with a problem much less severe than Helen Rynack's, but still very real and important. I had been invited to appear on Dorothy Gordon's radio program, *Youth Wants to Know,* because she was going to have four disabled teenagers and she wanted me to discuss their difficulties with them. Two of them had polio and one had asthma. My discussion with these three was rather routine. But I noticed the fourth, a girl about fifteen years old, wasn't saying anything.

Finally I said to her, "What's your problem?"

She hesitated for a moment, then said, "My problem is that I was born ugly. I was born with a big tumor on my face, and when I was very young they took me to Bellevue and cut it off. Now I have this long scar down my cheek and I have a speech impediment. You can hear how I lisp. I want to become a nurse, but nobody will take me into training. I've applied to several hospitals, and while they might not say it outright, I know what they're thinking. I'm so ugly I'd scare the patients. I've been turned down everyplace I've tried."

It seemed to me the discussion was getting too clinical and grim for the radio, so I said to her, "I'd like to talk to you after the program, but I'll tell you one thing right now. Don't let anyone take your lisp away from you. It sounds very attractive."

We met in the anteroom afterward and she told me the rest of her story. She had graduated from high school at the top of her class, but her family was very poor, and her father had left home. They were now on relief. She had a severely retarded sister, and her mother insisted she spend her free time at home taking care of the girl. Though she didn't mind doing so, she was worried about her future. She wanted more than anything else to become a nurse.

I said, "It sounds to me as if you would make a wonderful nurse." I invited her to come down to the institute the next day, and we gave her a job for the summer as a nurse's aide. But I couldn't deny that her appearance was bad. She had no make-up and she was wearing a very unattractive dress. I asked myself, What could I do about any of this? The girl's greatest problem was that she lacked self-confidence. I would hurt her terribly by telling her she looked terrible. Finally I remembered that a few months earlier I had met Elizabeth Arden. I wasn't sure she would remember me, but I called her and asked, "How would you like to make a princess out of an ugly duckling?"

As soon as I told her the girl's story, she took to the idea. "Send her up," she said, "and I'll see her personally."

When that girl came back from Elizabeth Arden's, she had a beautiful new hairdo, she had special make-up which almost concealed her scar, and she had stars in her eyes. There was never any question about her work. She was so good as a nurse's aide that we went to bat for her at Bellevue, where she had already been turned down for nurse's training, and we made such a fuss they finally accepted her just to get us off their backs. After graduating from Bellevue near the top of her class, she came to work for us as a nurse, first on our wards at Bellevue and later at the institute. By this time she had such a sparkle in her eyes no one ever noticed the scar on her cheek. She studied at night, got her master's degree, and became assistant supervisor of nursing. Today she's the head of nursing service in one of New York's best hospitals.

Disfigurement was a handicap too often ignored in those days. Today it's handled better, with plastic and reconstructive surgery, but the psychological problems of disfigured people still need more attention than they get. In the forties, almost nothing was done for such people, and apparently many of them were destroyed by neglect. Shortly after I came to New York, I had a call at my *Times* office from two boys who wanted to see me but couldn't come until after dark. Would I agree to wait and see them after 6 P.M.? I did.

They came into my office looking like a pair of gunmen, with their coats buttoned to the top, mufflers covering half their faces, and hats pulled down.

I sensed their problem. When they took off their hats and mufflers, I was confronted by two of the most horribly disfigured faces I had ever seen. They had come to me simply in the hope that I might help them get jobs in the *Times'* distribution department, which were night jobs and would allow them to work from eight or nine in the evening to four or five in the morning.

"Then we could get home while it's still dark," one of them explained, "so no one would see us."

I said something to the effect that they shouldn't feel that way. The other boy shook his head and said, "You don't know how often people have screamed when they looked at me in the street."

I wish I could say now that I did something dramatic for those boys, but aside from helping them get jobs, I couldn't think of anything to do.

Job placement is, of course, a very important part of rehabilitation, and one in which we quickly became involved. We received a big boost in 1949, when Orin Lehman of the New York banking and brokerage family took the leadership of a new committee called Just One Break, or JOB. Lehman had lost a leg in the service during the war and soon was one of our friends and benefactors. The JOB committee which he helped to found was a group of business and professional men who met at the institute every two weeks to interview patients and try to help them find suitable work when they were ready for it. There were six hundred thousand physically handicapped Americans looking for jobs in 1949. Lehman and the JOB committee, which included Thomas Watson, Jr., of IBM and Robert Samstag, a New York industrialist, had trouble making a dent in this dismal statistic. But they did help publicize the fact that it was good business to hire the handicapped; at the same time, they also found jobs for a lot of "disabled" people who might not otherwise have had a chance to prove they were still able.

One of these was a young Italian named Ernest Della Donna who had worked in a sausage plant. About a week before the war ended he caught both hands in a grinder and lost them just above the wrists. He felt that this had been some kind of retribution because he had not served in the armed forces during the war. There was, of course, no reason for him to feel this way; nevertheless he was full of guilt. An orthopedic surgeon fitted him with an old-fashioned pair of "show hands" which looked fine but were completely useless. With a wife and three children to support, he was absolutely desperate when he came to see us. He couldn't feed or dress himself, and he couldn't travel alone because he couldn't make change.

We fitted him with hooks, taught him to fish out a dime for the bus (we soon had to re-teach him because the Transit Authority pulled a dirty trick on him and raised the fare to twelve cents), and started him on job training as a combined handyman, file clerk and messenger. Then Lehman's JOB committee set out to place him. Actually it was Henry Viscardi, whom I had met in Washington during the war and who was then director of JOB, who found a job for Ernie— as a mechanic's helper at the Ford Instrument Company on Long Island. He would have to maneuver boxes of tools that weighed about fifteen pounds, so we trained him at the institute, by making him move around boxes that weighed twenty pounds to make sure he could manage the job. When he started work two weeks later, the foreman was worried that it might upset the other workers to have a handless man among them, but actually the effect was just the opposite. Ernie was accepted immediately, not only because he was a nice fellow, but because he did the job well. He had one difficulty, however. There was one round, slick-steel doorknob at the plant that he found hard to open with his hooks. His fellow workers noticed this, and one day when he returned from lunch, it had been replaced by a square doorknob which he could open easily. But instead of being grateful, Ernie was absolutely furious. He said to his co-worker, "I don't know who changed that knob, but whoever did it did me no service. I don't want any special favors around here."

Ernie's children are now through with school and his daughters are married. Every few months, he still comes to see me and tell me that life is good. And one day his wife told me: "Before Ernie lost his hands he was an ordinary kind of fellow. Since he lost his hands he's a great man."

While we were fighting to launch our rehabilitation programs here in New York, I was also fighting for rehabilitation on the national level. In 1947 I wrote a memo to President Truman pointing out there were twenty-three million disabled people in the country, and proposed a nation-wide attack on the problem. The President was sympathetic to this goal from the beginning. Later, he made a speech in New York City, saw me in the audience (I had known him since my Missouri days), pointed me out and repeated the statistic about the twenty-three million disabled people. Referring to me in connection with rehabilitation, he said, "You know, he and I are nuts on that subject."

Unfortunately, I'm afraid that many people did think we were "nuts" in our campaign to establish rehabilitation on a national scale. President Truman had been a driving force in the formation of the Veterans Administration rehabilitation program, and he appointed me chairman of the National Health Resources Planning Board, partly to further the cause of rehabilitation among civilians. As a result of our work with Federal Security Administrator Oscar R. Ewing, one of the health recommendations made by the administration in September 1948 was the establishment of a program "to rehabilitate the 250,000 men and women who become disabled through illness or injury every year, so that they can be restored to the most nearly normal life and work of which they are individually capable."

Despite the President's support, however, we encountered resistance, not only from congressmen who thought it was too expensive, but also from some medical men who didn't have much faith in rehabilitation, or who were concentrating their support on other worthy endeavors. Our hopes were damaged also by the Korean War which, from 1950 on, demanded such heavy federal expenditures that it was hard to get appropriations for anything else.

There is one story about President Truman that has nothing to do with rehabilitation, but which is an interesting footnote to history. As everyone knows, he was a plain-spoken man and when he got angry, he didn't hesitate to show it. I had an appointment with him at the White House on the morning of April 9, 1951, and at that time he was furious with General Douglas MacArthur; as supreme commander of our forces in Korea, MacArthur was showing less than full respect for the orders of the Commander in Chief in Washington. When I arrived at the White House the President's appointment secretary, Matt Connelly, said, "I hope you're not in a hurry. The President has some small fry in there with him. He'll be busy for a while." When the door of the Oval Room eventually opened, I was somewhat startled at the identity of these "small fry" Connelly had mentioned. There was what looked like the entire cabinet, the Joint Chiefs of Staff, Vice President Alben Barkley, and several congressional leaders including the Speaker of the House, Sam Rayburn. After they had gone, I went into the President's office and found him standing by the window, gazing out toward the grounds, apparently lost in thought. I sat down and waited for him to notice that I was there.

Within a few minutes, he turned and saw me. "Oh, Howard," he said, "I didn't hear you come in."

With his quick, brisk step, he came over to me and shook hands, but it seemed to me from the start that he had his mind on something else.

Finally he said, "Howard, have you ever had to fire God?"

I was quite taken aback. I said, "I don't know what you mean, Mr. President."

"I mean just that," he said. "Have you ever had to fire God?"

"No, I guess not," I said.

"Well, I have to do it," he said. "I'm going to fire the 'so and so' this afternoon." Later that day President Truman relieved the popular general of his command and thereby brought upon himself a storm of protest.

But to get back to our main subject—while we weren't doing very well for rehabilitation in the political field, we took comfort from our progress in New York. The Bellevue and Goldwater programs were running smoothly by late 1950, and the capacity of our temporary institute on Thirty-eighth Street was now fifty-one beds. We had even taken some rooms in the nearby George Washington Hotel, to which we were transferring patients when they became semi-ambulatory. This allowed us to take new patients at a faster rate. It was not fast enough, however. We were being swamped with referrals, and I think it would have driven us crazy were it not for the fact that work had begun on our $2 million permanent institute at Thirty-fourth Street and First Avenue as the first unit of the projected New York University-Bellevue Medical Center. We had collected almost all of the necessary funds; the old laundry building previously on the site had been cleared away and the construction was progressing at a rapid rate. Time after time, I used to sneak down there by myself just to watch the work crews on the job.

CHAPTER

. . . .

VIII

. . . .

ON JANUARY 25, 1951, WE OPENED our permanent institute.
It was the first unit of the great New York University Medical Center that now stretches several blocks down First Avenue. We held our dedication ceremony in the ground-floor
lobby, and among those present were Bernard Baruch, Mrs.
Bernard Gimbel, Winthrop Rockefeller (who was then president of the NYU Medical Center's board of trustees), and
our dear friend Sam Leidesdorff who later was chairman of
the board of the medical center and continued to be one of
our greatest supporters. I learned later that he insisted that
the foundations of the institute be strong enough to carry
four more floors should they be needed later. When he was
told that funds were not available for such extra-strength
foundations, he guaranteed the funds for their construction.

But the star of the day was a nine-year-old girl named
Margaret Ann Flick who cut the ribbon for us after the
speeches were made. Margaret Ann was the daughter of a
friend of mine in Washington, D.C., and she had come to us
after polio crippled both her legs. On the day she cut the
ribbon she was still confined to a wheelchair, but she was as

determined as she was cheerful, and before she left us she was walking beautifully. The last time I heard from her she had finished college, had married and was living a normal, happy life.

Before the ceremony, there was a parade of wheelchairs down First Avenue from our temporary quarters on Thirty-eighth Street. Passersby must have been astonished as we pushed all those wheelchairs down the street. Some of the patients could walk, of course, so behind the wheelchairs came a squad on crutches, and for those who were not yet in condition to brave the winter air, we had cars. Sandwiches and hot coffee were waiting for us when we arrived around 11 A.M., and before the day was done, all the patients had been assigned to their rooms and resumed their training programs.

The building had four floors (three more floors and the research wing were added later), and while we could accommodate twice as many patients as we had at Thirty-eighth Street, we were filled beyond capacity within a few days. Aside from the crowding, our facilities were wonderful. On the ground floor we had a library, a cafeteria and our general offices. On the next floor were the patients' quarters; on the floor above that, the physical therapy unit, given to us by Irving Geist, who was one of the institute's greatest friends until his death in 1970. There was also a therapeutic swimming pool and gymnasium and on the top floor the occupational-therapy department with the Psycho-Social and Vocational Guidance Department. We were very proud and happy, especially when our fund chairman, Nevil Ford, announced that we had raised all but $131,000 of the $2,055,000 needed to build the place.

We had our growing pains, and we made our share of

mistakes. I remember one which might have been amusing in a way but which was also sad, because it deprived three men of the good we could have done them. In an effort to learn more about the impact of spinal-cord injuries we were conducting several studies, including one on the sex problems of the paraplegic. Up to that time, people used to assume that spinal-cord victims were both impotent and sterile, and many a doctor used to tell this to his patients. We now know this isn't necessarily true. While such injuries do lessen potency and fertility, we've had scores of males with severed spinal cords who fathered perfectly normal children, and hundreds of women who have given birth to normal children. But in those days the evidence was still inconclusive, so we had a very fine social scientist, Georgia McCoy, conduct the study for us. It included a questionnaire—serious and scientific—which she passed out to all of our paraplegics. Unfortunately, among our patients from the United Mine Workers at the time there happened to be three men from a small, isolated community in West Virginia who were horrified by it. This community had been started about a hundred years earlier by the members of a fundamentalist religious sect, people who had come to the new country from England so they could isolate themselves from the sins of the world. One of the most awful of those sins was sex, and our three patients felt it was a dirty subject, never to be discussed. For a week after they saw the questionnaire they were quiet, withdrawn and troubled. Finally one day they simply signed themselves out of the institute and went home to West Virginia. They wanted nothing more to do with us if we had such filthy minds. We had not, of course, tried to force them to fill in the questionnaire. All they had to do was disregard it, but they couldn't do so. Their early training had been so rigid they were unable to overcome it. I felt sad when they left because I was certain we could have helped them.

Our research in those early days was rather catch-as-catch-can. We had little money and no laboratories. Nor was anyone devoting himself entirely to research. We all did what we could. Then we began to get small grants here and there. We launched a study of cerebral palsy at the behest of Dr. Deaver, who had always taken a special interest in the disease. Then he began a program to improve the design of braces and of wheelchairs. We knew the wheelchairs then available were not satisfactory, and we believed that a chair could be as meticulously prescribed as a drug or a diet for each individual patient. Or perhaps I should say, each patient should have his wheelchair fitted to him as he would a suit of clothes. We had only two areas, a space twenty by twenty feet, to use for this kind of research, and this was borrowed from NYU.

From our experience we gradually learned what companies made the best braces or artificial limbs for the least money, and what companies were willing to tailor-make them for individual patients. Eventually, for difficult cases, we began making our own braces and devices, but not then. It must be remembered, however, that the basic thing which makes rehabilitation work is the patient's own desire and determination. A short time after we opened on Thirty-fourth Street, we took in a New Hampshire high school student named Gilbert Provencher, who had broken his neck the previous year by diving into a shallow swimming pool. (Diving accidents and auto accidents are still the most common causes of spinal cord injury.) Gilbert was paralyzed from the upper chest down with no sensation. He had no motion in his hands but could move his wrists, his elbows and his shoulders.

After he had been with us awhile, and passed through the worst phase of that horrible depression which attacks almost everyone in such circumstances, he said to me, one day, "Do you know what I'd like to do, Doctor? I'd like to paint."

I was so surprised I said, "Paint what? You mean paint pictures?"

"That's right, sir."

I hoped he didn't notice my disbelieving reaction. My surprise had made me violate the cardinal principle of rehabilitation, which is that a patient should never be told he can't do something until he's had a chance to try it. In an effort to recover I said, "Have you ever painted?"

"No, sir."

"Well then, it's about time you got started."

We designed a double-strap apparatus to go around his elbow and attached a paint brush to it. Then we gave him a set of oils, propped him up against a tilt-board, and I told him, "If you want to paint, paint."

After three weeks of torturous labor, he finished his first picture: a typical New Hampshire winter scene with a tall birch tree in the foreground. In the next two months he did six more paintings, and people at the institute began to wonder if there might be more to this for him than rehabilitation. He was creative and talented. His family was very poor, so he put the six paintings up for sale at the institute; six understanding people bought them for a hundred dollars each. An art critic told him that his work had some of the qualities of a Grandma Moses, and a friend of the institute gave him a year's tuition in the Famous Artists School correspondence course.

Gilbert left us in September 1951, and by then he was reaping a significant income from his paintings. He moved his family to Florida, where, with the help of many institute friends in Palm Beach, he held an annual show at the well-known Findlay Galleries. The shows were very successful, and Gilbert continued to paint every day of his life until he died fifteen years later. He found wonderful fulfillment for himself, and you might say it was because of, not in spite of, his handicap. He also left the institute a great heritage. Our conference room at the institute is lined with his paintings, and it's a wonderful lift for new patients when we point out to them that they were done by a quadriplegic.

While we weren't successful in obtaining national assistance for the rehabilitation movement, President Truman used to ask me from time to time to undertake special assignments. With Admiral Robert Dennison and Dr. Arthur Abramson (a paraplegic since the Battle of the Bulge in World War II, when his spinal cord was cut by a shell fragment) I headed a committee to try to straighten out a mess in a California Veterans Administration hospital. As a result of that committee's work, a study was done to reorganize the health services of the entire V.A. While working with that group, I noticed that there was no way the various health officials—the Army, Navy and Air Force surgeon generals, and the medical directors of the V.A., Indian Affairs Bureau, Civil Service, Public Health Service, etc.—could get together and talk out their common problems. All their communications had to be on paper. I mentioned this to the President, and he sent me down to see Stuart Symington, who was then chairman of the National Security Resources Board. Stu was an old friend from St. Louis; I had been his family's doctor. Before I knew it, I was the head of a new group called the National Health Resources Advisory Committee, and I found myself traveling to Washington, at first for a three-day meeting every other week, then eventually twice a month for two days. In addition to our formal meetings we had an informal sandwich luncheon once a month where all the surgeons generals and directors of government medical services could get together and exchange ideas. We dealt with such matters as medical manpower for the armed services, reorganization of the various government medical services when needed, and civil defense in case of war.

In our governmental reorganization function we worked closely with the second Hoover Commission. Robert F. Kennedy was the commission's number one staff man, and I've never seen anyone more eager to learn than he was. He never missed a single luncheon as long as the job lasted, and his interest in our problems was intense.

When General Eisenhower became President in 1953, he asked me to remain as chairman. I held the chairmanship for seven and a half years. Then one day I went in to see the President and told him I felt I had made my contribution. There were other men who could do the job as well or better. He graciously relieved me.

In 1951 I had a distressing disagreement with Bernard Baruch, and I think it was the only time we ever differed on an important health matter. The argument grew out of our attempt to get rehabilitation recognized as a full-fledged specialty in medical practice. Even in 1951 most doctors still considered it a boondoggle, although Dr. Frank Krusen, a colleague of mine and director of the Baruch Committee, had succeeded in getting the American Medical Association to at least recognize "physical medicine" as a specialty. This was a remarkable accomplishment, but I felt it was not enough because it did not take into account the important nonphysical aspects of rehabilitation—the emotional, social, educational and vocational training which were an integral part of our programs. The A.M.A. subcommittee which dealt with this subject was meeting in Chicago that summer, and I was granted permission to come and be heard, even though I was not a member. It was a frightening experience because, aside from Dr. Krusen, all the members were physicians from other specialties. They knew little about rehabilitation and cared less. I spent a full day on the witness stand and effected a compromise in which the specialty would henceforth be called "physical medicine and rehabilitation." But in the process, I made remarks before the subcommittee that upset Mr. Baruch. I had observed what must seem now a truism —that the psychiatrist was an invaluable member of a rehabilitation team, and that in certain cases he was more important than physical-medicine experts.

Mr. Baruch had always been averse to psychiatry. When he read a copy of my testimony before the A.M.A. subcommittee, he was furious, and asked me to come see him.

"I just want to tell you this," he said. "If your program has anything to do with psychiatry, then you've lost me."

After all that Bernard Baruch had done for us, it is easy to imagine how I felt. Yet I could hardly back down on something so important. "Mr. Baruch, I hate to tell you this," I said, "but I feel it so deeply I can't compromise. If a patient came to me with a leg off and he was suffering from a deep emotional anxiety as a result of it, and I couldn't get him the proper attention for his emotional disturbance, I wouldn't be a good doctor. If rehabilitation is going to ignore the emotional problems of the disabled, then I'll go back to internal medicine, which is my first love. I was the second doctor in this country to take the examination in internal medicine when that specialty was established in 1930. I'm proud of that and I could very well go back to it. But I'm also proud of what we're doing in rehabilitation and I want to see the concept grow, not diminish."

We had a long discussion in which I explained again that rehabilitation was neither a purely psychiatric nor a purely physical-medicine concept; it was a total concept to meet the total needs of a disabled person.

Finally he said, "All right, I understand now how you feel. I can see the need you're talking about and I won't belabor the point." He was a strong man and also very wise, and he knew how to listen.

Our progress in New York, though satisfying in many ways, was still painfully slow. As late as 1952, New York City was the only community in the country that offered comprehensive rehabilitation services in its municipal hospitals. In addition to the Bellevue and Goldwater programs, the city had opened units at City, Metropolitan and Kings County hospitals, and more units were scheduled to open at Fordham, Queens, Bronx, and Bird S. Coler hospitals. Our organization, which was in charge of general planning for all these units, now had thirty-five young doctors in training in the department, with a corresponding number of nurses, therapists and other specialists. But even with all of our growth, we could only accommodate a fraction of the people who needed rehabilitation. All those units in the city's municipal hospitals together came to only 349 beds. A questionnaire sent out to sixteen hundred general hospitals throughout the country indicated that only sixty-five of them could offer organized rehabilitation services.

We were also having less than complete success in finding jobs for our rehabilitated people. The JOB (Just One Break) Committee, under the guidance of Henry Viscardi, Jr., and Orin Lehman, was remarkably successful. It had found work for several thousand amputees, paraplegics, cerebral palsy and polio victims. But there were still a great many people the committee could not place because the severity of their handicaps had prevented them from developing any skills. Viscardi used to pace back and forth on his own artificial legs, stewing about these people. One day in the summer of 1952, he decided that if no one else wanted them, *he* would hire them. There was just one technicality: he didn't own a company.

Henry was not deterred by such a small matter. He borrowed eight thousand dollars, rented a vacant garage in West Hempstead, Long Island, and pronounced himself the president of a company called Abilities, Inc. The only other member of the firm in the beginning was Arthur Niernberg, the "plant manager," who was paralyzed from the waist down as a result of polio. He borrowed some card tables and chairs and began interviewing prospective employees while Henry began visiting the executives of Long Island's large corporations, among whom were Preston Bassett (president of Sperry Gyroscope Corporation), Raymond Jahn (president of Ford Instrument Company) and Arthur Roth (president of the Franklin National Bank).

In September, Abilities, Inc., launched its first assembly line with five workers lacing cable assemblies. There was only one good leg among them, and it belonged to a boy whose other leg was off at the hip. But they had seven usable arms among them and five good heads.

Within two years, Abilities, Inc., had 160 employees and

a backlog of four hundred thousand dollars in contracts. Since then it has continued to grow and prosper, and, the last I heard, it had 450 employees, almost 90 percent of whom had never before held jobs.

Though it seemed obvious to me that it's good business to hire the handicapped, many employers still didn't believe it. So in the early fifties we started a campaign to show businessmen and labor leaders that physical wholeness and ability were not synonymous. Survey after survey showed that disabled people, when properly trained and placed, had high production rates, lower accident rates, lower absentee rates and nine times less turnover than the so-called normal people working beside them.

At the same time, we were preaching to doctors the medical value of rehabilitation—also with only partial success. In those early days I made so many speeches I hardly had time to see my own children, and I am eternally thankful that they had a mother like Glad to look after them. After a full day at the institute, I would drive from fifty to three hundred miles to make a two-hour speech, then answer questions for another hour and finally get home at two in the morning. I know how hard this was on my family, but they seldom complained, because they believed in the importance of what we were trying to accomplish.

I could smell out a medical meeting hundreds of miles away, and I learned all the tricks of taking advantage of my friends to get invited. I also learned a lot about speechmaking at the expense of the poor doctors who had to listen to me. I found that if I went into a meeting cold, and used the word "rehabilitation" in the title of the speech, it was like giving sleeping pills to the whole audience. But before long I hit upon a title so ambiguous that unless they already knew me, they couldn't tell exactly what I was going to say. The title was "Sick People in a Troubled World." Once I began my story, I had no trouble holding them.

I learned a great lesson the first time I was invited to speak before the American College of Physicians. I had worked long and hard on that paper. I filled it with references and historical data. I had the subject down pat, but a few minutes after I began to speak, the audience was wandering in and out of the room, talking, and drinking Coca-Cola. I was a complete flop. It was ten years later before they invited me to address them again. This time the meeting was in Boston, and I had flown all night from another meeting in Dallas to get there. I was tired and I had no time to prepare anything, so I began my speech like this: "There isn't a man in this audience who doesn't have at least forty patients of the type I'm going to discuss. Patients who are being completely neglected in the matter of their basic need, which is to get back into life. I'm talking about the two million people in this country who have suffered strokes and are now sitting around, waiting to die because no one is helping them to live. I'd like to tell you today about a few simple things you can do for many of these people, right in your offices, or in the home at the bedside." I told them how to prevent painful hips by sandbagging the patient's leg. I told them how to sandbag a shoulder so it wouldn't become what we call "frozen" and require several weeks of painful therapy and stretching to get it back to normal. I took out some props and showed them how they could make an exercise device for arms and shoulders of stroke victims simply by using a window pulley and six or eight feet of clothesline. I pointed out that a patient could help himself more with this device than a therapist could help him because, by doing it himself, he could sense the pain threshold and therefore stretch farther than a therapist would dare to try. I talked about aphasia, the speech difficulty stroke victims suffer, which seems to me one of the most frustrating problems of all. It's like not being able to say an old friend's name, multiplied to infinity. As I talked, this time I noticed there was absolute silence in the hall, and instead of seeing people leave, I noticed that more people kept arriving until, by the end of my presentation, they were standing in the aisles.

Afterward, I was practically mobbed by a score of doctors, all of whom were confronted with problems like those I had mentioned, either among their patients or within their own families. Where could they send people for rehabilitation? Where could they get more information about what I had told them? One young doctor said, "My father is also a doctor, and he's just suffered a stroke. I came here three days early and I've walked the streets of Boston looking for a hospital or an agency or somebody who could give him really effective therapy. Especially for his speech. Do you know, I haven't been able to find anyone."

Today Boston has a number of excellent programs, including a splendid one at Boston University directed by Dr. Murray Freed, who trained with us. But Boston, like every American city, needs more rehabilitation centers. It was from the Boston area that Robert Heist came to us just five years ago. Heist is the young man who broke his neck while water-skiing, and whose story began this book. Now we're accustomd to success stories like his. But when we first began our program, the successes of our patients seemed almost like miracles.

I remember the case of Paul Francolon, for instance, a French jockey who broke his back and became a paraplegic when a horse fell on top of him in a race at the famous Paris track, Longchamp. The shape he was in when we found him convinced me that his survival was nothing short of a miracle. I've already mentioned the meeting in Paris where one of our first paraplegic heroines, Jamie Coffman, performed so beautifully before an audience of French doctors. After that meeting, I noticed a young French woman, about thirty years old, very pretty but with a sad, apprehensive face.

She was standing apart from the crowd and she waited until everyone else had gone, then came to me and said, "My husband is a paraplegic. Could he learn to walk like Jamie?"

"I would have to know more about him," I said.

"He's a wonderful man," she said, "a very strong man. He was a jockey until a horse fell on him and he's been an invalid ever since."

"Where is he now?"

"Right down there," she said, pointing to the fourth row of the now-empty theater. Huddled in one of the seats was a shrunken gnome of a man. When I went down to greet him it was obvious I couldn't examine him there, so I picked him up and carried him to a table on the stage. He had the strong arms, shoulders and hands you would expect of a jockey, and he was a typical paraplegic, unable to move from the waist down.

After a short examination, I turned to his wife, whose name was Nelly, and said, "Yes, he can learn to walk just as well as Jamie. There's no reason why he shouldn't. But I don't think there are any full-scale rehabilitation institutes here in France. Do you think you can get him to the United States? If so, we'll do everything we can for him."

"I'll get him there," she said, and we soon learned that when Nelly Francolon decided to do something, she didn't rest until it was done. She pulled every string she could. The World Veterans Federation helped. His racing friends assisted, too. Paul had not been a run-of-the-mill jockey. Among his victories were the Grand Prix de Paris and the Prix de l'Arc de Triomphe. Now that he needed help, the French National Federation of Racing Clubs staged a special race for his benefit.

The Paris newspapers publicized the story and the French public also got behind him, but not unanimously. A group of French physicians raised a fuss about the case. In a letter to one of the papers, they declared that the whole thing was an insult to French medicine, that French doctors were perfectly capable of taking care of French paraplegics, and that they had special knowledge of how to treat bladder and bowel malfunctioning in such cases—knowledge that presumably doctors in other countries did not have.

Despite their protest, the necessary money was raised, and when Paul reached the institute he was in a condition which can only be described as deplorable. His catheter had not been changed for many months. His bladder was packed with stones and so was one kidney. We had to operate, and when we did so we found more than one thousand stones in his bladder.

It took him a month to recover from this operation. Then we fitted him for braces and got him on his feet. He was one of the hardest-working patients I can remember, and because of his strong forearms and shoulders he made wonderful progress until an attack of jaundice laid him low. Undaunted, he fought that off and got well again. Once more his progress was rapid. He did so wonderfully we were able to schedule a date in advance for his discharge, and when that news reached France, a great welcome was prepared for him. He could hardly wait for the day when he would walk off the plane at Orly Airport into the arms of Nelly, his wife. Then, three weeks before his scheduled departure, while practicing his technique of walking up and down stairs, he fell and broke his left leg. He healed quickly, however, and when he did return home, it was to start a new life and a new job. Between himself and Nelly, who had a little business of her own, they did very well.

About three years later, when I visited Paris, I gave them a call. Paul was driving a car, so he and Nelly came to my hotel to see me. In the course of our visit he asked me if there was any special thing I would like to do in Paris.

"Yes, there is," I said. "The one thing I'd rather do than anything else on this trip is to go to Longchamp with you."

The smile left his face and he paled. "I haven't been there since the day I broke my back," he said, "but if you want to go, I'll take you."

I had suspected his fear. I had always been a horseman and a horse lover myself, and I knew how a fall from a horse could turn a person against horses. I remember when my son Howard, who was about six or seven years old and just learning to ride, steered his mount into a stone wall and fell head over heels. I could see he wasn't hurt, but he was very frightened. I said to him, "Get back on that horse." He said, "I don't want to." I said, "I don't care what you want. You're getting back on that horse." Since I was bigger than he was in those days, I won the discussion and by the time we finished our ride that day, he had practically forgotten his fall. Needless to say, I had no intention of trying to get Paul back on a horse, but I did want to take away from him that dread memory.

We went to Longchamp on a Sunday. Paul and Nelly

picked Glad and me up at the hotel in their car, with him driving. When we entered the parking lot at the track, things began to happen. The attendant looked into the car and cried out, "My God! Paul Francolon is back!" He shouted to another attendant, "Paul is back!" and we were quickly surrounded. By the time we got to the track restaurant, there was a crowd around us, greeting him, and you could see how excited but also how nervous he was. The head steward came and invited him to the paddock, and one of the track officials insisted that we go up and sit in the president's box, where we could drink champagne while we watched the races. Again Paul showed discomfort, and when we got to the stairs, I understood why. The president's box was up four very steep flights, and there was no elevator.

Paul moved one crutch so he could hold the hand rail, and he started up those stairs with absolute determination. Neither Nelly nor I made any move to help him. We both knew better. By the time we got to the top he was drenched with perspiration, but he had an enormous smile of accomplishment on his face. "Now, where's that champagne?" he said. It was a great afternoon.

My weekly column in the *Times* had become accepted. Even though I often preached the gospel of rehabilitation, it wasn't meant to be used solely for that purpose. It was a general medical column, so I was always on the lookout for medical stories.

It had been reported in the general press that Winston Churchill had suffered a stroke. I decided to do one of my Sunday columns on strokes, using Churchill as an example. I described the symptoms, which include paralysis and aphasia, and pointed out that with modern rehabilitation techniques there was new hope for the stroke victim. I filed the column and took off for Korea. This was August 1953. Two days later General James Van Fleet, who had joined us, let me see his copy of the Sunday *Times*. I searched every page and the column wasn't there. It was the first time this had ever happened and I was upset. On my return to New York I went to see the managing editor, Turner Catledge. He stopped me before I could even say a word. "I know what you're going to say. What happened to the column? You were out of communication and we couldn't talk to you, so I had to kill it because it had never been announced officially or admitted by Churchill or his family that he had had a stroke." I said, "Well, but it appeared in the press." Turner said, "Maybe the general press, but not *The New York Times.*"

Churchill recovered from his stroke, and two years later, in the House of Commons, he confirmed what I had wanted to print. During a debate, he got angry at an opponent, and shaking his finger with Churchillian emphasis, he told him that two years earlier he had been paralyzed and unable to speak, but that he had fought this disability with all his strength, so that now he walked and talked again, and that he was prepared to fight his political opponents with equal determination.

Churchill must have had as much determination as any man in history. Everyone knows the historic importance of his determination to defeat the Nazis. Apparently he brought the same quality to everything he did. Bernard Baruch, who was one of his close friends, and with whom he used to stay when he came to New York, told me a story about one of Churchill's last visits here. Shortly after the former Prime Minister returned to England, Baruch said to me, "I was glad to see Winnie get out of town this time. We both love gin rummy, and I made the mistake of getting sixty dollars ahead of him the first two days he was here. So for the last three days he woke me up at six o'clock every morning so he could win it back."

Even in death, Churchill's determination seemed to hold. First of all, his medical record was almost as historic as his political record. In spite of the fact that he broke all the known rules of health—chain-smoking cigars, drinking champagne and brandy like water, keeping irregular hours, disregarding his excess weight, and working under constant tension—he lived to the age of ninety-one. In his last days, when he knew the end was near, he expressed the wish that he might die on the day of his father's death. Shortly thereafter, he went into a coma, but continued to live for another twelve days and actually died not only on the date of his father's death but at almost the exact hour.

Churchill was an outstanding example of a man who proved that mind could overcome matter. And every day at the institute we see dozens of our patients, armless, legless or paralyzed, who are proving the same thing. I have a special feeling for one such person, a girl named Denyse Winters, who arrived at the institute in 1953. She was then three years old. She had been born with no arms and only one leg, but the big, open smile on her face would make you think she was starting life on a par with everyone else.

Since her one leg was the only extremity she had, she learned first how to use it in place of her missing hands. She became exceptionally adept with that foot, learning how to feed herself and even write with it. In the meantime we fitted her with an artificial second leg, with which she learned to walk as if it were a real leg, and then she got her artificial arms, with hooks for hands. I've seen a lot of normal children who couldn't use their hands as well as Denyse learned to use those hooks. She could even crochet and do needlework with them.

As the years went on, we saw a great deal of Denyse. She was with us for quite a while, and when she was not with us we would still see her periodically. She would visit the institute for checkups or just because it was like home to her. She did well in elementary and high school and grew up to be a beautiful young woman. When she reached college age, she already knew what she wanted to do. She went to the Erie County Community College in Buffalo, New York, where they were beginning the first course ever offered in the profession she had chosen—occupational therapy.

After her graduation, Denyse came back to the institute and is now on our staff, in the occupational therapy department. She lives like any other career girl in New York, keeping an apartment, battling the traffic and crowds on her way to and from work, and coping with all the inconveniences of big-city life. In other words, she has the same problems as the rest of us. But to those who know her, she gives the impression that even with only one leg and no arms, she has fewer problems than the rest of us.

CHAPTER

....

IX

....

SHORTLY AFTER GENERAL EISENHOWER won the presidential election in the fall of 1952, his Secretary-of-State-designate, John Foster Dulles, suggested that to alleviate conditions in Korea, which had then been torn apart by two years of war, America should do something for the country on a people-to-people basis besides what we were doing on a government-to-government basis. As a result of this suggestion, Dr. Milton Eisenhower, the President-elect's brother, accepted in December of 1952 the chairmanship of the American-Korean Foundation. This group had been formed the previous summer by the Korean ambassador to America, Dr. You Chan Yang; Dr. Roland De Marco, president of Finch College; and financier O. Roy Chalk. But it didn't really get off the ground until Dr. Eisenhower joined it. They asked me in January to go to Korea and study the health problems there.

I was scheduled to be in Hawaii on a mission and proceeded from there with a small task force to do a crash study of the problem and make appropriate recommendations to Dr. Eisenhower. No airlines were flying into Korea at the time, so we flew in from Japan on an Air Force plane. We were met at the Seoul airport on an extremely cold, blustery day by U.S. Ambassador Ellis Briggs and a committee of prominent Koreans.

That afternoon we were received by Korea's President, Syngman Rhee, at his residence in the Blue House. He had struggled for Korea's independence for forty years, and during World War II he had been a prisoner of the Japanese. While we talked he blew occasionally on his fingertips, because during his imprisonment his jailers had driven bamboo slivers under his fingernails so many times that his hands had become permanently sensitized. He had found the blowing on his fingers was like blowing cool air on a fresh burn, giving him a few seconds of relief from the constant pain.

As a nation, Korea was equally tortured. The city of Seoul had been won and lost in three vicious battles and it looked awful. The countryside was even worse, however, and the health conditions we saw were appalling. Out of a total population of twenty million people, an estimated two and a half million had tuberculosis and a hundred thousand were known to have leprosy. Skin diseases and intestinal parasitism were universal conditions. As for hospitals, what there were proved to be inadequate and obsolete. There were only two hundred so-called beds for tuberculosis patients in the whole country—and these consisted of two blankets placed over a straw mat on the floors of unheated rooms. Worse, there were pitifully few doctors, and those there were, had been poorly trained. It was a frightening situation.

In the average Korean town of twenty-five thousand people, for example, one third of its buildings were completely destroyed and one third unroofed. Families had only enough fuel during those bitter winters to make one hot meal a day, and only as much water, which was usually polluted, as could be carried from the nearest stream. In a town of that size, twenty-five hundred people would have tuberculosis and almost everyone would have some kind of skin disease. There would be one doctor and perhaps one nurse to meet the town's health needs. Korea had already lost a million people in the war—more than the United States had lost in both world wars and the Korean War combined—yet these people had not lost their will to fight. One day we visited the country's Finance Minister in his cold, battered makeshift office. He said, "We need help and we need it badly, but you Americans are too kind sometimes. Last week you sent us a whole carload of peaches. Canned peaches. We hadn't tasted peaches for years. They were delicious, but don't send us any more peaches. We can't afford to develop the appetite for them. We'll eat rice until we're free."

We visited as many hospitals as we could all over the country, including military hospitals, which were reasonably good because the U.S. Army had furnished them with materials and personnel. But while our Army could help the Korean military, it had neither the resources nor the authority to do much for the civilian population. I'll never forget one leprosarium in the mountains. When we arrived on foot through the snow, we were greeted by a little band with ancient and battered instruments playing "Nearer, My God, to Thee," and never have I heard more appropriate music. Those people, adults and children alike, were standing barefoot in the snow. Leprosy was still looked upon with all the old-fashioned prejudices. The lepers were locked in their compounds, and children were taken from their parents as early as possible, since children are more susceptible to the disease than adults. But in fact, leprosy is not an easily spread disease. Its infectious ratio is very small compared, for instance, with tuberculosis.

That trip was a shocker to me, because I had never before seen people endure such suffering. What I had seen behind the Iron Curtain during my trip to Poland in 1949 was not comparable in any way. I remember driving through the streets of Pusan, a city near the southern tip of the Korean peninsula. Pusan had swollen from a normal three hundred thousand people to nearly a million. When the North Korean Communist Army made its initial thrust south, pushing refugees in front of it, many had ended their flight in this city, within the armored pocket where the Americans made their first stand of the war. Hundreds of thousands of these refugees were still in the city in 1953, and as we drove along we saw scores of corpses on either side of the streets—bodies of people who had frozen to death the previous night. When we reached the Maryknoll Sisters' Clinic, we found almost four hundred women who had been sitting all night on the frozen sidewalk with their sick children huddled in their padded, Chinese-style robes, waiting for whatever medication the sisters would give them.

In this clinic, I saw something I had never before seen. These Maryknoll sisters (two of them were physicians; the others, nurses) were treating tuberculous meningitis on an out-patient basis. It was either that or nothing. There were no beds—even for children who were that sick. The mother would bring the child in and the nuns would do a spinal puncture, inject streptomycin into the spinal canal, then give the child back to the mother, who would take it home for a week before returning it for a repeat treatment. Without this program, the mortality rate among these children would have been 100 percent. But these nuns, with the help of a few

Korean doctors and nurses, had reduced the rate to 10 percent, which would be an enviable record in a modern American hospital today.

Though I had gone on this mission just to make a survey, I came back—like everyone else in our party—full of fire and determination to do something to help improve the health conditions in Korea. The first thing was to go to Washington and report to the President. When I arrived at the White House, I was still so horrified at the prevalence of tuberculosis in Korea that I made a very unscientific suggestion. A drug called isoniazid had been discovered less than a year earlier in a research project sponsored by Mrs. Albert Lasker and David Heyman. When its discovery was announced at the New York municipal hospital on Staten Island, there was a great wave of skepticism about it all over the country. It was supposed to prevent or even cure tuberculosis, but a lot of doctors didn't believe in it. Though it did need more testing, the results up to this time had been so spectacular, and the need for help against TB in Korea was so immediate, I didn't think there was any time to waste. So I said to President Eisenhower, "If I were running the health program in Korea, I'd saturate the whole country, right now, with isoniazid. I know there are no doctors or nurses in the rural areas, but this is a medication which can't cause any worse harm than nausea or a little rash. I'd send a supply to the mayor of every little community and tell him to give pills every week to anyone who had a chronic cough or was losing weight or spitting up blood. Whatever side effects it might have can't possibly be as bad as the tuberculosis they're suffering."

President Eisenhower replied, "That makes sense to me." Then with a chuckle he added, "Why don't you try it out on your colleagues in the Public Health Service?"

But when I mentioned it to my scientific friends in the Public Health Service, I was told that my suggestion was heresy. You couldn't possibly treat tuberculosis without before-and-after X-rays, long-range follow-ups, etc.

"But do you know how few X-ray machines they have in Korea?" I asked. "And how primitive they are? And how badly these people need any help they can get?"

It made no difference. All the Public Health Service did was to set up a small, meticulously scientific program with four hundred tuberculosis cases in Seoul, and this has always rankled me because the usefulness of isoniazid has now been proven beyond doubt. In 1969 the Public Health Service announced the results of the study they had conducted among Alaskan Eskimos over a period of many years. One group of TB victims and their families had been given isoniazid routinely as a prophylaxis. Another group of TB victims had been given no isoniazid, and this second group developed ten times as many new cases of tuberculosis as the isoniazid group. Looking back to 1953, I am saddened to think of how many Korean lives could have been saved by an isoniazid saturation campaign.

My report to President Eisenhower, however, had one unexpectedly good result. After our meeting, but before I left Washington, I learned that he was scheduled to confer with the presidents of all the American railroads the next morning. I called and asked him if he would be willing to arrange for me to speak to them for a few minutes when he finished. He agreed. I told these men what I had seen in Korea, and they promised to organize a Help-Korea train which would travel across the country collecting contributions of goods from the people here to the people there. This campaign started with one train in New York and ended up with four trains full of goods from all corners of the country. It included everything from pencils and paper to used locomotives, used buses, farm equipment and even livestock. Not just a few cows but a shipload and a half of livestock. Altogether, it came to four shiploads of material.

The American-Korean Foundation was established by this time and I was all wound up in it. Through the years, the work of the foundation has continued to expand and I've been back to Korea eight times. With the help of the World Health Organization and the United Nations International Children's Emergency Fund, millions of Korean children have had tuberculin tests and have received B.C.G. vaccine. Each year the foundation sends several hundred thousand dollars' worth of donated merchandise to Korea, including a wide range of drugs contributed by pharmaceutical companies. One year, Dow Chemical not only contributed sixty-four thousand vials of influenza vaccine valued at $225,000, but also paid the cost of shipping by air.

I think this generosity by the drug companies grew out of a luncheon President Eisenhower had for the nation's forty top pharmaceutical manufacturers shortly after I returned from my second trip to Korea. He asked me to tell these men what I had seen there, then he asked them to help in any way they could, and through the years, almost all of the big drug companies have been very responsive. An incident three years ago is a case in point. The Korean Health Minister, passing through New York on his way to a World Health Organization meeting in Geneva, dropped in to see me one day.

"I have one great dream in life," he said. "I want more than anything else to stamp out polio in my country. But it would take more than a million doses of vaccine to inoculate all the children who need it, and I have enough money in my budget for only fifty thousand doses."

I just couldn't forget his anxious face, so after talking to him I called my good friend Eugene Beasley, president of the Eli-Lilly Company, and said to him, "Gene, wouldn't it be a wonderful thing if one company, by itself, could eradicate polio from an entire country? Just think what it would mean to be able to say, 'Because of my company, there's a whole country where children aren't going to be crippled any more.' "

"It's a very intriguing thought," he said. "But is it possible? How much vaccine would it take?"

"A little over a million doses."

"We're having a board meeting next week," he said. "I'll present the idea to them."

About ten days later he called back and said, "We're ready to furnish one million two hundred thousand doses. Just tell us where to send it."

They not only furnished it free, they flew it over as refrigerated cargo. And today, polio is no longer a threat to Korean children. A short time later, Elmer Bobst, a giant in the pharmaceutical industry, established a school of pharmacy at Chung Ang University in Seoul. Drugs, vaccines and other supplies continued to pour in from the whole industry.

The livestock contributed during the Help-Korea drive came mostly from 4-H Clubs throughout the Midwest and South. We used it to organize 4-H Clubs in Korea, and with such success that they now have six hundred thousand members over there—the second largest membership in the world.

The program also has had an enormous effect on Korean agriculture. It helped South Korea prove it could be self-sufficient, even though much of Korea's industry is in the North. In recent years the 4-H Clubs have taken on a special project. Because much of the land is rugged and mountainous, and the fertile soil has been washed downhill, millions of acres have always been unproductive. Those kids, six hundred thousand strong, are now bench-terracing the hillsides, filling in the crevices with rock, then carrying soil up those steep grades in A-frames on their backs. They've reclaimed thousands of acres and converted them into fertile farmland.

Koreans are now doing the same thing with the sea. Using modern technological methods, they have built many dikes which protect the precious topsoil that would otherwise have floated away and been lost. Such a project is now under way in Kunsan, one of the country's poorest provinces but an area of special interest to us because the foundation has two very important installations there—the Gordon Seagrave Memorial Hospital and the Lucy Moses Children's Home.

The story of Dr. Seagrave, the Burma surgeon, is well known. He founded a hospital in Burma which was accidentally shelled and destroyed by American forces during World War II. Afterward, he came back and rebuilt it, reestablished his nursing school, and spent the rest of his life trying to improve health conditions for the Burmese people. In spite of this, when he died the political situation was such that all of his colleagues were ordered out of the country on very short notice. The Seagrave Foundation, an American fund which had been organized to give him financial support, had at that time about $150,000 left, with which its members wanted to do something in his memory. After looking all over the world for a suitable site, they chose Kunsan in Korea and planned a hospital and nursing school there. The development of good nursing was one of Seagrave's continuing concerns, and any place in Asia today where you find a

Seagrave-trained nurse, you can be sure you've found a good one. The money the Seagrave people had was not sufficient, so the American-Korean Foundation launched a campaign and raised almost a million dollars. The result is that relatively unprosperous Kunsan now has one of the most modern hospitals in any rural Asian community—the Gordon Seagrave Memorial Hospital—splendidly equipped and with a hundred beds.

At the same time, Mrs. Henry Moses, a dedicated New York philanthropist, became interested in the plight of children in this same province and financed the building of a hospital for orphans which now bears her name. It is a beautiful modern home for two hundred children, an installation big enough to meet the needs of the whole province. Children live there until they reach the age of five or six, after which they are returned to the community, usually in foster homes. It has become a model for the entire country in handling the problem of parentless children.

The problem of the orphans in Korea was particularly acute and we were most fortunate to have Dr. Leonard Mayo, director of the Association for the Aid of Crippled Children, as a special consultant.

The American-Korean Foundation has also helped many Korean students come here to study in the last eighteen years, and it's gratifying to see how well they have done, especially in music. I took a particular interest in one student because of how I met him. While we were visiting an Air Force base in Pusan during our first trip to Korea, we walked through an enlisted men's day room. As we approached the room I heard piano music. At first I gave it no thought. Then it dawned on me that we were hearing magnificent classical music.

All of us were so astonished we tiptoed into the room. And whom did we find at the piano? Not an American soldier, but a little nine-year-old Korean boy playing like a concert artist.

Here was a child from whom you couldn't just walk away. We were introduced to him and found out that his name was Tong Il Han. He was well known in the area as a child prodigy, and he played every day in the recreation room because it had the only available piano. All the other pianos in the area had been destroyed by the fighting, and Tong's father, who worked on the base, had requested permission for the boy to practice there.

Not long after that, the Air Force men on the base took up a collection and sent Tong to the United States for a musical education. He arrived when he was ten or eleven, lived with a Korean family in New York, won a scholarship at Juilliard and spent five years there. By this time, the American-Korean Foundation had taken an interest in him and was also helping to sponsor him. After he finished at Juilliard, Tong went on to study under the great masters in America and Europe, and he has since launched upon a most promising career on the concert stage.

When I go to Korea now, it is not with that dread I used to feel on earlier trips, but with eager anticipation to see what new things the Koreans have accomplished. Though it is still not a wealthy country, its exports have increased in the last five years from an annual fifty million to nearly a *billion* dollars. New businesses are developing rapidly throughout the country. The people are beginning to prosper, but to me, the most satisfying development is reflected in a statistic about the nation's health. The average Korean's life expectancy now is 63.8 years. When I first visited Korea in 1953, it was 31 years.

On the way back from Korea in 1953, I also visited Hong Kong, and then India for the first time. Hong Kong was a dreadfully crowded refugee city in those days, worse than today. But even with two or three million Chinese living in shacks made of flattened beer cans and other debris, the British government had done an excellent job in controlling disease there. The malnutrition and crowding did cause occasional outbreaks of cholera and tuberculosis, but there were excellent hospitals, including one founded by a prominent businessman named Dhun Ruttingee and another, the Granthham, which was named for the very popular British governor. The guiding genius behind the Granthham Hospital was the superintendent of nurses there, a lady named Shila U. She was one of the most efficient nurses I've ever met, and she ran one of the finest hospitals I've ever seen.

During this Hong Kong visit, I met two doctors who have worked together through the years in the cause of rehabilitation, and who soon became my friends. One is Dr. A. R. Hodson, a British professor of orthopedic surgery at Hong Kong University and dean of the medical school. The other is Dr. Harry Fang, a Chinese orthopedic surgeon whose human qualities match his skill. When his brother died several years ago, leaving eight children orphans, Dr. Fang immediately adopted all of them. They have both continued through the years as great leaders in the field.

Thanks to people like these, we found the Hong Kong medical situation in 1953 much better than we had expected it to be. But we were disheartened by the situation in India. When I met the Minister for Health and Social Welfare, I soon realized that while the Indians understood the philosophy of rehabilitation, they were not practicing it in their hospitals. I suggested that the Minister choose two or three bright young doctors and other personnel, then send them to us in America for training.

"With this small nucleus," I said, "you could start a pilot center."

The Minister was much more ambitious than that. "We can't start just one center," he said. "We must start at least twenty centers."

"How can you do that?" I asked. "You have no trained people."

"We must do it," he said. "We don't have time to wait."

Since India had waited throughout its history without anything of the kind, it seemed that it could now wait long enough to make sure that when a rehabilitation program was launched, it would be launched correctly. In fact, nothing happened at all until two years later, when one young Indian doctor came to train with us, but of his own volition, not with government support. Since then we've trained about twenty Indian physicians. Many of them didn't return to India because as they invariably explained, there were no facilities there. It would be very difficult to start new facilities, and even with their special training it would be difficult simply to make a living. Thus most of these Indian doctors went to Canada or England after training with us.

It would be unfair to say, however, that no one in India cares about rehabilitation. Many do and very deeply. Several years ago a paraplegic woman doctor named Mary Vergese, who trained at the institute, set up the first rehabilitation center in Vellore. Another lady, Dr. Rah Kumary Amrit Caur, who was once Mahatma Gandhi's secretary, fought all her life in an effort to build health and social service systems in India. When Jawaharlal Nehru was Prime Minister, he took a special interest in the mentally retarded child of an

Indian consular official in the United States, and I met both him and his daughter, the present Indian Prime Minister Indira Gandhi, when they came to New York to visit this child. We were then evaluating the child in the hope that we could help, a hope that we could not fulfill.

At that first meeting, I found Mrs. Gandhi a charming, vivacious young woman deeply devoted both to her father and to her country. She never lost interest in this retarded child, who was placed in the Institute of Logopedics at Wichita, Kansas. Every time Mrs. Gandhi came to this country she went to visit him there. During the last year of her father's life, in 1964, she asked me to come to India to try to set up a rehabilitation program for soldiers who had become casualties of the border war with China. Many of the casualties were amputees who had lost their legs as a result of frostbite. The Indian Army had been so poorly equipped, these men had been sent into the mountains of northern India without winter clothing. Hundreds of them had suffered frostbite, which then turned into gangrene. Mrs. Gandhi told me that even when she used the influence of her father's office, it would often take her two years to get an artificial limb for someone in whom she was personally interested. She desperately wanted to correct the situation, so she set up a meeting between me and a young lady who was then the Health Minister, Dr. Sheila Sushila Nayar. I'm afraid I was no more successful with Dr. Nayar than I had been with her predecessor several years earlier. First she was irate because I said I could spare only five days in India. She said I should spend at least six months, which was impossible inasmuch as I was engaged in the management of our still-new, growing institute in New York and we were helping projects all over the world. I did repeat, however, my suggestion that the Indian government send a few doctors to America for training, and she seemed inclined to accept this. At least we got the nucleus of a program started. Unfortunately, it did not flower. Nothing really happened until 1968, when a man named Juan Monros of the World Rehabilitation Fund arrived in India to set up a training program for prosthetic technicians.

Meanwhile the progress of our program continued, thanks especially to people like Miss Mary Switzer who had become, in 1950, the director of the federal government's Office of Vocational Rehabilitation. Mary Switzer was a magnificent woman who came from New England to enter government service in 1921. After beginning with the Treasury Department, she switched over to the Federal Security Agency, where she distinguished herself as a very skillful liaison agent between the government and the American Medical Association, two rather stubborn giants which were not getting along very well with each other in those days. One of her first acts when she took charge of the Office of Vocational Rehabilitation was to launch a study of the nation's rehabilitation needs, which were staggering. With facts in hand, she then set about making herself felt in Congress, and the result was a law passed in 1954 which aimed at the rehabilitation, through federal funds, of two hundred thousand disabled persons a year by 1959. (In 1954, the government was providing such services for only sixty thousand people.)

A study done that year proved again the economic value of rehabilitation. It traced eight thousand people who had removed themselves from the public-assistance rolls as a result of rehabilitation, and it was found that this group had earned more than fourteen million dollars during the first year of employment and had paid one million in federal taxes. Until she died in 1970, Mary Switzer was the real keystone in the development of rehabilitation in the United States.

As I look back on those days I wonder how, with all my running around, I ever got to know any of our patients at the institute. But we were getting a lot of very interesting people, some of whom I'll never forget. Marion Kaufmann, for instance, was a beautiful girl who came to us in 1954. Though she was only twenty-eight years old, she had graduated from the Bellevue School of Nursing and had already become a nurses' instructor in pediatrics at Bellevue. Before that, she had been, among other things, a night-club singer, radio actress, model and color consultant. She had also found time to marry and was the mother of two beautiful children, aged five months and two years.

In September of 1953, when she was already pregnant with her second child, she contracted polio while driving through Tennessee with her husband. For the next several months, she lay in a Nashville hospital, paralyzed from the head down. In this condition she gave birth to her second child and then came to us. Within three months, she had regained the use of her hands and arms, and by that time she was also helping our chief nurse in Bellevue's training program for student nurses. A few months later, despite her quadriplegia, she was back home with her husband, helping to raise their children. She later became a top administrator at the Magee Rehabilitation Center in Philadelphia.

In 1955, we met a young fellow who must have been just about the unluckiest, but also one of the pluckiest men alive. His name was James Harrall; he was about twenty-five years old. At the age of two, he had fallen from the porch of his parents' home in Drumright, Oklahoma, landed on his head and become a deaf-mute. Eventually he was sent to a school for the deaf, where he learned sign language but did not learn to lip-read. He became the school's star football player, and after graduation, won a two-year art scholarship at a college in Kansas—the first deaf-mute ever to win this scholarship. After graduation he went back to live with his parents, who were impoverished, and helped support them by working as a commercial artist and a handyman. Then, as if life had not already dealt him enough blows, he was in an auto accident in November of 1954 and broke his neck, becoming completely paralyzed from the neck down. I'm not sure any of us can grasp the full horror a mentally alert young man must feel when he realizes he can't move, can't speak, and can't hear when someone speaks to him. I wish I could end the Jim Harrall story by describing a remarkable recovery climaxed by his walking out of the institute under his own power. But there was only a limited amount we could do for this unfortunate young man. We did teach him to lip-read. We also worked on his muscles until he got back some use of his right arm, and we worked out some self-help devices so that he could do a lot of everyday things for himself. Had he been able to hear and talk, we could have done much more. But his problems were so great he made us face up to the fact that rehabilitation, like everything else, has its limits.

That same year, though, we met a nine-year-old boy named Juan Yepez who helped stretch those limits. He had been born in La Paz, Bolivia, with no arms or legs, but with tiny four-finger hands growing out of his shoulder joints and normal feet growing out of his hip joints. His mother had died and his father's whereabouts were unknown. The La Paz Rotary Club "adopted" the boy and he was admitted to the American Hospital, directed by Dr. Frank Beck, who became his lifelong friend. There he came to the attention of Dr. Terry E. Lilly, an American plastic surgeon. Dr. Lilly, impressed by Juan's intelligence and strength, wrote me a letter asking if the institute could do anything for him. We did not at that time have enough money to help, but I left the letter on my desk and one day it was seen accidentally by Miss Mary Boyle, who was Bernard Baruch's secretary. A short time later a fund was established by Miss Boyle personally to aid in Juan Yepez' rehabilitation and education.

When he came to us, Juan was already a phenomenon. Though he couldn't walk, he could roll and tumble his little body along the floor or the ground with such speed and dexterity that someone had already made a newsreel short of him playing baseball in Bolivia. While lying on his side, with the ball grasped in his hand, he could twist his shoulder so fast that he could pitch accurately to the plate. And if the ball was hit within three or four feet of him, he could get to it, catch it, and throw it to first base. I wouldn't have believed it were it not for the fact that I saw the newsreel footage and I also saw Juan repeat the performance in person.

The only English he knew when he got here was "Okay," "Thank you" and "Goodbye." Within less than a year, he was speaking both English and Spanish (previously he had spoken only Quechua), and he had become what you might call the captain of the children's division at the institute. Whenever a newly arrived child showed signs of distress or homesickness, it was Juan who would produce exactly the right joke or crazy antic to cheer him up. On the other hand, if one of the kids got out of line, he dared not assume that Juan's lack of arms or legs would make him helpless. In Bolivia, Juan had worked out his own techniques, not only for playing baseball but for self-defense, which he perfected at the institute. When he rolled up to another boy and attacked him in the legs, that boy went down. And once he had a boy on the ground, Juan was on better than equal terms with him, since the ground had always been Juan's natural habitat.

One of our biggest jobs was to get him off the ground. William Tosberg and Dr. Allen Russek in our prosthetics department began designing experimental crutches and legs for him. They were able to fit him with an arrangement that was like a bucket seat perched on mechanical legs. Then they went to work developing special crutches, which he could manipulate despite his lack of arms. Conventional crutches, though they fit into the shoulder socket, are manipulated by the arms. Juan would have to manipulate his with his hands, which would be so near the tops of the crutches he would have very little leverage.

But Juan was absolutely determined that he would soon walk. I was in the children's division one day and overheard a conversation between him and two other boys. One of the boys announced proudly that he was going home next week. Then he said to Juan, "When do you go home?"

Juan ignored the fact that he had no home. He said, "I only go home when I walk home."

It was not long before our prosthetic experts developed the ideal lightweight crutches for him, and he was walking. Clumsily, at first, but then, as he developed his own techniques, with amazing speed and agility. He had a way of swinging himself when he walked, so that he moved along with what sometimes seemed to me dangerous speed. But his balance was so natural and perfect he never fell. (The prosthesis designed for him became the models for those used later by thalidomide children.) A few months after Juan began to walk, he suggested to some of the other children at the institute that they all walk over to the Empire State Building, about five long blocks away. When it came time to return, the others took a bus, but not Juan. He walked all the way and, thanks to New York traffic, beat them home.

As soon as Juan was mobile, we enrolled him in the Sacred Heart Primary School near the institute. He walked back and forth every day. He also became one of the best students in his class, but that didn't surprise anyone. He was cheated in arms and legs, but he had more than his share of brains. When he finished elementary school, we decided to send him to a junior college in Pomona, California, where he could continue his education. Though we had all come to love him, we didn't think permanent residence in an institution like ours was the best thing for him. In California he finished high school and a two-year course at Pacific College. Then he came "home" to the institute, as a good-looking young man, and we gave him a series of aptitude tests which indicated he would be an excellent computer programmer. He took a three-month IBM course in the subject and graduated with honors. He was ready now to go out into the adult world and make a living for himself, but first he wanted to fulfill an ambition that had grown in him through the years—to walk down the street in the city where he was born, La Paz, Bolivia. Before he returned home we were able to place him through the United Nations as a computer programmer in the nationalized tin industry. He had a difficult time adjusting to his new life when he first returned home, but he conquered the adjustment problems with the same courage with which he had overcome his disability. I hear from him often, and I wish all the "normal" people in the world could be as happy and successful as Juan Yepez.

CHAPTER

· ·

· ·

WHEN GENERAL "WILD BILL" DONOVAN (who headed the Office of Strategic Services intelligence network during World War II) was ambassador to Thailand in the early fifties, he got in touch with me and said he was facing a difficult political situation. The Thais were cynical about America, and something needed to be done to make them feel we were interested in them as people. Since there was no such thing as rehabilitation in Thailand, Donovan thought that if we could bring a team of Thais to America, train them here, and send them back to launch a rehabilitation program there, both countries would benefit from it.

Needless to say, he didn't have to sell me on the idea. He found the money, brought over a team of people from Thailand, and we trained them. After their training, they returned home to start a very successful program. It was so successful that on one of his trips back to the United States, Donovan and I discussed with our great friend and sponsor Mrs. Albert Lasker the possibility of continuing and enlarging this type of program. The conclusion was that we shouldn't limit the idea to Thailand, but that we should organize a nonprofit rehabilitation agency to help launch similar programs all over the world. The usual channels through which such things were done—the Department of State, the United Nations, the World Health Organization—worked too slowly. They gave such a low priority to rehabilitation that it usually took a year to get anything done through their efforts. What we needed was an agency that would be free to move quickly when someone asked us for help. As a result the World Rehabilitation Fund was organized in December of 1955. Its basic aim was to sponsor international projects which would help the handicapped and create a better understanding of them and their problems.

One of the first people I went to see when we were planning to launch the W.R.F. was former President Herbert Hoover. When I explained our purpose to him, he said, "Yes, I think that's a very good idea. It ought to be done. But what can I do about it?"

I said, "You could be one of our first honorary chairmen."

"If you think my name will help," he said, "go ahead and use it. But I can't work. I'm just too old."

"Don't worry," I said. "We'll do the work."

Then he asked me who the other honorary chairmen would be. I said we weren't yet sure, but that we planned to ask former President Truman, Dr. Albert Schweitzer and Bernard Baruch.

Mr. Hoover nodded his approval and smiled. "If you have trouble getting any of those other fellows, I'll talk to them for you."

Fortunately, we had no trouble getting any of "those other fellows," and we began with as distinguished a board of directors as we could have wanted. Our first step was to develop a system of training fellowships sponsored by American industries. Among the first to help were Sinclair Oil Company, American-President Lines, IBM World Trade, General Electric, General Foods, the pharmaceutical companies, American Express and many others. The fund-raising for the W.R.F. was not an easy task. We tried to hire a professional fund-raiser but none of the good ones would touch it. One man, who was then engaged in raising money for the International Rescue Committee and the American Association for the United Nations, told me, "I wouldn't take your account for any consideration. It doesn't have the kind of broad public appeal that would be successful." He felt we could raise money only by making personal calls on leaders of industry, labor and the various foundations.

That's what happened. I became a door-to-door salesman. I tried to make two calls a week. It was difficult to find that much time, but I was spurred on by the knowledge that each fellowship I "sold" meant that one more doctor could come here from a foreign country and train in rehabilitation. Fortunately, it worked. The combination of human rehabilitation and international understanding had a certain appeal for most businessmen. Over the years I don't think I was turned down more than three times.

At the outset, a fellowship cost only five thousand a year. It was always our policy to pay foreign doctors in training the same stipend we paid American doctors, and in those days this was the going rate. The stipend has more than doubled now, and that's as it should be, because the pay of residents and interns was pitifully low in the old days. I can remember how difficult it was for me to get along on twenty-five dollars a month when I was an intern in St. Louis. I also remember reading the rules for residents and interns in one

New York City hospital in those early days. No doctor could be appointed if he or she was married. If a doctor got married during his training period, his wife could not live in the same city; he would be allowed to visit her only on his day off, which was once a month. Thank God all that has changed. As a result, I think we're attracting many high-caliber people into medicine who otherwise couldn't afford it. The new young doctors have great ability. I know of one senior medical student who recently worked out a method of reducing dangerous blood clots that can develop in various parts of the body after open-heart surgery. His discovery is now in general use. This same young doctor, as a first-year resident at Bellevue, answered a 5 A.M. emergency call in a New York City sewer, and when he found that a seriously injured man was pinned under a dangerous pile of rubble, he crawled right in, administered Demerol, and gave the man emergency treatment which was credited with saving his life. His name is William Brenner; he's the husband of one of my former secretaries who helped him get his medical education.

You can't pay enough money for dedicated service like that, but you can at least provide enough dollars so young doctors like these can live normal, dignified lives while they're in service to the hospitals. It has been estimated that more than 75 percent of all medical students are deeply in debt when they finish their training. No one can deny that once they begin to practice, their income increases rapidly and medicine is now among the best-paid professions, but I don't think anyone need apologize for this. If a doctor does his job well, he should be paid well. The incidence of coronary disease among doctors is higher than in most other professions. We've had a lot of doctors come to us for rehabilitation training in their late forties and early fifties, and they almost always say the same thing: "I'm making plenty of money but I work a seventy-hour week. I never see my family. I'm tired all the time and I don't want to be hit by a coronary. In a field like rehabilitation, I can work and survive." Some of the best doctors we have in rehabilitation today come from this group.

While I ran around looking for money, the really difficult work of getting the W.R.F. on its feet was done by Jack Taylor. He was the administrator, the planner, the letter writer, the person who made the policies and the program work. And the quality of his administration has been such that through the years, W.R.F. has been able to get much more done per dollar spent than any governmental agency could hope to do. Taylor was responsible for the communications system which has kept rehabilitation people throughout the world informed about new methods and advances. We didn't want to lose touch with the doctors we had trained after they left us and returned to their own countries, so he worked out a policy by which every physician who took our training course became a fellow of the Institute of Rehabilitation Medicine. This means that four times a year he receives, wherever he may be, a packet of the latest literature to keep him up-to-date on his specialty. We now send out more than five hundred such packets every three months.

A few years later we had an idea about establishing our own shortwave radio station, with a special band like a ham radio, over which we could broadcast throughout the world a monthly symposium conducted by various rehabilitation experts. I blithely sailed over to Rockefeller Center and put this idea to a man who had long been a friend of our program and a member of our board, R.C.A. Board Chairman David Sarnoff.

I thought he would never stop laughing. "Howard," he said, "you may know a lot about rehabilitation, but you don't know a thing about communication. I'll send you one of my most experienced people in the field. You tell him what you want and we'll see what he can work out."

A few days later, a senior R.C.A. vice president came to the institute and explained to me why the idea wouldn't work. "But let me tell you about another possibility," he said. "R.C.A is now coming up with a new tape recorder and playback machine with two-hour unerasable tapes. With these, you could record your symposia here at the institute."

It sounded good except for one thing. "All right," I said, "suppose we cut tapes and send them out. How will our people all over the world be able to play them? They don't have machines."

He smiled. "I think you might find Mr. Sarnoff fairly generous about that."

Mr. Sarnoff was indeed generous. He gave us a hundred and thirty-five tape recorders and all the tape we would need for three years. With this we started a program of recorded clinics on every possible subject. Whenever an expert in a special field happened to be in New York, we would ask him for two or three hours of his time for a taping session. He would make a presentation, then a panel of our fellows would ask him questions. These tapes went all over the world and became the property of the centers to which they were sent. They were translated into almost every language, and are now the real foundation on which rehabilitation is taught in many countries. We've also made more than a hundred single-concept 8mm films on every subject, from management of paraplegics to the treatment of bedsores, and these have been very useful in the United States and other countries.

However, in less affluent countries, film has its limitations, because many rehabilitation centers can't afford to spend money on special projectors. I envision a day, however, when film will be our best world-wide training aid.

Through the years the World Rehabilitation Fund has kept broadening its program. Training doctors is only one aspect of the W.R.F.'s work. Another enormously important field is the training of artificial limb and brace makers all over the world. Twenty-five years ago, most of the less developed countries in the world had nobody making artificial limbs and braces for the handicapped. Now that has changed. The person most responsible is Juan Monros, mentioned earlier, a native of Spain who had been a professional soccer player until he decided he wanted to do something more important.

In 1957 Juan came to us, and the W.R.F. gave him a four-year fellowship to study prosthetics. He completed his studies in 1961, and since then he has traveled nearly two million miles, circling the globe at least ten times while visiting sixty-three different countries to show people how to make artificial limbs and other prosthetic devices. He has been decorated by several governments, and has received awards from countless organizations, including the U.S. Agency for International Development, and the People-to-People Program. When he goes into a country, Monros not only trains workers, he helps set up prosthetics shops and he builds management programs to make sure they continue to run efficiently after he leaves.

We have done a lot of traveling for the W.R.F. One of our most satisfying trips was to Guatemala in 1956, where one of our graduates, Dr. Miguel Aguilera, had inspired and directed the growth of a remarkable program. We then went to see how our graduates were doing in Portugal, and I don't think there's a finer center today in the entire world.

Our next stop was Finland, where, in Helsinki, I saw an excellent children's hospital which many Finns called the Coffee House. After the war there was an acute need for such a hospital, but no funds with which to build it. There was also at the time a lively black market in coffee, which the Finns love even more than the Irish love whisky. A distinguished doctor named Arvo Ylppö, whose wife was also a pediatrician specializing in cerebral palsy, was leading the crusade to build the hospital. He finally went to the government and said, "If you give us the monopoly on coffee, we'll build you the finest children's hospital in all of Europe." The government agreed, whereupon the good doctor immediately dropped the price of coffee a penny below the black-market price. Every time the black-market price dropped, he would drop a penny lower. Soon the black marketeers went out of business, the coffee monopoly began making money, and the hospital was built.

We flew from Helsinki to Leningrad and then to Moscow. We were taken on the usual guided tours of the countryside, seeing model farms, rural health clinics and an old people's home, which was very impressive. I wanted to see what the Russians were doing in rehabilitation, but for most of our stay I couldn't get any answers to my questions. Then two days before we left, I found out why: rehabilitation services were under a different ministry. I never did get to see how much of a program they had, or how it worked.

But I did manage to see an artificial-limb center, which was concerned more with research than production, and I asked a rather unpopular question when I was there. I asked, "Why do I see so many amputees on crutches in Moscow, without artificial legs?"

My guide was equal to the question. "Those are all

people from the country," he said, "who have come in to have their limbs fitted."

I judged from the old, worn look of their crutches that it had taken most of them a long time to get in from the country.

This mission to Russia was not very productive, but one good thing grew out of it. Shortly after our return Dr. Paul Dudley White, who headed the mission, and I decided to invite some Russian physicians here as our guests to observe what we were doing. We sent the invitation through the necessary channels, and about a year and a half later, on twenty-four hours' notice, four Russian doctors arrived— two women heart specialists who were to spend six weeks with Dr. White, and two men, a psychiatrist and a neurologist, who were to spend six weeks with us. The men were dressed, identically, in heavy blue serge suits, dark gray neckties, and even heavier blue fur-lined overcoats with fur collars. They had no idea what they were about to see and I think they were nervous about what kind of reception they would get. They needn't have worried. We treated them exactly as we did all the doctors from other countries who were training with us. We have no secrets. We gave them all our literature and taught them as much as they could possibly absorb in such a short time. We also arranged for them to meet some nice families and see all the sights in New York and Washington which were not restricted to Russian visitors. They were fine doctors and fine people. We were delighted with them. We had a dinner for them at the Overseas Press Club the night before they left at which we gave them gifts to take back to their wives and families, and at that dinner, the older doctor, the psychiatrist, said to me, "There are many things Americans have that I wish we had in

Russia—the cars, the refrigerators, the shops full of goods. But there is only one thing I truly envy you. That's the kind of homes you have. I'm a senior physician, but my wife, two children and I have to share a three-room apartment with two other families, and there is just no chance for privacy." It was a poignant remark. Of course, that was fifteen years ago, and I trust things are better now in Russia.

In recent years we have had many more Russian visitors at the institute, and we get along beautifully with them. Physical handicaps know no national boundaries or political ideologies. In our field we have a common language, which is the best possible tool for bridging gaps of human understanding.

I went to the Pan Pacific Conference on Rehabilitation in Australia in October 1956, and on the plane from Auckland to Sydney I met an interesting man who had lost both arms at the shoulders. On one side he had a three-inch stump, on the other side nothing. He was fed by a very nice-looking lady who was with him. He was going to the conference because he wanted to demonstrate an apparatus he had designed—a huge wooden arm fastened to the top of a table and operated by his foot. With it he could pick up a cup, knife or fork, and meet some of his other needs for daily living. When we arrived in Australia he demonstrated the apparatus and proved to be very skillful with it, but the thing weighed at least two hundred pounds. It was very clumsy and the only place he could use it was in his own home. I was so impressed with him as a person, I said, "If you can just get yourself to the United States, maybe we can design something better for you." Because he had only the one short stump to direct the movement of an artificial arm, I knew it would be difficult to do anything for him, but I also knew that Bill Tosberg, who ran our prosthetic service, was a genius, and I felt sure he could come up with something.

Several months after my return from Australia, I was surprised to get a phone call from this man announcing that he and his new bride were in New York. He had married the lovely lady who had been with him on the plane, and they came to the institute, where Bill Tosberg went to work on him. In less time than I would have expected, the man was fitted with very workable hooks. He was a good patient, working hard and learning fast. In eight weeks he was ready to return to Australia, and the day before he left he demonstrated his skill for a group of reporters. Sitting in a chair beside my desk, he took a pack of cigarettes out of his pocket, lit one, and holding it in one of his hooks, smoked it so carefully that the inch-long ash did not fall off. Then onto a piece of paper he carefully knocked this section of ash, and with his other hook, picked it up so delicately that it did not break. It was something I could not have done with my fingers. He returned to Australia and now makes his living there as an artist.

During that trip to Australia I met another fascinating man, an Englishman named Douglas Bader, who had been a legless group captain and fighter ace in World War II. He had lost both legs in the R.A.F. before the war. When the war began, he applied to reenter the service as a fighter pilot. His application must have caused some laughter at first, but he wouldn't give up. He pointed out that it would be almost an advantage to be legless in a crowded fighter-plane cockpit, and that the rudder of a plane, usually controlled by the pilot's feet, could easily be controlled by his hands. Finally they accepted him; he went back on duty, began shooting down German planes, and became an ace pilot. One day he was shot down over Holland, fell into the hands of the Germans, and was placed in a prisoner-of-war camp. When the British found out where he was, they asked the Germans if they could drop his legs into the camp by parachute. The Germans agreed. Three nights after his legs arrived, Bader escaped from the camp and was at large for a week before the Germans recaptured him. A short time later, he escaped again, only to be recaptured again. To prevent a third escape, they took his legs away from him every night, allowing him to use them only in the daytime. After the war, he joined the Shell Oil Company, for which he worked as a roving ambassador.

Two years after this trip, I went again as a guest of the Australian government to help plan a rehabilitation program. One of the most interesting places I visited that time was a geriatric community conceived and established by an Episcopal minister named Father Tucker, who believed people should continue living usefully after retirement. It was on a large piece of property, where everyone was invited to do his own thing. You could live in a modern specially designed apartment or if you wanted to build your own house, they would assign you a plot of ground and let you go ahead. They had the best small supermarket I had ever seen, founded and run by a widow who came to the community desolate after her husband died. Before the dedication of a new building took place, my wife and I admired the beautiful landscaping as we walked through the grounds, and when we made a special fuss over some of the flowers, Father Tucker said, "I'll tell you about those flowers. Old Joe, our eighty-six-year-old gardener, transplanted them day before yesterday. He worked very hard that day to get everything ready for the dedication, and after he had the garden in perfect condition, he went to bed feeling, as he said, 'pretty tired, but very happy' with the job he had done. That night he died in his sleep." Father Tucker spoke of Old Joe wistfully and poignantly. "When people come here, they live until they die." Father Tucker was a remarkable man and he created a remarkable community.

A very wise American doctor named George Morris Piersol, a great leader in rehabilitation, once said something similar in different words. Speaking of the responsibility of the medical profession in the field of geriatrics, he remarked, "Now that we've added years to people's lives, it is also our responsibility to add life to their years."

Advances in medicine have indeed complicated our geriatric problem. An economist recently calculated that if such advances continue during the seventies as they did in the sixties, we'll find that by 1980, every able-bodied worker in the country, besides having to support his dependent family, will have to produce enough to take care of one chronically ill, or physically disabled, or mentally handicapped person. Many economists doubt that our economic system can support this burden.

I think that one way to relieve the problem will be to discard the whole notion of compulsory retirement at the age of sixty-five. It's absurd to say a person is able to do his job when he's sixty-four years and three hundred and sixty-four days old, but not the day after that. Retirement robs many people of life by robbing them of their feeling of being wanted and belonging. Retirement should not be decided on the basis of an arbitrary age basis. Age is physiological, not chronological. Some are young at eighty and others are old in their forties. If Winston Churchill had retired at sixty-five, he would have taken no part in World War II, and the crucial

Battle of Britain might have gone the other way. Our society should be able to design an equitable plan whereby those who want to work can continue as long as they are able, and those who want to retire from their vocations can find useful and fulfilling avocations.

One of my most rewarding experiences in geriatrics has been my association for the last twenty years with Mother Bernadette, a senior member of the Carmelite order, whose primary mission is care of the aged. I met Mother Bernadette through my associate at the institute, Dr. Edward Lowman, when the Carmelites were trying to launch the Mary Manning Walsh Home in Manhattan. Its origins are interesting. The building on Fifty-ninth Street used to house an orthopedic hospital which merged with Columbia Presbyterian Hospital and moved uptown. The Salvation Army bought the building for $350,000 in the hope of using it as a hospital, than abandoned that hope and sold it to Cardinal Spellman, Catholic Archbishop of New York, for a handsome profit, which qualified the Catholic Church as one of the world's great contributors to the Salvation Army. But the Church got a sound, beautiful building big enough to house four hundred patients. It needed only to be refurbished. One day while Cardinal Spellman was trying to think of where he would get the money to finance all this, a tall white-haired man named Thomas J. Walsh came to see him and said he wanted to do something in honor of his deceased wife. The Cardinal immediately told him about this geriatric center that he was trying to help the Carmelites establish.

Mr. Walsh, who was a shy man, said he would very much like to contribute to such a cause, but that he didn't think he had the kind of money that might be needed. "I can only give you a million dollars," he apologized.

Cardinal Spellman, telling me the story later, said that when he recovered from the shock, he stood up and told Mr. Walsh, "For a million dollars we'll name the whole institution after your wife."

The Mary Manning Walsh Home opened in September 1952, and today it is one of the finest geriatric homes in the world. Because Mother Bernadette did not want it to be just another old folks' home, we designed a special rehabilitation program for it and trained several of the nuns at the institute. Mother Bernadette also put together a very able medical board of advisers and worked out a full program of activities to keep the residents busy. The rates were reasonable. You had to be sixty-five or over to get in, but you didn't have to be Catholic. All were welcome. Though you were encouraged to take part in the great range of activities offered inside the home, you were also encouraged to get out as often as possible and keep up all your old friendships.

One of the features of the place I have always liked best is the little bar, which opens at five o'clock every afternoon and is manned by bartenders from the neighborhood pubs who come and contribute their time. I remember getting out of the elevator at the home late one afternoon and being approached by an old, apparently Irish lady who looked as if John Barleycorn had been a dear friend of hers for many years.

She said, "For God's sake, you're not leavin' us at a time like this, are you?"

I said, "I'm afraid I have to."

"But didn't you know the bar is about to open," she said, "and it's the finest bar in the city of New York. They charge you only a quarter for a big drink, and if you don't have a quarter they charge you only a dime, and if you don't have a dime they don't charge you anything at all. Come in for just a half an hour. I've got an extra quarter."

It takes a great person to run a home for old people where they can feel as much at home as that, and Mother Bernadette is a great person. She has taken part in every White House conference on problems of the aging, and she is one of the major reasons why the Carmelite order now has thirty-five splendid geriatric centers throughout the world.

By 1956, our Institute for Rehabilitation Medicine had become so crowded we had to build three more floors. Those were the worst days we ever had, because while the work was in progress we had to use our student dormitories for patients and push them through the slush and snow back and forth to our torn-up building every day. Both the expense and the inconvenience were murderous. Thanks to inflation, it cost us more to add those three stories than it had cost us to build the original institute, just five years earlier. But when the work was done, we had the capacity for twice as many patients, and that made it worthwhile.

In December of 1956 we gained a great measure of financial stability for the institute, but in doing so, we lost a wonderful friend—Louis Horowitz, who, back in 1949, decided to leave the bulk of his fortune, estimated then at about six million dollars, to the institute. After he died, his bequest turned out to be more than eleven million, an endowment which has enabled us to provide patient care for hundreds of people who could not otherwise afford it, and also to enlarge very significantly our research and training programs.

Louis Horowitz was a great humanitarian. During his last years he suffered from cancer, and when I heard that his condition had become grave, I immediately flew down to Florida, where he was spending most of his time. When I arrived he was deathly sick and his mind was wandering. But as soon as he saw me, he began to talk very lucidly. He reached out, took my hand, and said, "Howard, I'm happy about what I've done because I know it's going to help a lot of people." Those were the last words he ever said to me.

One of the first people helped by Mr. Horowitz's patient fund was a young German engineer, whom I shall call Herman. He was the only man I ever saw that became a paraplegic twice. In Hitler's Germany, he had been put in a concentration camp for anti-Nazi activity, and during his imprisonment a guard had beaten him brutally and caused a severe hemorrhage of the spinal cord. For three months he was paralyzed from the waist down. Then time healed his condition; he regained the use of his legs and escaped to France, where he fought with the French underground. After the war he went to Mexico as an engineer, married a girl from the United States and became a father. But one day his car turned over on a mountain road near Guadalajara; his back was broken and his spinal cord severed. This time he was paralyzed permanently.

After three years on his back, he wrote us in desperation. He and his wife, by doing every possible odd job, had saved a few hundred dollars. Presuming that his rehabilitation would take only a few weeks, he thought he now had enough money to come to New York and pay his own way at the institute.

Though we knew better, we told him to come anyway. He arrived in critical condition, with numerous pressure sores and infections of the bones and kidneys. In the months that followed he underwent more than a dozen surgical operations. And when he was well enough to begin training, his overconfidence and zeal caused him to fall and break his leg. That didn't stop him. As soon as his leg healed, he got back on his feet again, finished his training, and returned home to his wife and little daughter.

I still have a Christmas card I received from his wife a year or two later. "Everything continues as it should with us," she wrote. "Herman remains wonderfully fit in spite of working like an idiot. After a full day at the factory, and when there's nothing more interesting to do, he puts on the braces and bounds around to the tune of the 'Cha-Cha-Cha.' He never ceases to amaze everyone."

Another memorable Christmas card came from Adlai Stevenson. It carried a quotation that drew such a strong reaction from our patients it has become, in effect, the "creed" of the institute. Stevenson was a man so sincere he went to great lengths each year in an effort to find a quotation which would be unusual, but exactly right, for his cards, and for the Christmas of 1955 he chose the personal prayer of an unknown Confederate soldier in the Civil War. He found it, I believe, in an old church in South Carolina. It goes like this:

I asked God for strength, that I might achieve
    I was made weak that I might learn humbly to obey . . .
I asked for health, that I might do greater things
    I was given infirmity, that I might do better things . . .
I asked for riches, that I might be happy
    I was given poverty, that I might be wise . . .
I asked for power, that I might have the praise of men
    I was given weakness, that I might feel the need of God . . .
I asked for all things, that I might enjoy life
    I was given life, that I might enjoy all things . . .

I got nothing that I asked for
　　—but everything I had hoped for
Almost despite myself, my unspoken prayers were answered.
　　I am among all men, most richly blessed!

One of our patients, when he read this, tossed it over to a boy with severe cerebral palsy and said to him, "You know, this man is talking about us."

When the boy's father came to see him that night, the son showed it to him and then repeated what the other patient had said, "This man is talking about us."

The father said, "He's talking about me, too." The father was so impressed he had the prayer cast in bronze and it now hangs on the wall of the institute lobby. Thousands of patients and their families, after reading it, have asked for copies. It has been translated into several languages and you'll find it now in rehabilitation centers all over the world. People everywhere seem to find in it a message of hope.

Around this time we watched the culmination of a touching romance. We had a nurse training in rehabilitation medicine, a Dutch girl named Gertrude Vis, who had come to us from Holland in 1954 because she wanted to be an expert in rehabilitation. The real reason for her ambition was not apparent when she arrived, but after she had been with us awhile, she told us that she was in love with a man back in Holland who had been a paraplegic since 1945, and she wanted to be able to do everything for him that could possibly be done. The man's name was Henk Geluk, and she had met him in 1953, when he was admitted for surgery at the hospital where she then worked. During his postoperative recovery she was his nurse and before long they were engaged. It was her dream, not only to marry him, but to get him back on his feet and help him really live again.

With the help of friends we brought him to New York, and at the institute Geluk's training developed without complications. So did his romance. Within four months, he was not only ready to walk out of the place, he was ready to get married. So he and Trudy decided not to wait any longer. They had their wedding at the Church of the Sacred Heart of Jesus over on Thirty-third Street, and I gave away the bride. It was a lovely ceremony, attended by a sizable crowd of our patients who had by this time become friends of the Geluks. Afterward they returned to Holland and lived happily for several years until Henk died from an illness unrelated to his paraplegia.

At the annual meeting of the International Labor Organization in Geneva in 1958 I met for the first time Mr. David Morse, who was then the director general of the I.L.O. He is now, I'm happy to say, associated with us in the World Rehabilitation Fund. At the same meeting I also had the pleasure of seeing again two of our most remarkable former patients. One was Paul Francolon, the French paraplegic one-time jockey whose story I have already told. The other was a Greek named Steve Kalkandis who had been a patient of ours at Bellevue in 1947, and was now back in Athens living a very active life.

Kalkandis had been a flier in the Greek air force during the war. One day, when he pulled his plane out of a dive he suffered some kind of paralysis in his arms and legs, but it gradually went away, so he went back to flying. A few weeks later, after a similar dive, he suffered complete paralysis and this time it was permanent. Through the efforts of a dedicated Greek priest, he was brought to New York for surgery at one of our large medical centers, but when they operated they found he had extremely large varicose veins in the spinal canal.

The pressure on these veins precipitated by the airplane dive was the cause of his paralysis.

Removal of the varicosities was impossible. His doctor wrote a letter to the priest saying there was nothing that could be done for him and that he should be taken home as soon as possible because he probably wouldn't live more than another six months. Inadvertently Steve saw the letter. He said, "No, I'm not going to die. I'm going to do something with my life."

At that time, in 1947, we were just getting started at Bellevue. The priest, hearing about the program, came and asked if we would examine his friend. I'll never forget it. His limbs were so spastic, any kind of pressure would cause him to go into severe spasms. The first day we fitted him into braces, it took four men to stretch out his legs so we could get the braces on. But he worked hard and the exercise had a great effect in reducing the spasticity. Eight months after his admission, he walked out of Bellevue with two short leg braces and two canes. When he got back to Greece, he received so much publicity for his victory over paralysis that he became a national hero. He was soon the unofficial spokesman for Greek war veterans. When Glad and I visited Athens in 1951, he met us at the airport and drove us to our hotel. Since that time he has become Mr. Rehabilitation in Greece. In a recent letter he reported he had been promoted to the rank of general and was walking without braces or canes. He gave us due credit at the institute, but stated passionately that prayer and God had saved him. I think he was right.

Both he and Paul Francolon gave wonderful performances at the I.L.O. meeting at Geneva in 1958. They walked on and off the stage, told their stories and demonstrated what they could do. David Morse was so impressed, the rehabilitation program in the I.L.O. took on new dimensions that day. It has now grown into a world-wide network of rehabilitation centers. When the I.L.O. won the Nobel Prize in 1969, the citation made special mention of its efforts in the field of rehabilitation for injured working men.

One of our most famous patients came to us in 1958—Roy Campanella of the Brooklyn Dodgers, who had been the best catcher in the National League until the night of January 28, when he was driving to his Long Island home and his car overturned on a slippery road. He fractured his fifth cervical vertebra and severed his spinal cord, which made him a quadriplegic. When he came to us from the Glen Cove Long Island Community Hospital in May, he had slight movement in his wrists and could extend and bend his arms, but could not move his fingers. After six months of hard work he was ready to go home. While there is no way in which a quadriplegic can learn to walk, Campy was then able to get himself from wheelchair to automobile and take care of his daily needs. But instead of describing his experience secondhand, I'll put it down in his own words as he told it to New York *Post* columnist Milton Gross a few days after he returned home.

"The two toughest times for me," Campy recalled, "were lying in the wrecked automobile, afraid it would go on fire and there was nothing I could do but just burn up in it. And the other time was when I developed pneumonia [after surgery] and I couldn't breathe. They had to get a tracheotomy tube into me. They had to cut my throat.

"For five months I lay in that Stryker bed [a special frame designed to support a patient and hold him in place during traction] and when I couldn't feed myself I'd wonder if I ever would. I'd keep asking the nurses if there was anybody else like me in the institute who could feed himself. 'You'll feed yourself,' they'd say. 'Don't worry about it.' "

The nurses were right. Gradually, as the summer progressed, Roy Campanella learned to feed himself and do all kinds of other things. Then came World Series time, which was naturally difficult for him because he had starred in so many World Series. The Yankees, who were in the series that year as they were just about every year then, invited him to attend the New York games as their guest. After some hesitation, he accepted.

"Everything went along fine," he said, "until it came time to put my wheelchair in the aisle and they found the aisle wasn't wide enough. I had no idea they'd pick me up and carry me. Maybe I wouldn't have gone if I had known that.

"Tears came to my eyes. I heard the comments as I was being carried down the aisle. I was proud of the recognition the fans gave me, but at the same time it hurt me that I had to be seen the way I was. And I was worried whether I could sit in the seat. You worry about everything that's new."

Despite his worries, he sat through the whole game and came back again the next day. After that, he went to the trotting races at Yonkers and a basketball game at Madison Square Garden. One night he had dinner with singer Nat King Cole at the Copacabana.

"I learned that you have to get around," he said. "If you just sit down and sulk and not go anyplace, it's bound to worry you. I've come through some close times and just to be able to talk about it shows the progress I've made."

A measure of the progress he made was illustrated by his account of a little incident which took place just before he left the institute. "There was a young fellow in the room next to mine. He had dived into a foot and a half of water and broken his neck. He lay there with tongs in his head."

Recalling the five months he had also lain, completely immobilized on a Stryker frame, Campy knew exactly what was going through this boy's mind. By now, Campy was moving around the hospital like any other patient in the final phase of rehabilitation. Without waiting for an invitation, he went wheeling into the boy's room and introduced himself, meeting at the same time the boy's parents, who were also there, looking worried.

"I wanted him to see what I could do," Campy said. "And it was the most wonderful thing in the world when he and his mother and father realized I could actually feed myself, get around, and do all the things I was doing."

In our institute, the best psychologists are the patients themselves. They show each other, as Roy Campanella showed this boy, how many things are possible in spite of their handicaps.

· ·

XI

· ·

THE CAMPAIGN TO GET the international health and medical research act through Congress involved a struggle from 1959 to 1961 that dramatized the enormous complexity of our legislative process. The purpose of the Act was to establish an international health program that would help expand medical research all over the world. The money would come from America's surpluses in the currency of other countries, primarily from payments for surplus commodities, for at that time we were enjoying favorable trade balances. The "Health for Peace" bill seemed an ideal way to get something good for the whole world out of these excess funds, which had to be spent in the country in which they were located. The bill went sailing through the Senate by a vote of 63 to 17 under the sponsorship of Lister Hill of Alabama and Hubert Humphrey of Minnesota, who was at that time Democratic whip. When it reached the House of Representatives, however, it had a rough time. It first had to pass through the Interstate and Foreign Commerce Committee, whose chairman, Representative Oren Harris of Arkansas, was a very astute politician but not very internationally minded.

The American Medical Association, which had supported the bill in the Senate, indicated surprisingly that it would not support the bill in the House. The A.M.A. simply refused to comment on it before the Harris committee, which was like pronouncing a death sentence. The A.M.A. had one of the most powerful lobbies in Washington, and someone of considerable influence in the medical profession had apparently decided he didn't like the bill. It was impossible to guess who this might be.

I was concerned because I was scheduled to testify in favor of the bill and it looked as if I would have a bad time. After thinking about what possible influence I could bring to bear, I went to see Representative Clarence Cannon, who came from Elsberry, Missouri. My mother had been his first teacher in the little primary school there and he had always been fond of her and of our family. He was then chairman of the Appropriations Committee, which made him one of the most powerful figures in the House, since that committee controlled the purse strings. He was also conservative, especially with money, so I explained to him very carefully the advantages of the international health bill, and at the same time I said I expected trouble before the committee the next day.

"I've never met Mr. Harris," I said. "I wish you'd come over and introduce me to him."

Cannon said, "Howard, I'd be delighted. You be in my office at a quarter of nine tomorrow morning."

When he led me into that chamber the next day, I got more than my share of attention. Representative Harris spoke about what a great honor it was for the chairman of the Appropriations Committee to visit his committee; it was unprecedented. Then Cannon gave a peroration about his colleagues, about Missouri, about me, and even about my mother. It was embarrassing, but it was also effective up to a point. When I testified, everyone listened attentively and no one attacked me.

However much good I might have done with the committee members, I had not swayed the A.M.A. As the hearing continued, it became evident that nothing was going to happen. The bill was not called out of committee to the floor of the House.

I then began looking around for people who might be able to help. Since Representative Harris was from Arkansas, we found other people from that state whom we knew he respected, and got them to talk to him. One of them was Senator J. William Fulbright, whom I had known as a lad because he was born in Mendon, Missouri, not far from Brookfield. When I began practice in St. Louis, his mother had been my second private patient. She was a very brilliant woman. The family had then moved to Fayetteville, Arkansas, where they owned a bank, a bottling company, the local newpaper and other interests. After her husband died, she had stepped in and run them all. So I'd known Bill Fulbright for a long time, and he very willingly spoke to his fellow Arkansan about the health act. But Fulbright didn't seem to have any more influence with Harris on that subject than he was to have later with Lyndon Johnson and Richard Nixon on the subject of the Vietnam war.

Finally, I remembered a patient who had spent some time at the institute a few years earlier, a lady from an influential cattle-breeding family in Arkansas. She had broken her neck and her daughter had brought her to us. I couldn't forget the daughter because of the absolute, unshakable determination with which she had worked and fought for her mother. After her mother's rehabilitation, which was limited by the fact that her paralysis was from the neck down, the daughter went back to Arkansas and began campaigning, with charm, persistence and great success, for the establishment of state rehabilitation service there.

In desperation I called this young lady and told her something which was really only a suspicion in my mind. Silly as it seemed, I had a feeling that Representative Harris' negative reaction to the bill was at least partly prompted by a powerful and extremely conservative country doctor in Arkansas, whom I knew by reputation but not in person. He was apparently a fine, dedicated man but quite provincial.

My friend, after talking to me, got in her car with a friend of hers and drove three hundred miles to see this doctor. When she found him, she spent an hour explaining the bill to him as no one else had ever before bothered to explain it. As soon as he understood it, he said, "I believe in that. What do you want me to do?"

"It might be helpful," my friend said, "if you would send a telegram to Representative Harris."

He did, and that was the key. The bill came out of committee and was soon passed into law by the House. But for more than a year, that one country doctor in Arkansas had exercised enough power to bottle up a measure which was of concern to the whole world.

In 1962 we had a patient for whom, I'm sorry to say, we were unable to do as much as we hoped. That was Joseph Kennedy, Sr., the father of President John F. Kennedy. I had first met Joseph Kennedy when he appeared in my office unexpectedly one day in 1959 and said, "I've heard of this place and I'd like to see it."

When we returned to my office after a tour of the institute, he explained why he had come. "I'd like you to help me reorganize the Kennedy Foundation," he said. "My son is planning to run for President next year and I don't want anyone to say the foundation has made a contribution to a hospital or a community or any other agency for political reasons. We've decided we want the foundation to work basically in the field of mental retardation. Could you take a reading on this and give us your recommendation?"

I told him I would put together a small committee of the best people I knew and we'd study the matter. I then got together an excellent group: Dr. H. Bernard Wortis, head of the NYU psychiatric department; Dr. Francis Braceland, a senior consultant to the Navy in psychiatry who had then organized the Mayo Clinic program before becoming director of the Institute For Living, at Hartford, Connecticut; and Dr. Kenneth Appel, head of the Psychiatric Institute in Philadelphia. We made our recommendations to the Kennedy family and they seemed very appreciative. They had done a lot of serious thinking about the matter themselves and they settled on what has turned out to be an excellent program to help the mentally retarded. At our last meeting with the family, Joseph Kennedy, after explaining to us how the new setup would work, turned to me and said, by way of thanks for my efforts, "I very much admire the work you're doing, and if you could use a twenty-five-thousand-dollar check for the institute, it will be in the mail this afternoon."

I spoke to Joseph Kennedy only casually on a few occasions between then and the day in late 1961 when he had his devastating stroke in Florida. After the tragedy, the family asked me to go down for consultations; I made seven trips back and forth. We helped set up a rehabilitation program for him first at the hospital, then at his home in Palm Beach.

But after several months it seemed wise to bring him to the institute. He was paralyzed on his right side, with very little function in his hand but about 40 percent use of his leg. He had to wear a brace on the leg, and with it he could walk, but he hated the brace and fought it like a tiger.

Mr. Kennedy, as I think most people know, was a man of strong will. The one very helpful thing he liked to do was swim, which he did regularly. But his greatest disability was aphasia, the speech handicap from which so many stroke victims suffer. His mind was perfectly clear, yet he could not put the right word with the right object. It is just about the most frustrating thing that can happen to a person, and Joseph Kennedy had always been so successful in achieving what he set out to do that his frustration point was low. This inability to speak properly was something he just could not accept.

When he agreed to come to the institute in May of 1962, we flew to New York together on the *Caroline*, the family-owned jet plane which became famous when his son used it during the Presidential years. We landed at La Guardia and, to avoid reporters, parked way out at the end of a runway where an ambulance and cars were waiting. When we were ready to leave the plane, Mr. Kennedy insisted on walking down the stairway himself, which he could not do. I was set against it because at that stage it would have been very dangerous if he fell. There was a little portable chair in which he could easily have been carried down the stairs, but he absolutely refused to get in it. The more we cajoled, the more adamant he became.

After about a half hour, I finally said, "I don't know any other way you can get off this airplane, Mr. Kennedy. I have a lot of patients to see, so I've got to go in to the institute.

But the ambulance will wait here. When and if you decide to come, we'll welcome you."

There was no mistaking the fierce anger in his expression, but finally he said, very softly, "No," which, because of his aphasia, meant "Yes." If he said, "No! No! No!" with great emphasis, that meant "No." But if he simply said, "No," softly, that meant "yes." He accepted the chair, and the trip to town was uneventful, but he was so angry, he wouldn't speak to me for two days.

For security reasons, since we knew the President would often be coming to see him, we set him up in a little house adjacent to the institute which we call Horizon House. Ordinarily we use the house for teaching, as it was specially designed as a house that would meet the needs of wheelchair living. It has ramps instead of steps, wide doorways, a centralized vacuum-cleaning system and kitchen appliances easily used by a person in a sitting position. We made Mr. Kennedy comfortable there and one of my young colleagues, Dr. Henry Betts, became his personal physician. Dr. Betts did a fine job and got along very well with the whole Kennedy family. (He is now the director of the Institute of Rehabilitation at Northwestern University in Chicago.) Mr. Kennedy stayed with us about two months and President Kennedy made several trips from Washington to see him. They would sit on the porch of Horizon House and talk. The President would tell his father about his problems in the White House, and Mr. Kennedy would always respond vigorously, despite his difficulty in communicating. The entire family came to see him regularly. They're a very devoted family, and they did everything possible for him, but there wasn't much that we could do to help. He was so strong-willed that he found it impossible to surrender himself to the training. I understood this and could sympathize with his frustrations. But I very much regretted that the extent of his rehabilitation was so limited. All we could do was set up a program for him at Hyannisport, where he swam in a warm pool and walked in his brace on rare occasions. He also liked to go out on the family boat and be with his grandchildren. I saw him from time to time, and I was in close communication with his sons Bobby and Teddy.

When President Kennedy was assassinated Mr. Kennedy was not told immediately of the events of those awful days. Although the family kept him away from the devastating scenes on television, he sensed that something was terribly wrong. It was Teddy who sat down beside him to tell him the tragic news, and when he heard it, I understand he sobbed from the bottom of his heart, then rolled his wheelchair to the window and looked out at the sea. Joseph Kennedy was an extraordinary man, a sad and silent giant.

After we met through his father, President Kennedy and I became friends, and when he put together a commission headed by General Lucius Clay to study our foreign-aid program, he named me to it as a medical representative. It was an interesting assignment, but I often felt like Little Orphan Annie because the problems of international finance the committee frequently discussed were far over my head. Sometimes I also felt like a terrible nuisance. Whenever someone else talked money for too long a time, I would bring the discussion back to people and the vast numbers of them all over the world who suffered from such awful needs. I'll never forget the first day the Clay commission met in the President's office; I was three hours late getting there. It was very cold and the weather was so bad, I didn't want to risk flying, so I had taken the midnight train from New York and when I awoke at sunrise we were parked on a siding some-place in Delaware. The meeting was scheduled for 8:30 A.M. and I was in a complete stew by the time the train reached Washington around eleven. How does one walk gracefully into a meeting with the President three hours late? I was still worrying about it when, fortunately, as I got off the train, I ran into General Clay and three other commission members in the same situation.

In the field of mental retardation great progress has been made in the last fifteen years, and the Kennedy Foundation has been responsible for much of it. This was a largely ne-glected field before the Kennedys began to take a vital inter-est in it. They made funds available for many projects that have proven that retarded people can do much more for themselves than they've ever been given a chance to do.

On a smaller scale, Henry Viscardi's company, Abilities, Inc., which I described earlier, conducted a project that proved the same thing. He induced a Long Island bank to turn over its simple accounting, checking and recording procedures to his company. Then he hired a group of re-tarded people, taught them uncomplicated computer pro-gramming, and showed them how to do routine bank work. At the end of the first year, the bank found it was not only getting the job done more cheaply than before, but more important, the retarded people were making fewer mistakes than the "normal" people who had previously done it. The retarded workers were not bored by the routine tasks, they appreciated the opportunity.

The speech therapist who tried so hard to help Joseph Kennedy with his aphasia was Mrs. Martha Taylor, director of our speech department at the institute. She and neurolo-gist Dr. Morton Marks in the late 1950s were struck by the abysmal ignorance of the public on the whole subject. As a result, Mrs. Taylor wrote a simple little book called *Understanding Aphasia*, which set out to explain in plain words the nature of the affliction and how much could be done to overcome it. The book exploded the widespread belief that people with aphasia were *non compos* and they pointed out how the condition could be helped by proper therapy and understanding. We printed only a few thousand of these little books, thinking the demand for them would be limited. That was in 1960. *Understanding Aphasia* is now in its tenth printing and has been translated into fourteen languages. It is still available through the institute.

A few years ago, another colleague, Dr. Albert Haas, wrote a similar booklet entitled *Living with Pulmonary Emphysema*. Patients with pulmonary emphysema have difficulty breathing because of a dilatation of the air sacs in the lung. Just before the booklet was to come out, I decided to do a column about it in the *Times*, and when I asked Dr. Haas for some details, he said, "I'm afraid I've made a terrible blunder. I got overenthusiastic and had five thousand copies printed. We'll never get rid of them." In the two weeks after that column appeared in the *Times*, we had requests for ten thousand copies. This book, which has now been reprinted seven times and translated into six languages, is also still available through the institute.

In May of 1964 I returned to Hong Kong. I was delighted to see that while there had been no rehabilitation centers when I first visited the colony eleven years earlier, now an 80-bed center was being operated by the Hong Kong Society for Rehabilitation of the Disabled and the 530-bed Aberdeen Rehabilitation Centre was about to open. A brace and limb shop had also been established at the Kowloon municipal hospital.

During this visit I was approached by a Hong Kong police sergeant who had a problem that was hard to ignore. His only child, a very bright little boy, suffered from a severe congenital heart condition called aortic coarctation. Without open-heart surgery, the child had only a short time to live, for in Hong Kong there were no doctors performing open-heart surgery. The police sergeant had saved enough money to pay the fare for himself and the boy to America, but he would then have none left over for the very considerable expense of the medical care involved. The kind of operation the boy needed would cost about seven thousand dollars in hospital costs alone. But I said to the father, "Come ahead. We'll do something."

When they arrived, we put the father in my own little apartment at the institute, and we admitted the boy as a patient. Dr. Frank Spencer, a professor of surgery at NYU, agreed to perform the operation without cost and I began scrounging among friends for the rest of the money. The little boy had a very hard time. He needed twenty pints of blood during and after the surgical procedure, but he did recover, and it was wonderful to see the depth of his father's love for him.

The two of them returned and I thought that was the end of it. It didn't occur to me that the news of their experience would soon spread all over Hong Kong. Before we knew it, we had requests to bring over four more children with similar need for open-heart surgery.

I began scrounging again and the four kids soon arrived. If you want to know the feeling of terrible responsibility, just take in four lonely children with severe cardiac disabilities, who don't speak a word of English, all of them facing surgery that carries a mortality rate of 20 percent. We were fortunate in the medical center to have several nurses who spoke Chinese; we arranged their schedules so at least one was always available in the intensive-care and recovery rooms. Fortunately, all four of these children survived, and shortly after they returned home, I was in Hong Kong once more. We had a party for them and their families with ice cream and candy and all the things kids love. It was a deeply moving experience; there were laughter and tears—tears of joy.

We also had another party on this trip. The police sergeant was at the airport to meet us and announced we were going to dinner in a floating restaurant at Aberdeen. That sounded fine but it turned out to be much more than that. He had planned it for some time and his fellow policemen had chipped in to help him pay for it. We were taken on a sampan out into these exquisite floating gardens and served a feast of every imaginable kind of seafood. Most of the guests had brought bottles of the finest liquor and we drank toast after toast to the guest of honor, the police sergeant's little boy, who sat in an elevated chair, smiling down on us. It was now six months since his operation; he had gained twenty pounds in weight and five inches in height. Today he is a normal boy with an excellent school record, and he and his family have emigrated to the United States.

As a result of all this, there were five happy children and their families in Hong Kong, but in solving their difficulties we had brought to light the problems of an estimated two hundred other children in Hong Kong who needed similar surgery. At seven thousand dollars per child, there was no way we could bring all of them to the United States. Dr. Spencer wanted to go to Hong Kong on a training mission to teach open-heart surgery to doctors there, but with the demand for his services here, he couldn't get away. A former associate of his at the University of Kentucky, Dr. Lester R. Bryant, was able to take three months off, however, and he took his family to Hong Kong, where he operated several times a day while a team of young Chinese doctors assisted and studied his techniques. He came back ecstatic about the capabilities of these young doctors. That must have been five years ago. Last year, after hearing about two Korean children who needed complicated open-heart surgery, I called him and asked him if he thought the doctors he had taught in Hong Kong could do it.

"Can they do it!" he cried. "They gave a report on fifteen cases at a conference in Singapore last month, and they were able to point out that they have a lower mortality and morbidity rate than we have in the United States."

After the death of President Kennedy, when Lyndon Johnson entered the White House, he set up a commission for the study of heart disease, strokes and cancer under the chairmanship of Dr. Michael DeBakey, one of the nation's outstanding vascular surgeons. The purpose of the group, which included twenty-five specialists in various fields, was to work out a master plan of attack against these three number-one killers and cripplers. As a member of this group I pointed out that while the basic approach should be prevention and cure, that wouldn't help people who were already victims of one or the other of these afflictions. Here I was arguing again for rehabilitation. Fortunately, the commission was composed of men with great understanding, and they established a subcommittee on rehabilitation in the fields of cancer, heart disease and strokes. When this subcommittee got into a detailed study of the problems, I was suddenly confronted with a fact of which I had been only dimly aware until then—that in the field of cancer almost no rehabilitation had ever been attempted. Of the more than two hundred thousand American handicapped people who had been rehabilitated in the previous year, less than five hundred had been cancer victims. One reason for this was that for many years it was erroneously assumed that a cancer victim's chance of survival was so slim, there was no point in spending money to rehabilitate him. If he had severe, mutilating surgery, the assumption was that he had only death ahead of him, and until recent years it was true. But by the early 1960s, the medical profession had demonstrated that with certain new drugs and surgery, certain kinds of cancer could be stopped. That meant an increasing number of patients were left cured but mutilated.

A most dramatic case of this kind came to us at the institute in December of 1964. The patient's name was James Cavorti. He lived in Ronkonkoma, New York, and he had been a clothes presser before being struck by cancer of the bladder in July of 1963. His doctors recommended surgery to remove the affected tissue, but two months after the operation the lower part of his body was racked by unbearable pain. In January of 1964 he was brought to New York City's Memorial Hospital under the care of Dr. Theodore Miller. After radical surgery, followed by X-ray treatments and every possible measure, cancer was still rampant in the lower half of his body.

At that point Dr. Miller contacted us before discussing the matter further with Mr. Cavorti. "This patient has only two alternatives," Dr. Miller said. "He can decide to do nothing more, in which case he faces a very painful death within six months. There is only one way he could avoid that: a hemicorporectomy. But we don't want to suggest it unless there's some chance that he can make a life for himself afterward. Do you think you could do anything to rehabilitate a man in that condition?"

A hemicorporectomy is an operation to remove the whole lower half of a person's body. To my knowledge, such extreme surgery had been performed successfully only once before, upon a young man in Minnesota. But there had been no attempt to really rehabilitate that man. When Dr. Miller mentioned such a possibility, we were at first overwhelmed. But the more we thought about it, the more we realized there were many things we could do. We called Dr. Miller and said we would be glad to undertake the rehabilitation of his patient.

He then confronted his patient with the dreadful alternatives. As Cavorti said later, "For three days I wrestled with the choice. I wasn't alone during that time. I had the help of my doctors, the hospital psychologists and my family." This included his wife, Elvira, and two sons—James, twenty, and Dennis, fourteen.

"Many questions haunted me," Cavorti recalled. "I knew I'd never be able to go swimming again. But could I go fishing? Would I ever be able to work? Or do anything but lie in bed? Fear tormented me at every turn. I worried about the effects on my family, too. But I realized that if I didn't go through with it, I would face lingering, painful death in a matter of months. And I decided it was better to chance being half alive than dead for sure. There was no turning back."

Before he made his decision, Cavorti and his family also held long conferences with the staff at Memorial Hospital who tried to make them realize exactly what to expect. He was amazingly brave. On September 23, the hemicorporectomy was performed. The amputation was made just below the rib cage at the fifth lumbar vertebra, removing his pelvis and lower extremities and leaving an artificial rectum in his right lower abdomen, and on the right side an opening for urinary drainage.

"When I came out of the anesthesia," he recalled, "I was missing from the ribs down. I felt completely helpless. It's impossible to describe all my feelings. Great waves of depression swept over me."

When he came to us three weeks later, he was a small third of a man, still anxious and distressed, lying there forlornly, the skin around the incision not yet healed. We had to wait several weeks for him to heal completely, but during that time, we began to strengthen his hands, arms and shoulders. We built a trapeze attached by a swivel beam to the headboard of his bed, and with this he soon learned to raise off the bed the sixty pounds that were left of him.

At the same time, our prosthetics genius, Bill Tosberg, and his staff made a cast of his chest and fashioned a shell into which he could fit himself. This shell was mounted on a board and placed in the seat of a wheelchair so he could sit and look the world in the face. Having learned to swing himself on the headboard trapeze, Cavorti now learned to raise himself off the bed and out over the wheelchair, then lower himself into the hollow shell, which fitted him perfectly.

As soon as he could sit up this way, and move around in the wheelchair, his entire outlook changed. He could look the rest of us straight in the eye from an upright position, he could wheel that chair anyplace he wanted to go. He was free at last from the bed. It was exciting to see him drop into that torso, put on his shirt, and wheel away. And it had all been quite simple. He was so courageous and so cooperative, I began to think we might be able to do even more.

One day in conference, I asked the staff, "Why don't we fit him with legs? If we can teach paraplegics to walk, why can't we teach him? The problems are similar. In some ways, he might have an advantage because he doesn't have any legs to carry around."

A short time later, Tosberg, using the socketlike prosthesis as a base, had designed a whole lower body for Cavorti, with full legs and feet. The legs could be bent at the knees and hips for sitting, or locked straight for walking. And the entire prosthesis weighed only fifteen pounds. We dressed it in pants, shoes and socks, so that when he lowered himself into it, he had only to attach the shoulder straps and put on his shirt. Sitting in a chair completely dressed, he looked like anyone else.

The question now was whether he could actually learn to walk. I don't think it occurred to him that he might be unable to. He became adept with crutches almost immediately. Sitting in his chair, he would straighten his legs and lock them onto his feet. He seemed to have no problem with balance. Not only did he learn to walk at a comfortable pace, he also learned to go up and down curbs, then up and down whole flights of stairs. But he wasn't yet satisfied. One day he came to my office and said, "You know, they took away my driver's license, and I don't think that's fair. With hand controls, I ought to be able to to drive as well as I did before."

After a half-dozen lessons, he was, indeed, driving as well as ever. He was also able to transfer himself from wheelchair to car. In May of 1965, eight months after he came to us, Mr. Cavorti went home to his family. I'll never forget the day. He got in the car with his wife, gave us a happy wave, and drove away. Today he lives contentedly with his wife, in a community not far from New York City, and we still see him occasionally when he comes in for a checkup.

James Cavorti gave us our first great encouragement in the rehabilitation of cancer patients. We have since trained several patients after hemicorporectomies. One was a coal miner who suffered such severe infection of the bones in his lower extremities, he was a total invalid. A young orthopedic surgeon in Waycross, Georgia, after reading about Cavorti, operated on this man and sent him to us. After seven weeks of training, he returned home and is now running his own little general store. Another was a nineteen-year-old soldier who had most of his lower body blown away in Vietnam. He was returned to this country and underwent surgery by the same doctor who operated on Cavorti. This young man was with us for sixteen weeks after his operation. He is now back with his family in the small New Hampshire town where he grew up, and has a full-time job operating a snowplow in winter and a tractor in summer, sitting in a molded saddlelike seat behind the wheel.

From this beginning we enlarged our scope, and in collaboration with Memorial Hospital for Cancer and Allied Diseases, launched a cancer rehabilitation program there. We were fortunate in finding an ideal director for it—Dr. Herbert Dietz. He had been a very successful surgeon in upper New York State until he said to himself one day, "There are plenty of surgeons but not enough doctors helping people after surgery." It was the same conclusion to which the great rehabilitation pioneer Dr. Henry Kessler had come many years before. Dr. Dietz moved to New York City, spent two years studying rehabilitation, especially can-

cer patients, and was all ready for us when we began planning the unit at Memorial. He and his staff have had great
success, especially with women who have had breasts
removed, people with ileostomies and colostomies and other
disabilities. The cancer rehabilitation program now operates
most successfully as an independent service program.

Our experiences in cancer rehabilitation during this
time were another reminder to us that what we knew
about rehabilitation was only a fraction of what we didn't
yet know. The need for serious, long-range research was
so acute we began in the 1960s to envision a large research wing which would be an adjunct of the institute.
We were eager to enlarge our studies in such fields as language impairment, congenital limb deformities, *spina
bifida* birth anomalies, the dystrophies, behavior patterns
of brain-damaged children, braces and prostheses, emphysema, cardiac problems and many others. All this
would require a staff of perhaps two hundred people in a
building almost as big as the institute itself. It would also
require about four million dollars, which seemed to put it
out of range. But fortunately, we were not without
friends. People at the National Institutes of Health listened with interest and respect when I explained the importance of this dream. And in August 1964 the Division
of Health Research Facilities and Resources of the U.S.
Public Health Service granted us $1,355,000 toward the
construction of a research building. Though it would be
another four years before we had enough money to complete our research center, we at least felt assured that
when that government grant came through we would be
able to manage the rest. Today, it is a reality.

XII

I REMEMBER A STORY SENATOR LYNDEN JOHNSON told me shortly after his recovery from a severe heart attack, about 1956. Just before the attack, his tailor had measured him for two suits, one brown and one black. When he was in the hospital later, Mrs. Johnson told him the tailor had called to ask what should be done about the suits. Mr. Johnson said to her, "You may as well have them both made up. I can use the black one whatever happens." Fortunately, he recovered completely and after he was elected President, he summoned me to the White House in September 1965 because he was disturbed about the health situation in Vietnam, especially among the refugees. He knew about the assistance we had given Korea, through the American-Korean Foundation and the World Rehabilitation Fund as well as the government, and he hoped we might be able to start similar programs in Vietnam. I was, of course, deeply disturbed about the Vietnam war and I welcomed a chance to do whatever was possible in my field for the Vietnamese people. I had never been in Vietnam, so I could make no medical recommendations without taking a look at the situation there.

A few days later, I took off for Vietnam with my associate, Jack Taylor, Juan Monros and Abba Schwartz of the State Department, who was in charge of the refugee program. Our number one host in Saigon was Major General James Humphreys, a most capable doctor whom I had known in the Air Force. He was then on loan from the Air Force to AID (Agency for International Development) and was trying to establish a health program for Vietnamese war veterans and civilians. At the time there was only one facility in that country involved in rehabilitation. This was an artificial limb and brace shop that was producing six limbs per month and repairing forty or fifty broken limbs or braces. Yet there were an estimated thirty-five thousand amputees in South Vietnam, and one could not walk the streets of Saigon or any of the provincial capitals without being impressed by the number of people who needed artificial limbs.

Juan Monros, our prosthetics expert, met us in Saigon and we paid our first visit to the pathetic little limb factory which was destined to be enlarged so dramatically under his guidance. Afterward we left Saigon and flew south by helicopter to Cantho, on the Mekong Delta, escorted by two armed helicopters. When we landed at Cantho, about 7:30 A.M., we went directly to a hospital where a team of Philippine physicians was providing as much medical care as was possible under the circumstances. There had been a skirmish with Vietcong raiders from across the river the previous night. It was described as a minor affair with sporadic fighting, but it was no minor affair to the half-dozen wounded people we saw in the emergency room. Two young men who looked as if they were still in their teens had lost legs. A child had a severely lacerated face. A woman had been shot in the abdomen. When I looked at them, the full impact of the Vietnam war in all its horror suddenly hit me. We inspected the hospital and found it pathetically primitive. There was no running water and only sporadic electric current, but everyone was working hard and doing the best he could.

From this hospital we went on to a base near a large refugee camp about fifteen minutes away by helicopter. The base, which housed a detail of only a half-dozen men, was commanded by an Army captain from the Midwest whose tour of duty was scheduled to end the following month. He had just come to the difficult conclusion that he couldn't leave the people in that refugee camp, so he had signed up for another year of duty. We went with him to the camp in which there were an estimated thirty to forty thousand people who had been driven from their homes by the fighting. Action had been heavy in the delta during the previous weeks, and it was the policy of the American and South Vietnamese military to drop leaflets warning people that their village was to be a target area and telling them to evacuate. Those who did were placed in the "safety," if you could call it that, of the refugee camps. They would stay until the fighting abated, then returned to their homes, or what had been their homes before the action began.

The plight of these people was so tragic it was difficult to walk among them. The camp reminded me of the Korean refugee establishments I had seen twelve years earlier, but with a difference. Most of the Korean refugees, having been driven down across the 38th parallel, could not go back to where they had once lived, so they adopted a more or less permanent mode of life. The population in a Vietnam refugee camp fluctuated daily as the fighting and bombing moved from place to place, with one batch of people leaving the sheltered area as another came in to take its place. We found this particular camp well provisioned with rice, and as we walked the streets of the little village adjacent to it, we saw some good-looking pigs billeted on the front porches of the houses. These pigs, we learned, had come through an AID agricultural program the previous year. But in the entire camp there were no hospitals and no formal medical treatment available. There was a sick call for anyone who needed treatment—a gigantic sick call, conducted not by physicians but by Medical Corps sergeants who had received a few weeks or months of rudimentary training. These sergeants each carried a big black bag which contained about thirty drugs ranging from aspirin to penicillin, anti-malaria preparations, salves for skin diseases—the simplest kinds of remedies that could be applied with some precision by a person with limited training. A team of these sergeants would come to each dispensary two or three times a week. At the dispensary we visited, about three hundred people were standing in line waiting for care. In cases of severe injury or difficult diagnosis, the patient was sent to the nearest provincial hospital, which would be a primitive facility but which at least had a few doctors. The entire setup was woefully inadequate, but I must say I have great respect for the sergeants with the black bags. Under the circumstances, they were doing very well. Nearly all the people who came to them had some kind of intestinal parasite; malaria was endemic; tuberculosis was rampant; and I saw cases of leprosy, cholera, plague, typhoid and an assortment of other exotic tropical diseases.

In this camp there were many children who had suffered polio, but the immunization program was not yet under way. When I asked one of the sergeants if they were administering the Sabin vaccine, he said they had it in Vietnam, but they couldn't give it at the camp because there was no electric power and therefore no refrigeration. The vaccine would deteriorate before it could be administered. The same situation prevailed at most of the other provincial hospitals in Vietnam.

One other malady was common in this camp—tetanus, or lockjaw as it is often called. Its prevalence was due to the fact that when someone in the village was injured, the witch doctor applied a poultice of fresh cow manure to the open wound. Fortunately, the sergeants with the black bags were later joined by public health technicians, and together they set up tuberculosis and malaria-control programs and taught such simple but important public-health concepts as sewage disposal, latrine digging, and food preservation. They tried to make people understand the importance of boiling their water, which came from polluted streams. Inadequate as the program was, they saved thousands of lives in a country where the general population was accustomed to virtually no medical care and no public-health programs.

In Vietnam at that time there were less than a thousand doctors to meet the needs of about sixteen million people, and two thirds of these doctors were in the armed forces. Aside from our sergeants and small numbers of other U.S. health personnel, and seventeen medical teams sent by other countries, there was just no care for the Vietnamese civilians. These medical teams were doing splendid work under pathetic conditions. During that first trip to Vietnam, I visited an outpost area where a Korean team had taken over a deserted five-room building and with their own hands had built examining tables and laboratory benches. After scrounging for supplies, they had opened this little hospital, and I remember the great pride with which the head of their laboratory told me about his procedures. After making diagnoses on serious diseases, such as tuberculosis and leprosy, he would send the slides to the Pasteur Institute in Saigon for verification, and even though they included some diseases which were quite rare, his diagnoses had been correct in every case. In one place after another, we met men like this, totally dedicated to their work. But despite their valiant efforts, the overall health picture in South Vietnam was grim.

Wherever we went, we ran into disabled people—especially amputees. While it seemed pointless to dream of full rehabilitation for all these people, Juan Monros and I agreed that at least an artificial limb and brace program was feasible. With this in mind, we returned to Saigon and asked Ambassador Henry Cabot Lodge to arrange an audience with Nguyen Cao Ky, who was at that time Prime Minister. When we entered Ky's office, I found him to be a very slender, alert and firm-looking man with a somewhat furtive manner. His eyes seemed to dart in all directions. I told him that I thought the country needed a crash program to equip amputees and other crippled people with artificial limbs and braces; that the program should be launched in Saigon, both for civilians and soldiers; and that it should become, as soon as possible, a nation-wide program.

He readily agreed and when I left him it was with the understanding that the program would be announced the following day. Actually, it took several weeks for the announcement to go through all the government formalities and become public.

After the audience with Prime Minister Ky, we visited a large Vietnamese military hospital in Saigon and found it a very well-run institution. The wards were clean and orderly, the surgery rooms well equipped and the X-ray labs efficiently managed. When we concluded our tour of this facility, I noted that we had seen no paraplegics, and since I was certain that an army at war had to have a sizable number of them, I asked our guide where they were kept.

He said, "We've set up a special program for them in an old French summer resort, a lovely watering place, Vung Tau, about twenty minutes from here by helicopter."

When I asked if I could visit the place he said, "Certainly, but it might take a while to get the helicopter ready."

The reason for the delay was evident when we took off. We had waited for the arrival of three armed escort helicopters which flew at tree-top level below us watching for snipers. I learned later that this entire area was heavily infiltrated by the Vietcong. We landed at an isolated enclave which was strongly held by the military. It had an excellent little hospital, entirely staffed by Korean doctors and nurses, but there were no paraplegics here. They were at a place called the Vung Tau Convalescent Center.

The Center was permeated with an atmosphere of hopelessness and death. It had no doctors or nurses, and only a small staff of attendants to try to meet the basic needs of about seventy paraplegics. The men had no braces or wheelchairs, and they were getting no treatment. The only "equipment" I saw was a pathetic little device one of the patients had worked out for himself. He had attached gauze bandages to each of his big toes, and by pulling these he was able to move his paralyzed legs. The air was fetid with the stench of bedsores. The patients were so hopeless they wouldn't even look up at us.

Returning from Vietnam, I reported to President Johnson at the White House. It was obvious that the refugee problem was too big for private agencies to handle. An estimated six hundred thousand people had been displaced and only a government agency like AID could possibly cope with their pitiful condition. But at the same time I favored a large person-to-person voluntary campaign to aid the Vietnamese, which would be coordinated by a nonprofit organization similar to our American-Korean Foundation. My feeling was that such an organization should concentrate on rehabilitation of both civilian and military war victims.

This brought me to the subject of the awful paraplegic center which I had been unable to put out of my mind. I described its patients in detail to President Johnson and he was immediately concerned.

"What can we do about them?" he asked.

I pointed out that there was not much we could do about them if they remained in Vietnam because there were no specialists available there. "We can either pick them up in a big airlift and fly them here, or we can let them die," I said. "And that won't take long. In their condition, ninety percent of them will be dead within a few months."

President Johnson said, "I'll send a plane tomorrow."

"Mr. President, not tomorrow," I replied. "First we'll have to have them sorted out and determine which ones are strong enough to make the trip."

"All right, we'll send the plane whenever you say so."

"And at the same time," I suggested, "I think we should bring some Vietnamese doctors and technicians so we can train them in rehabilitation. The whole country is in desperate need and nothing will happen until the Vietnamese themselves are ready to start it."

President Johnson's cooperation was complete. An old veterans hospital at Castle Point, New York, across the Hudson from West Point, was prepared and staffed expertly to accommodate the Vietnam paraplegics. On November 9,

1965, they arrived by air, fifty-six of them, to be greeted by General Maxwell Taylor, several Army officials from Washington, several of my colleagues at the institute and me. They had made the trip in twenty-two hours on board a giant C-141 transport and not one of them had even asked for a sedative. It was bitter cold, and there were shocked expressions on their faces as they emerged from the plane for their first taste of subfreezing weather after living their entire lives in the tropics. But a few minutes later they were being warmly received in the comfortable hospital, where two spotlessly clean wards were ready for them. Within a half hour they were laughing, listening to the radio and eating a typical American lunch, to which had been added rice and an odoriferous fish sauce called *nucman,* an essential ingredient of the Vietnamese diet.

Eighteen months after these men arrived, all but four had returned to Vietnam. Their training had required more than two hundred and fifty surgical procedures and thousands of hours of work on their part, learning to walk and take care of themselves in every possible way. All except five or six of them walked off the plane when they got back home and are living today with their families. As part of their rehabilitation they had received vocational training, and most of them are now supporting themselves in Vietnam.

Of the four who did not return with the others, three went to the Joseph Bulova School of Watchmaking and became watchmakers. These three are now back in Vietnam teaching at a vocational school and doing watch repair. The fourth man who remained was a young officer who spoke no English when he arrived, but who learned to speak it so fluently during his rehabilitation that he was able to earn a scholarship at Long Island University. After his first year there, he came to me to report his progress.

"I didn't do as well as I hoped," he said.

I was sympathetic. "English is a new language to you," I reminded him, "and I'm sure that must still be a great problem. What kind of grades did you get, anyway?"

He said, "I got three As, but in my fourth subject, I only got an A-minus."

He went on to graduate with honors, and he's now on a full scholarship while working for his Ph.D. in English at the University of Missouri.

The team of Vietnamese doctors and nurses who came to America with the paraplegics also completed training and returned to launch the first modern rehabilitation center in Saigon. In the meantime Juan Monros had launched for the World Rehabilitation Fund a very effective program to teach Vietnamese technicians the art of making artificial limbs. The Volkswagen Company's factory in São Paulo, Brazil, which was then mass-producing limb parts very cheaply for the rehabilitation center there, contributed two thousand component parts for the Vietnam program. With the help of a grant from AID, Monros had trained fifty technicians and increased the output of the Saigon center from six to three hundred limbs per month. A second center was built at Danang, a third at Cantho, and in 1969 the Canadian government financed, built and staffed a fourth center at Quinhon. The American Friends Service Committee has now also established an excellent center at Quangngai. When Juan Monros returned from a trip to Vietnam in January of 1971, he reported that the limbs being manufactured in the shops there now are as good as any in the world—and cost less than a quarter of the price in the United States.

AID also has helped establish an excellent medical school in Saigon and staffed it with a rotating faculty from many of the best medical institutions in the United States. A campus of new buildings was provided by U.S. government money, and the school soon began turning out a hundred and fifty graduates per year. At the same time, the American Medical Association started a program under which doctors could volunteer for short tours of duty in Vietnam, during which they would work in regional hospitals. This was especially attractive to older, retired doctors, and it was found that such doctors, especially if they had been general practitioners, seemed to do better in Vietnam than some of the younger, highly specialized physicians. The older men had more patience, and perhaps from long experience, they were better able under difficult conditions to make do with what they had.

The World Rehabilitation Fund, in addition to its artificial-limb program, helped launch several other projects in Vietnam, including one for the mentally ill. This began when W.R.F.'s director in Vietnam, a brilliant young psychiatric social worker named John Wells, went to visit the country's only mental institution at a place called Bien Hoa, about twenty miles outside Saigon. Being half Indian and a native of Oklahoma, Wells had seen his share of suffering on reservations there, but as he reported to us, he had never seen anything like this so-called mental hospital. More than two thousand inmates were jammed together in locked wards in a building designed to house eight hundred. The rooms had dirt floors and there was no water, no plumbing, no drugs and practically no clothing. The institution's only equipment was one electric-shock machine, which was used merely to subdue the most violent patients.

After visiting this place, Wells cabled us in New York to

say he was going to try to raise money in his Oklahoma hometown with which to buy emergency drugs for this hospital as a first step in a campaign to improve it. Instead of allowing him to do that, I called the heads of six big pharmaceutical companies and described the situation to them. Within twenty-four hours, fifty thousand dollars' worth of drugs was on the way, and within a few weeks conditions at Vietnam's only mental hospital began to change.

Ironically, we learned later that the drug shortage at the hospital had been completely unnecessary. There was no shortage of drugs in Vietnam. The whole supply organization was so chaotic, it was often impossible to get the drugs to where they were needed. This has since been corrected. But drug supply was only one of many problems at this hospital. Fortunately, a doctor named Hermann Steinmetz soon took an interest in it. He was a German psychiatrist who had fled Hitler, worked for many years with his wife among the natives in the jungles of southern Colombia, then come to the United States, earned his citizenship and gone to Vietnam under the A.M.A. volunteer program. After a few months there, he was so disturbed by medical conditions that he joined the W.R.F. staff and stayed for two more years. When he returned, he immediately went to work and took charge. He removed the locks from the wards, soothed and pacified the patients by judicious use of the drugs which had been sent, then launched a campaign for clothes. He picked out the able-bodied patients and put them to work digging sewers, installing water pipes and stringing wires for electricity. In a few months he had an open hospital with only a fraction of the patients requiring locked-ward care. The place was clean and the patients had begun a sizable gardening project to provide themselves with fresh vegetables.

Dr. Steinmetz also recruited a number of dedicated nurses, whom we sent to Malaysia for a six weeks' course in psychiatric nursing. Then he found two excellent Vietnamese psychiatrists who began contributing their time, and he encouraged medical students to come and observe, in the hope that he might lure a few into this field which so badly needed recruits. In the three years he served there, Dr. Steinmetz converted a pathetic, dirt-floored hovel into one of the best mental hospitals in Asia.

The World Rehabilitation Fund, under contract with AID, also launched a training program for the blind in Vietnam. It taught them how to walk the streets safely, how to arrange their household items and furniture to simplify their daily living, and most important, how to support themselves despite their handicap. America has had such programs for some years, but no one had ever tried to train the blind in Vietnam and make them self-reliant. A bright young professional named Rodney Kossick went over to direct the program, at considerable sacrifice to himself, because he had a wife and four small children who were not allowed to live in Vietnam but had to be billeted in Kuala Lumpur. He spent eighteen months in Vietnam, and besides training several hundred blind people, he trained a group of Vietnamese teachers so they could take over the program when he left. The first time a blind man walked the streets in Saigon alone with a cane he stopped traffic because no one had ever seen such a sight. That school is still operating and it has made hundreds of blind Vietnamese self-supporting as Morse-code operators, telephone operators, X-ray technicians, and in a variety of other jobs at which the sightless are most adept. Tragically, there are thousands more who need such opportunities.

Such stories of assistance and progress in Vietnam should not, however, obscure the fact that a terrible war was still in progress throughout the country and the general medical situation remained dismal. In 1967 President Johnson asked me to visit Vietnam again, not only to survey medical conditions there, but also to inquire into charges by a distinguished group of doctors, clergymen and other public figures that countless numbers of Vietnamese children were being burned by American napalm bombs. This group, the Committee of Responsibility, was establishing a program to fly such children to America and Europe for medical care; the press gave it much publicity. The President asked me to evaluate the problem and recommend what should be done for them. It was a disturbing assignment, which I approached from a strictly medical viewpoint.

Major General James Humphreys, who was in charge of American medical efforts for civilians in Vietnam, was a man I had known and respected for many years. He organized for me a tour of twenty-seven hospitals from the Mekong Delta in the south to the Demilitarized Zone in the north. I questioned every doctor I encountered and asked to see every burn patient in each of those hospitals. Though no one could deny that Americans were using napalm in Vietnam, I must report that of all the burn patients I saw, none could be identified as napalm victims. The overwhelming majority of severe burns, according to the doctors and the patients themselves, resulted from explosions of gasoline used in cooking. Black-market gasoline had become a popular cooking fuel, but people didn't know much about how to use it, and their stoves were ill-suited to it. In all of the institutions, I saw almost four hundred cases which one could identify as gasoline burns or the ordinary type of burn (chemical burns are readily distinguishable from the usual type of burn). I also saw five cases of phosphorous burns.

I'm certain that in consultation with my medical colleagues from the United States and the teams from other countries, I diagnosed the cases I saw correctly. While I am sure there are napalm-burn cases in Vietnam, I didn't see any. Possibly they didn't survive to get to the hospitals. But when I reported this on my return to America I was criticized by the Committee of Responsibility, which charged that such cases had been hidden from me, that I had gone to the wrong places to look for them, and that I was naïve. I could only report the facts as I had seen them, and I did not believe cases had been hidden from me because it was inconceivable that all of the hundreds of doctors to whom I spoke were involved in a conspiracy of silence. As much as I sympathized with the humanitarian aims of the Committee of Responsibility, I could not give false testimony.

Nor could I endorse, after my tour of Vietnam, the committee's plan to fly hundreds of burned children to America or other parts of the world for treatment. The more hospitals I visited, especially in the hinterlands, the more convinced I became that it would be an additional and unnecessary shock to these children to uproot them from their culture and friends and relatives (if any were left) for as long as it would take to do the necessary surgery. It might take months or even years. Many of these people had lived so deep in the jungle, they knew nothing but the most primitive conditions, and were completely bewildered whenever they were removed from their immediate surroundings. I was familiar with the case of one woman who had lost a leg and had been flown to our W.R.F. center in Saigon where she was fitted for an artificial leg. The helicopter which returned her to her home landed in a clearing about a mile from her village because there was no closer spot available. We learned later it had taken that woman several days to find her village because in all her life she had never been a mile away from it. I felt the best answer to the problem of treating Vietnamese burn patients was to send plastic surgeons to Vietnam immediately, and as quickly as possible, have them train Vietnamese plastic surgeons.

Because the Committee of Responsibility was not satisfied with my conclusions, I readily concurred with a suggestion that the State Department arrange for the group to send its own representatives to Vietnam to assess the situation and to search for napalm victims. This was done, and after a three- or four-week tour there, the committee's emissaries were able to claim only that they had found thirteen children who were napalm victims. I felt vindicated by the fact that they had found so few after expecting to find so many.

Shortly after my return from Vietnam in 1967 a committee of American plastic surgeons, headed by Dr. Arthur Barsky, organized a program to establish a modern plastic surgical hospital in Saigon, staffed by American volunteer doctors, where children who had suffered burns could be brought for proper care. Through a grant from AID, this supermodern, well-equipped, air-conditioned facility was soon built, and today it is operating most successfully. It has expanded its scope to handle not only burn cases but all kinds of plastic surgery. Vietnam has, for instance, an exceptionally high percentage of children born with cleft palates and harelips. This is considered such a social stigma that parents are willing to do almost anything to have a child's harelip repaired. They now have a modern hospital where it can be done, either by American plastic surgeons, who rotate on assignment, or by young Vietnamese surgeons who have become expert after studying under the Americans.

It would be untrue to say, however, that Americans have done enough to alleviate Vietnamese health problems. A look at the amputee situation illustrates the point. In 1965, when I first went to Vietnam, there were an estimated thirty-five thousand people who had lost limbs. This was not just the result of the war. The cases had been accumulating for more than twenty-five years because there had never been a program to serve them. It was accepted that if your leg was off you spent the rest of your life on a peg leg or crutches. If you were a victim of paralysis from polio, accident or disease and had no braces, you simply accepted crutches or crawled on all fours. After five more years of war, in 1970 (when better statistics were available), there were an estimated hundred and twenty-five thousand amputees in Vietnam, and by then the World Rehabilitation Fund and other agencies were producing about twelve thousand artificial limbs and braces per year. Obviously, that is not enough. The Vietnamese people are not getting enough of anything in the medical field. Their country has been torn by war for twenty-five years now, and their plight is so tragic that it is impossible to describe. In the years to come, they deserve maximum opportunities for health and education as at least some compensation for their suffering.

SENATOR STUART SYMINGTON, whom I've known since my Missouri days, once told me about an incident that happened when he was Secretary of the Air Force. At Fort Benning, Georgia, he watched an airborne maneuver in which two thousand paratroopers jumped. As his party was returning to base headquarters from the maneuver area, they came upon one of the paratroopers who had apparently just landed and was trudging along with his parachute under his arm.

The Secretary's car stopped to pick up the soldier, and as they continued on, Symington said to him, "Do you jump much?"

"Yes, sir. Today was my two-hundred-and-sixty-ninth jump."

"You must like to jump."

"No, sir, I hate to jump."

"Why?"

"Because I'm scared to death every time I jump."

Symington was puzzled. He asked the soldier, "How long have you been in the paratroops?"

"Five and a half years, sir."

"I don't understand you," Symington said. "If you hate to jump, if you're scared to death every time you jump, why don't you transfer out? You don't have to stay in the paratroops."

"Well, sir," the soldier said, "I've given that a lot of thought. And I've come to the conclusion that I'm the kind of fellow who likes to be around the kind of fellow who likes to jump."

That's the feeling I have whenever anyone asks me why I get such satisfaction out of working with disabled people. You don't get fine china by putting clay in the sun. You have to put the clay through the white heat of the kiln if you want to make porcelain. Heat breaks some pieces. Life breaks some people. Disability breaks some people. But once the clay goes through the white-hot fire and comes out whole, it can never be clay again; once a person overcomes a disability through his own courage, determination and hard work, he has a depth of spirit you and I know little about.

I've now been around such people in great numbers for almost thirty years. I never get tired of them, never stop learning from them, perhaps because after all this time I know that I still have so much to learn from them. Rehabilitation is one branch of medicine in which the patient has more power than the doctor in setting the limits and possibilities. The doctor can tell the patient what to do, but only the patient himself can decide how much he's going to do. In making these decisions, patients are constantly teaching us doctors new things about rehabilitation by proving that they can do more than we had presumed possible.

Thanks to such patients and to a growing number of dedicated doctors, as well as a select group of financially generous people and many understanding, dedicated public servants, the concept and practice of rehabilitation have made a good start in the world. But while public acceptance increases every day, we still have made only a start. We've come through the cold winter, as it were, and reached the spring; the long summer of growth toward total acceptance is still ahead.

At the end of World War II when I came to New York, the Institute of Rehabilitation Medicine was merely an idea, and certainly not a very popular idea. There was no facility anyplace else in the world quite like it in scope and concept. Many people, even in the medical profession, considered it foolish to spend money or effort on such a "frilly boondoggle." It wasn't that they disapproved of getting disabled people onto their feet and back into the mainstream of life; it was just that they didn't think it possible. We started proving otherwise in the two bare wards the City of New York assigned to us at Bellevue Hospital. We're still proving it—more conclusively every day—in Bellevue and the two other New York hospitals where our New York University Department of Rehabilitation Medicine manages units (there is now a rehabilitation unit in every municipal hospital in New York City). A final proof is in our own institute, a unit of NYU Medical Center just up the street from Bellevue. We have room for a hundred and fifty-two in-patients, plus several hundred out-patients, at the Institute of Rehabilitation Medicine and I wish we had room for many more. We're always full. In our first quarter century, at least two hundred thousand people have learned at the institute how to overcome their disabilities and get back into life. And the emphasis is always on the patient doing it himself, by learning, learning, learning.

When a new patient arrives at the institute, feeling low and helpless, it often happens that he finds a potted plant or flower by his bed. It's a kind of welcome but it's also more. After he's been there a day or two, he begins to see that the earth around the plant is getting dry. It needs watering. In most cases, he will eventually say to the nurse, "How come nobody waters this plant?" And the nurse will reply, "Well, it's your plant. Why don't you water it?"

What she is saying to him is that the institute is not a place where you lie around doing nothing. If you want something accomplished, you've got to do it yourself. That's why the place does not look like a hospital. It is a tempest inside four walls, with wheelchairs flying past, people on crutches, kids on tricycles—doctors, nurses and visitors rushing up and down the halls. Nobody spends the day in bed unless he's actually ill. Disability is no excuse for inactivity. The patient goes to work the minute he arrives, and that's what accounts for the high-spirited atmosphere of the place. We don't give people time to brood about themselves. There are more severely disabled people in this building than in any comparable building in the world, yet almost every visitor who comes here mentions the cheerful expressions on the faces of the patients. It's a happy place.

We like to think of the institute today as a place of opportunity and hope for the severely disabled. Throughout the complex there are many small oases of comfort and beauty. There is a therapeutic greenhouse where patients can get their hands in the soil and work with growing things, which is not only good occupational therapy but good for the soul too. We call it the Garden of Enid because it was given to the institute some fifteen years ago, and supported by Mrs. Enid Haupt, who loved flowers and beauty and recognized their healing qualities. The patients' library has all types of books available—from textbooks to whodunits. There are more than two thousand pictures on the walls of the corridors, in the classrooms and in the patients' quarters. These two programs were conceived and supported in the very early days by Mr. and Mrs. Robert Haas.

On the East River side of the institute is another garden —trees, fountains, comfortable benches, where patients can sit in the sunshine in the beautiful quiet atmosphere that seems far from the hustle and traffic noises of First Avenue. At the entrance is a bronze plaque which reads as follows: "This garden is a gift to the patients of the Institute of Rehabilitation Medicine from Alva and Bernard F. Gimbel."

On the roof there is a special patients' recreation area called the Rainbow Roof, honoring one of our most respected and beloved volunteers, Miss Gretchen Green. Here activities are at a "Go-Go" pace—everything from rock 'n roll to cook-outs.

The institute simply could not operate without its magnificent auxiliary, composed of more than four hundred dedicated men and women who give hundreds and thousands of hours each year in dedicated service to our patients. Our volunteers work in the library, the gift shop, gymnasium, recreational programs and in many, many other activities. They guide the more than one hundred visitors weekly who come to learn about rehabilitation; they bring the life outside the institute inside, and share their world with our patients, which is an invaluable therapeutic tool. They sponsor our annual garden tour, theater benefit, and help in many ways to provide funds for our patients' services program. They give with their hearts.

Conceived and organized more than twenty years ago by Mrs. Margaret Hillman Purnell is another group that must be mentioned. It is our Special Placement Committee, which is composed of labor leaders, industrialists, lawyers, bankers, personnel experts and civil servants. They meet once a month and, after a sandwich lunch, see the patients that no one has been able to place because they are so severely disabled. Then they go out personally and help them to get jobs. Through the years they have placed about forty such patients annually. And the earnings of these patients have averaged more than a hundred and fifty thousand dollars a year. I pointed out at the annual meeting that the committee had met ten times for twenty hours. In these twenty hours it had produced a hundred and fifty thousand dollars, which is compensation of approximately seventy-five hundred dollars an hour. Everyone felt that this is not only good economics but that the joy of seeing these formerly hopeless people happy and productive again is compensation that cannot be calculated in dollars.

The whole program has changed enormously since the early days. Take, for example, the challenge we faced in rehabilitating paraplegics and quadriplegics. At the time we began, if anyone had asked me how much we could do for such people, I would have had to say that if we could get 10 percent of them back into some kind of life again, we would be doing reasonably well.

Five years ago, we did a survey on the 141 quadriplegics who had trained at the institute during the three previous years. These, of course, were people paralyzed from the neck down. We found that 53 percent of them were either back at work or back at school. In 1970 we did another survey on the 140 quadriplegics who had trained here during the three years previous to that. We found that in this group, 83 percent were either back at school or at work in a gainful occupation. I'm happy to say we've made the same progress with patients suffering from other kinds of disabilities, and with new knowledge through research, we expect in the coming years to increase that progress.

One reason for this expectation is that our research wing is now operating at full strength. Having opened in 1968 after almost five years of struggle and at a cost of more than five million dollars, it is now an eight-story structure dedicated to all kinds of study—from long-range, purely basic scientific exploration to the solution of immediate, practical problems. In 1969 we were most fortunate to be given a fully endowed professorship in rehabilitation medicine research by one of our great friends and supporters, Mr. Arnold Schwartz, and the Brookdale Foundation. This really solidified our whole research program.

On the ground floor we have a section for animal research and we have a hyperbaric chamber, which looks like a small submarine. Its purpose is to test the effects of oxygen under pressure on various physical disabilities, including circulatory impairment, burns, certain infections and wound healing. This program is still in the primary phase but the highly skilled specialists who conduct it have already made some promising observations. They've paid special attention to gas gangrene, because this type of infection usually necessitates amputation. Gas gangrene is caused by anaerobic bacteria— which means it cannot grow in the presence of oxygen. Our researchers can take a person who is moribund from this kind of infection, put him in the chamber, and have him sitting up, talking or eating a few hours later. We now are experimenting with the effect of hyperbaric oxygen on some types of circulatory problems in the brain. We hope that a direct infusion of oxygen under pressure will stimulate brain cells which may be dormant but not dead. It is still much too early to give an opinion on the outcome of this project. If it works, it will be a valuable therapeutic tool, but we don't yet know enough about it to make any predictions.

As you go up from floor to floor in the research wing, you come to a succession of different projects. One group of scientists is studying chronic obstructive lung disease, primarily emphysema, which causes the little air sacs in the lung to dilate and lose their contractility, so that a patient can take in air but can't exhale it properly. This project reflects a subtle change, or enlargement, in our whole approach to rehabilitation. When we started, we were concentrating primarily on orthopedic disabilities. But as the years passed, we found that the number of people disabled by such lung diseases as emphysema, chronic asthma and chronic bronchitis equals or even outnumbers those with orthopedic disabilities. We now know that with proper training, 40 percent of these lung patients, even the severely handicapped, can get back into some kind of work life, and another 40 percent can at least become self-sufficient at home. We're hoping our research will improve these figures.

On the same floor as the respiratory unit is an electro-diagnostic and electronic unit which is studying nerve and muscle physiology in the hope of developing new diagnostic and prognostic techniques. There is a great deal of research and interest in this field. On another floor we're doing a long-term study on various types of patients in the hope of identifying factors that lead to stroke and coronary ailments. If we succeed, we may have a formula by which we can predict these maladies early enough to prevent them.

We have units studying basic physiology of muscles and nerves. Other units are developing new types of limb braces and electronic devices for the disabled. There's a bio-mechanics section where we're studying the problems of lower-back disability, which is the most costly disabling factor in workmen's compensation. We're trying to work out new lifting methods and new tool designs. And at the same time we're studying new designs in surgical instruments.

Spinal-cord injuries occupy a large segment of our research; in this area we work closely with the NYU neurology, physiology and neurosurgery departments. An enormous amount of data has been collected, and we're now investigating reports that if a person's spinal cord has been damaged but not severed, refrigeration for a number of hours will increase the possibility of healing. Some new chemical research in this field indicates that if you can make certain changes in the patient's body chemistry, primarily the enzymes, it may be possible to promote healing in the cord itself.

We're conducting an extensive experiment with monkeys to learn more about brain damage. Techniques have been developed that can produce, by controlled oxygen deprivation at birth, a mentally retarded monkey or a monkey with cerebral palsy or simply a dull normal monkey who sits in the corner and never plays. But within a certain period after the oxygen deprivation, our scientists can prevent these conditions by administering certain electrolytes intravenously. These observations bring new techniques for the management of infant asphyxia at birth.

As a result of our special program of rehabilitation for *spina bifida* children, which I described earlier, we're also making a relentless effort to try to solve the problems of congenital deformities in children. *Spina bifida* is that unfortunate congenital defect in the vertebra which prevents the spinal cord from developing and makes it protrude in a sack filled with spinal fluid (myelomeningocele). The reader may recall the story of the little boy named Johnny who was our first *spina bifida* patient. Of the hundreds of *spina bifida* children who have trained at the institute since Johnny's rehabilitation here, more than 80 percent are now living at home with their families, and of these, about 90 percent are in school. Our research in this field has already paid off in teaching us better ways to manage such severely disabled patients, and we expect to keep learning from it.

I must point out that I have not described any of these research projects to raise false hopes. Handicapped people should not think that science is on the verge of solving all their problems. They should know that teams of scientists are working for them all over the world, but as yet there are no magic formulas, no pills or injections or operations that can be expected to create miracles for the disabled. These people must, and most of them can, create their own miracles by hard work and unflagging determination.

As a result of our achievement, more than two hundred and fifty thousand Americans per year have been getting excellent treatment. But anyone who thinks we should congratulate ourselves for this should stop a moment and consider that at least *ten million disabled Americans still need rehabilitation and are not getting it.* We'll have no reason to congratulate ourselves until the day when we assume that every disabled person has the right to rehabilitation, just as we now assume that everyone with a broken arm must have it set and splinted.

Before that day arrives, many thousands of young people in the health field must become dedicated to rehabilitation and choose it as a career. For this reason I'm very excited about my own granddaughter, Susan Sutphen, who, at the age of sixteen, wants to be a doctor. She has already spent two summers working as a volunteer in the children's ward of a hospital in a ghetto area, and her enthusiasm for the work is something marvelous to see.

Susan is the oldest of ten grandchildren of whom Glad and I can now boast. We've been wonderfully fortunate in the development of our own family. Susan's mother is our daughter, Martha, who lives with her husband, Preston Sutphen, and their four children, in a lovely old brownstone in New York City. Preston is in the international shipping business. Our oldest son, Howard, Jr., also lives in New York with his wife, Betsy, and their three daughters. He conducts his own business of fund-raising and public relations, primarily in humanitarian and health fields. Our younger son, John, is now a physician practicing psychiatry and teaching at Temple University in Philadelphia, where he lives with his wife, Anne, and their three children. I'm proud to have both of my sons working in fields which touch very importantly upon my own work.

Our summer student-training program at the institute is always most exciting. In the program we have thirty-five medical students who have just finished their first year and are happy to be out of the laboratory for a while and really work with patients. In addition, we have some two hundred senior high school and college students who think they might be interested in a career in one of the health fields. They are exposed to a whole panorama of opportunities. The last group are disabled youngsters, many from deprived areas who also feel they want work in some area of health service. The enthusiasm of these young people is most gratifying. In every field of health we need all the bright young people we can find. This is especially true, of course, in rehabilitation.

At the same time, if we have so far to go in this wealthiest of all countries, one can imagine how much still needs to be done in the world's less fortunate countries. It's for this reason that we've been traveling around the world since 1948, encouraging rehabilitation programs in South America and in Poland, Israel, Australia, Soviet Russia, Vietnam, India and more than a hundred other countries. It's for this reason we founded the World Rehabilitation Fund and launched our fellowship training program here at the institute. We have now trained more than a thousand doctors from eighty-five foreign countries, and almost all of those doctors are back in their countries conducting rehabilitation programs.

We have an average of about fifty doctors training with us at all times. We conduct continuing seminars and have become a clearing house for technical literature in our field. The message of rehabilitation has finally reached nearly every corner of the world. But available rehabilitation services lag far behind. Of the hundred and thirty or so member countries in the United Nations, only about ninety have any kind of rehabilitation programs. That represents a fantastic advance since the end of World War II when there were practically none. The International Society for Rehabilitation of the Disabled, the world's oldest organization in this field, has made great contributions toward this advance. The promise for the future is wondrous, yet even in many highly developed countries the work has just begun, and there is so much to be done that we take delight at evidence of any step forward.

Everywhere we go we see similar encouraging developments. Last year the World Rehabilitation Fund made a very important association which should hurry developments. At a meeting in October 1970, representatives of the United Nations and its member agencies voted unanimously to make the W.R.F. the liaison agency for rehabilitation activities for all the agencies within the U.N. These agencies include the World Health Organization, the International Labor Organization, The U.N. Education, Scientific and Cultural Organization (UNESCO), the International Children's Fund (UNICEF), and the United Nations Development Program.

This working agreement between the United Nations and the W.R.F. came about largely through the efforts of Mr. David Morse, whom I met in Europe when he was director general of the International Labor Organization. After twenty-one years in that position, he resigned in 1970 in order to return to his own country, the United States. He was quickly invited into law practice here, and was called upon for important consultations in labor matters because of his great expertise in that field. But he wanted to do something in addition and he had not forgotten the World Rehabilitation Fund. After counseling with his close friend David M. Heyman, who had been for many years a supporter of the Fund and a member of its board of directors, Morse decided this was exactly the kind of voluntary program in which he wanted to become involved.

We welcomed him with delight, not only making him a member of the board of directors but also putting him in charge of planning our future projects and policies.

We could not have made a wiser move. Morse was well acquainted with every important man in the United Nations, including Secretary General U Thant, Dr. M.G. Candau, director general of W.H.O.; C. Wilfred Jenks, then acting as Morse's replacement in the I.L.O.; René Maheu, director general of UNESCO; Henry R. Labouisse, executive director of UNICEF; and Paul G. Hoffman, administrator of the United Nations Development Program. Hoffman, fortunately, had also been a member of the Fund's board of directors for several years. He appointed Morse a special United Nations consultant to promote its rehabilitation program throughout the world, and he also helped arrange the meeting at which his United Nations colleagues decided that the W.R.F. should coordinate the U.N. programs and act as liaison agency with member governments.

This arrangement between the United Nations and the World Rehabilitation Fund has four main purposes, which David Morse spelled out very carefully at the first meeting: first, to improve efficiency for both organizations through increased cooperation, information sharing and joint planning; second, to take advantage of the W.R.F.'s ability to solicit financial aid from private sources; third, to try to increase funds for rehabilitation from the United Nations Development Program; and fourth, to encourage national governments around the world to build rehabilitation facilities as an important part of their economic-development processes.

Shortly before this agreement, we elected Mary Switzer vice president of the W.R.F., and induced her to take over management of our Washington office. Her great skill in dealing with members of the U.S. Congress and the Administration was a valuable asset to the cause of rehabilitation, not only nationally but internationally. Her untimely death was a great loss. In January of 1971 Mr. Francis Keppel, former dean of the School of Education at Harvard and U.S. Director of Education during the Johnson administration, joined the board of the Fund to help accelerate its world-wide program.

On October 20, 1971, the Fund held a luncheon in honor of U Thant at the Plaza Hotel in New York, shortly before his retirement as U.N. Secretary General. The event had great meaning for all of us because it was so significant for the rehabilitation movement. It was the first time U Thant had ever made a speech in the United States outside the U.N. complex when the General Assembly was in session, and two hundred dedicated, influential people came to hear him. The tables were decorated with a special collection of costumed dolls from all over the world—a collection which began at the institute when one of our foreign trainees, after returning home, sent us a beautiful little mannequin dressed in the costume of his country. Since then, many of the institute graduates send us dolls representative of their countries, and these together with the flags of United Nations countries which adorned the dais, provided very colorful decorations.

U Thant's remarks shocked many of the guests.

"There are today," he said, "some three hundred million persons in the world who require some kind of rehabilitation services and are unable to obtain them. . . . In some developing countries, such basic rehabilitation service as a well-organized prosthetic workshop is still lacking. . . . Even in the most developed countries, far too little is being done for the rehabilitation of those suffering from mental illness and retardation which, you will agree, is difficult to understand in a world which finds it possible to spend two hundred billion dollars a year on armaments . . .

"It is estimated that there are one billion persons in the developing world who are in the labor force. Of these, there are about three hundred million who are unemployed. There are an additional three hundred million persons with physical, mental and emotional disabilities who could become employable if they had access to adequate rehabilitation services. . . .

"If we break down the total sum being spent by the United Nations system on rehabilitation to a per capita figure, we find that it amounts to one third of one cent for each disabled person. Add to this the current annual contribution from the United Nations Development Program and all other international support—governmental and voluntary—and the figure still amounts to only one cent for each disabled person, or a total expenditure of three million dollars on the disabled in the developing world."

U Thant made his audience painfully aware of how little the world's nations are doing to rehabilitate their disabled citizens. But at the same time he proposed a new United Nations program to increase rehabilitation care around the globe. By the force of his persuasion, I think he brought us one step closer to universal recognition of the fact that we must revitalize handicapped people wherever they may be.

The concept has developed magnificently in the last quarter century. We've come so far that I am supremely confident this third branch of medical responsibility will one day be accepted and practiced as readily throughout the world as the first two branches, prevention and definitive care, are now practiced. The sooner the people of the world demand rehabilitation services, the sooner they will get such services.

If I sometimes become impatient at the slowness of total acceptance of rehabilitation needs, it is because millions of valuable lives are wasting away unnecessarily, because at this moment throughout the world millions of handicapped people lying helpless in their beds could be up and about, doing constructive things. It has now been proved beyond question that 90 percent of even the severely disabled have the capacity, if they get proper training, to take care of their own daily needs, and in many cases, to return to gainful employment in a competitive society.

To realize how important all this is, one should close his eyes and say to himself, What does it mean to me personally? What if I were suddenly paralyzed and needed help? How would I feel, lying on the pavement after an auto accident, when I realized my back or my neck was broken and I couldn't move? What could I then tell myself?

This is a question that people often put to me. What does go through the mind of an accident victim at such a catastrophic moment? I can't answer the question precisely because nobody can sense the true depths of such an experience until he himself has undergone it. But many patients have described to me this great fear that came over them the first time they tried to move their arms or legs and found they had no control. Most people in the early days of paralysis don't even ask questions. They don't want to hear the answers they subconsciously expect. Nature has strange ways of alleviating distress and pain. After such an accident, spinal shock soon sets in, followed by a general shock to the entire body which prevents the mind from interpreting pain with any great clarity. The full realization begins to come after the shock is gone, usually in a matter of days, and eventually the patient will be able to pose the question that fills his mind: "Will I ever be able to walk again?"

At that moment, all I can tell him is, "It's still too early to know. You may get back a little movement. You may get back a lot. The longer you remain without movement, the less you're likely to get back."

Whatever I may say, however, I don't actually expect it to sink in immediately. Acceptance comes only gradually to such patients, as Rob Heist pointed out in the opening pages of this book. Heist is a very strong and intelligent young man. Perception and acceptance probably came to him more quickly than to some patients. We find that most of them develop it, not from listening to the doctors but from watching fellow patients in the same condition.

How then should one feel when he does finally realize he will be paralyzed for life? What should you tell yourself if you ever find yourself in that situation? Thirty years ago, you would have had to face the fact that you were going to lie in bed for an indefinite period, months or years, becoming progressively weaker as you awaited death. If it happened to you now, you could tell yourself that in all probability, by working hard, you could still make a good life for yourself, even though it might be a different kind of life from what you had known and anticipated.

People also ask me from time to time what to do if there's an accident and someone is lying on the ground with a possible broken back. Even more important, what should you do if this happens to someone you love, someone in your family?

I should warn you in the first place that you may find yourself as frightened as the victim. But however you react, whatever you might want to do, remember that you should not move the patient until professional help comes. I've seen many spinal cords that were actually severed after an accident because of the way the victim was moved. If the person cannot move either leg, he probably has broken his back. If he can't move either arms or legs, he probably has sustained severe injury to his neck. If a person finds himself unable to move one arm or one leg, the chances are that he has had a stroke. But it is not your concern to diagnose. The best thing you can do is make him as comfortable as possible and get medical help fast.

After he has had emergency care, make sure he gets the best possible hospital care. And give him all the hope and love you can muster. There will never be a time when he needs you more. Tell him about the possibilities of rehabilitation, that there is hope. Then, most important of all, make sure he gets the opportunity for comprehensive rehabilitation.

Ultimately, the success of all rehabilitation depends on the patient himself. I have tried to introduce many people in this book who have proved this fact. And I can never forget a philosophical quotation that serves as a constant reminder of this truth:

> I hold the unconquerable belief that science and peace will triumph over ignorance and war, that nations will come together not to destroy but to construct, and that the future belongs to those who accomplish most for suffering humanity.

Those words were spoken by the great nineteenth-century scientist Louis Pasteur. Few people know that he suffered a serious stroke when he was in his forties, at a time when there were no medical programs as we understand them today. But Pasteur was a strong, dedicated man. He rehabilitated himself—working to the age of seventy-three—and many of his greatest scientific achievements came after his stroke.

Pasteur's words express what anyone working in this field must feel. To believe in rehabilitation is to believe in humanity.

Index

ABOUT THE AUTHOR

DR. HOWARD A. RUSK is Professor and Chairman,
Department of Rehabilitation Medicine, New York
University Medical Center. His pioneering work in the field
of rehabilitation has earned him international recognition;
among his awards are the Distinguished Service
Medal, U.S.A.; the National Medal of the Republic of Korea;
and three Lasker Awards in international rehabilitation,
medical journalism and public health. In addition to
heading the internationally known Institute of
Rehabilitation Medicine, New York University Medical
Center, Dr. Rusk has served as consultant in rehabilitation
to the United Nations and many other groups.

He has been President and Chairman of the Board
of the American-Korean Foundation since 1953, President
of the World Rehabilitation Found since 1955, and served a term
as President of the International Society for Rehabilitation
of the Disabled. Since 1945 he has been a contributing
editor to *The New York Times.* Among his many
honors and awards he has received sixteen honorary
degrees both in the United States and abroad.

Dr. Rusk and his wife, Gladys, live in Manhattan
and Armonk in Westchester County in New York.